Fate of the Union: America's Rocky Road to Political Stalemate

Hard Bargain: How FDR Twisted Churchill's Arm,
Evaded the Law, and Changed the Role of
the American Presidency

Riddle of Power: Presidential Leadership from Truman to Bush

None of the Above: Why Presidents Fail and
What Can Be Done About It

Promises to Keep: Carter's First 100 Days

A Question of Judgment: The Fortas Case and
the Struggle for the Supreme Court

The Detroit Race Riot: A Study in Violence (with Tom Craig)

THE DOUBLE-EDGED SWORD

THE DOUBLE-EDGED SWORD

HOW CHARACTER MAKES AND RUINS PRESIDENTS, FROM WASHINGTON TO CLINTON

ROBERT SHOGAN

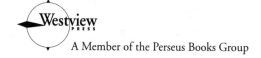

Westview
PRESS
A Member of the Perseus Books Group

Published in 2000 in the United States of America by Westview Press, 5500 Central Avenue, Boulder, Colorado 80301-2877, and in the United Kingdom by Westview Press, 12 Hid's Copse Road, Cumnor Hill, Oxford OX2 9JJ

Library of Congress Cataloging-in-Publication Data
Shogan, Robert.
   The double-edged sword : how character makes and ruins presidents, from
Washington to Clinton / Robert Shogan.
      p.   cm.
   Includes bibliographical references and index.
   ISBN 0-8133-6872-3 (hc)—ISBN 0-8133-6777-8 (pbk)
      1. Presidents—United States—Conduct of life—History.
2. Presidents—United States—Psychology—History.   3. Character—
Political aspects—United States—History.   4. Interpersonal
relations—Political aspects—United States—History.   I. Title.
E176.1.S565   1999
973'.09'9—dc21
[B]   98-39828
                                                                         CIP

The paper used in this publication meets the requirements of the American National Standard for Permanence of Paper for Printed Library Materials Z39.48-1984.

10   9   8   7   6   5   4   3   2   1

For the women in my life—
Ellen, Cynthia, and Amelia

CONTENTS

AUTHOR'S NOTE

When I told friends I was writing a book on presidential character, many smiled knowingly, referred to the seemingly unending controversies about Bill Clinton's personal conduct, and congratulated me on my sense of timing. Actually, though, I began thinking about the importance of presidential character long before Clinton entered the White House. The disastrous conclusions to the presidencies of Lyndon Johnson and Richard Nixon, following the landslide victories each had won, seemed rooted in their natures. And this suggested to me that any understanding of the presidency had to begin with understanding the relationship between presidential character and presidential performance. It is this connection that I have tried to examine on these pages.

Many people have helped me in this task. In particular, I am grateful to Charles Overby, head of the Freedom Forum. He encouraged me to pursue this subject and helped me to get a Media Studies Center fellowship, which made it possible for me to complete work on this book. I owe thanks to all my colleagues at the Media Studies Center, especially research director Lawrence T. McGill, who made sure that whatever resources I needed were made available; Monroe Price, for his encouragement, wise counsel, and friendship; and my researcher, Alina Oh. I am also grateful to the editors of the *Los Angeles Times,* where I have worked for more than twenty-five years, particularly to Doyle McManus, the Washington Bureau chief, for being flexible enough to allow me the time to finish this project, and to Don Frederick whose editing of my copy for the newspaper has helped me to better understand how to say what I mean; and to a number of my fellow reporters, especially Ron Ostrow and David

Willman. At Westview Press, I am indebted to Leo Wiegman for his early interest in the book and to Kristin Milavec and Michele Wynn for transforming the manuscript into reality between hard covers. Thanks are also due to my agent and ally Carl Brandt and to his colleague Marianne Merola. Once again, my greatest debt is to my wife, Ellen, who served as she has on past projects as first reader and best friend.

Robert Shogan

THE DOUBLE-EDGED SWORD

1

THE ULTIMATE
WEAPON

IF BOB DOLE EVER HAD A CHANCE of winning the presidency of
the United States, that opportunity came, and swiftly passed, during
his first televised debate of the 1996 campaign against Bill Clinton.
Did Dole believe, moderator Jim Lehrer asked midway through that
confrontation, that there were relevant differences between him and
Clinton "in the more personal areas"?

For a moment, anxious Democrats everywhere held their breath,
while Republican pulses raced with joy. The "character issue," the
jugular of Clinton's campaign, had been exposed, and Dole had been
handed a dagger. He only needed to drive it home.

But Democrats need not have fretted. Dole had no such intention.
"I don't like to get into personal matters," Dole said. "As far as I'm
concerned, this is a campaign about issues." Scolded by his aides,
Dole tried to revive the character issue in the second debate ten days
later. But his scattershot sniping at the president failed to carry out
its required objective of demonstrating Clinton's unfitness for the
Oval Office. Despite a new wave of scandal besmirching Clinton's
reputation in the closing days of the campaign, the outcome was
never in doubt.

This lost opportunity underlines one of the profound conun-
drums of presidential politics made evident by Dole's frustration and
Clinton's success. Franklin Roosevelt called the presidency "pre-
eminently a place for moral leadership." Walter Dean Burnham de-

scribes our chief executives as "the high priests of the American civil religion." Moreover, political professionals in both parties are unanimous in their belief that in a political system where the significance of substantive campaign pledges has been diminished by the repeatedly demonstrated inability of politicians to redeem their promises, character is the bedrock issue in presidential elections.

Here then is the riddle: How did Clinton manage to defeat Dole when countless polls provided evidence for the intuitive judgment that the vast majority of the electorate viewed the incumbent as less honest, less trustworthy, less likely to stand by his convictions—in short, as a man of weaker *character* than his challenger?

The answer to this question leads to another riddle, and it was suggested to me by none other than Clinton himself. Early in the 1992 presidential campaign, when I had the chance to talk to then Governor Clinton one-on-one, I asked him whether he thought a candidate's personal behavior was a relevant guide to his performance as president.

"That is a question that every American has to answer for himself," he said. "But the question I would ask back is to what extent is that the real reason the press pursues these matters with such relentlessness?"

That was a typically shrewd response, intended to put the onus for the so-called character issue on the press rather than on the candidate. Moreover, as the debate on character has raged on throughout his presidency, shifting from Gennifer Flowers and the draft to Whitewater, Paula Jones, the fund-raising abuses of the 1996 campaign, and ultimately to his bizarre dalliance with White House intern Monica Lewinsky, Clinton has continued to challenge his critics—even as he bends every effort to present himself as a paragon of middle-class values and virtues.

But the contradictions between Clinton's preachments from the bully pulpit of the presidency and the allegations of personal misconduct and political chicanery that have marred his tenure only serve to point to the importance of the tantalizing question that he raised in our conversation: What is the connection between presidential character and presidential performance?

More than half a decade after the numerous scandals surrounding Clinton clouded his quest for the presidency and more than twenty years after Jimmy Carter won the White House by promising never to tell a lie, that question still begs an answer.

What is badly needed and what this book will strive to provide is a clear explanation of how the so-called character issue and the intertwined issue of values, which together now color all public debate on politics, are linked to the political process and governance. It is this connection that I examine from two perspectives: First, by showing how the strengths and weaknesses of presidential character help shape presidential performance for good and for ill, and second, by exploring how presidents and their rivals on the political stage use the public's perceptions of presidential character and values to manipulate political audiences—the press and the electorate.

This book will demonstrate that character is a double-edged sword—an instrument that can discredit presidents and destroy their credibility but also one that presidents can use to establish their political identity and mobilize support. In sum, character, combined with values, is the ultimate weapon in modern American politics.

Of course, presidential character has been an important aspect of the Oval Office since George Washington and the cherry tree. The American people have always expected their presidents, and to a lesser degree other stewards of the public trust, to serve not only as political leaders but also as role models of personal behavior, setting standards for raising their children. Indeed, this book will show that it was Washington's character that provided the constitutional foundation for the office he was the first to hold. Without the framers' faith in Washington, they would not have granted the chief executive even the limited powers that devolved upon that office. And once inaugurated, Washington, through character, endowed the presidency with the prestige that has allowed the office to survive for more than two centuries, despite the dubious conduct of some who have worn Washington's mantle.

More than that, this book will show that in the case of each of Washington's most important successors, character not only defined their performances but also helped to redefine the presidency as an institution. Thus, Thomas Jefferson's sinuous nature lent a Machiavellian dimension to the presidency that endures today. Andrew Jackson's bellicose personality established the presidency's populist side, and Franklin Roosevelt's matchless self-assurance helped to make the nation's highest office a reality in the average citizen's life.

But as the new millennium nears, character and values have taken on a significance never contemplated by Washington and the Founding Fathers, as the strategies of both parties in the 1996 presidential campaign demonstrated. "Family values is one of those alarm clock phrases," Clinton's then secretary of labor, Robert Reich, asserted as the 1996 election approached. "It rattles people to attention whether we like it or not. The next election, I predict, will be a titanic struggle to define that term."

Reich proved to be prescient. In the campaign, Republican Dole denounced Hollywood for debasing American culture. And though Dole himself held back, his surrogates used every possible occasion to call attention to the incumbent president's personal frailties, while Democrat Clinton sought to protect children from the excesses of television and used his nominating convention to reaffirm his marriage and his parenthood.

And even after the campaign concluded, the turmoil over morality continued to roil the public arena, with questions surrounding the individual conduct of public figures and society's standards being raised painfully and conspicuously on all sides. In the months following the election, a candidate for chairmanship of the Joint Chiefs of Staff was forced to withdraw from consideration following disclosure of an adulterous relationship. And Massachusetts congressman Joseph Kennedy, the most prominent scion of America's most storied political dynasty, was obliged to abandon his plans to run for governor of his native state by the twin furors over his annulled marriage and his brother Michael's dalliance with a teenage baby-sitter.

"You run for office, and people pass judgment on your life from the day you were born," observed Representative Joe Moakley, one of Kennedy's Democratic House colleagues from Massachusetts. No one understands the consequences of that axiom better than Bill Clinton, who, after becoming the first Democratic president since FDR to win reelection, had to reorganize a fund-raising committee set up to finance the legal problems arising from the various allegations of impropriety against him, even as he was forced to submit to a deposition in the sexual harassment law suit brought by Paula Corbin Jones.

Still, for his first six years on the national political stage, as a presidential candidate and chief executive, Clinton seemed to lead a charmed life, as he won his party's presidential nomination and then two elections for the White House. "The people whose character is really an issue are those who would divert the attention of the people and divide the country we love," he declared when his character first came under fire, claiming that examples of misbehavior alleged against him were mere peccadilloes that had no bearing on his performance in office. And ever since, Clinton has used much the same argument—along with indignant denials of misbehavior—to shield himself from the intermittent firestorms of criticism. But then, as he began the second year of his second term, he was forced to confront the most serious character-related charge of his career—that he sought to obstruct justice to cover up an affair with a young White House intern. And the cumulative toll taken on his credibility by all the previous controversies seemed to place his presidency in extreme peril.

In a legal sense, everyone agreed with Independent Counsel Kenneth Starr when he pointed out that Clinton is entitled to the presumption of innocence. But in political terms, despite his strong showing in the polls in the months following the eruption of scandal, even Clinton's fellow Democrats worried over how long the public would continue to give him the benefit of the doubt.

The White House sex scandal both reflects and reinforces confusion among individual Americans about the moral standards they set for their elected officials, especially when it comes to sexual behavior. "People nowadays demand both the right to freedom and openness and acceptance in their sexual conduct, whatever it might be, and also the right to privacy," observed *Washington Post* columnist Meg Greenfield.

Defenders of politicians accused of misconduct decry the focus on the private behavior of presidents as akin to Peeping Tomism. And they argue that had the postpresidential disclosures about the philandering of Dwight Eisenhower and FDR been public knowledge when they sought office, the nation might well have been denied their services.

And it is true enough that behavior that flouts propriety is not necessarily relevant. But some is. Thus, the fact that Warren Harding, who led America into the Roaring Twenties, had a mistress, means little by itself. But the mistress's revelation made after Harding's death that their relationship reflected Harding's obsessive need for approval and affection might have served as a warning of the scandalous corruption that ultimately engulfed a president who would not separate himself from his crooked friends because he feared being without any friends.

Academic research offers further evidence of the increasing salience of presidential character and values in shaping campaign debate and voter decision. In the past, most political scientists treated the personal qualities of White House contenders as superficial fac-

tors, less consequential than party loyalty and the importance of issues in determining election outcomes. But the erosion of party allegiance and the haziness of campaign issue debate has led scholars to
put greater weight on the traits of individual candidates. A landmark
study of voter assessments of presidential candidates, based on data
collected by the National Election Studies covering nine presidential
elections starting with Eisenhower's victory in 1952, concluded that
at least five dimensions of an individual candidate's makeup have an
important part in influencing which lever voters pull on election day.
Besides competence, these include integrity, reliability, charisma, and
personal, a sort of grab bag of miscellaneous factors such as a candidate's age, demeanor, and background.

These judgments are of course highly subjective and are made more
so, as the study notes, because in evaluating these individual traits,
voters draw on their own well-established conceptions about individual behavior and presidential performance. As Walter Lippmann
pointed out in his celebrated *Public Opinion,* "We do not so much see
this man and that sunset; rather we notice the thing is man or sunset
and see chiefly what our mind is already full of on these subjects."

The authors of the study, Arthur H. Miller, Martin P. Wattenberg,
and Oksana Malanchuk, conclude that "people have a preexisting
knowledge structure or scheme concerning what a president should
be like, and judge real candidates according to how well they meet
the elements of these schemas." Moreover, they point out that the
impact of character traits on the campaign is the result of a dynamic
process that feeds on itself. "Voters abstract from their experience of
past presidents those features and behaviors they associate with political success, and then evaluate other candidates with respect to
these same characteristics." For their part, candidates during the
campaign emphasize certain of their characteristics in ways intended
to get favorable reaction from the voters. "Voters in turn respond to
these campaign messages not only because they are relevant to their
scheme for presidential candidates but also because these are the
terms in which the political dialogue is conducted."

Admittedly, even under the light of scholarly research, character
and values remain amorphous terms, subject to misinterpretation.
For the purposes of this book, here is how I define them:

Character: The sum of a politician's psyche and personality; the
internal drives that provide motivation and focus. Character

has many facets and is not simply the equivalent of morality. In deciding between Clinton and Dole, voters had to balance Dole's reputed rectitude against Clinton's supposed compassion.

Values: The principles and beliefs that shape behavior for individuals and for society and that have taken on new prominence in the political arena. Presidents rely on private values to guide their own conduct and often use public values, such as freedom and equality, to rally support—if these values are consistent with their characters.

Character and values are the most powerful tools we have for political communication. Whether they are good or bad depends on how they are used—or abused. During the Reagan-Bush era, Republicans seemed far more adroit at using them—and abusing them—than their Democratic opponents. But Democrats can play this game, too, as FDR showed years ago in the midst of World War II by promulgating the celebrated Four Freedoms—freedom of speech and worship, freedom from want and fear—as emotion-laden symbols of American beliefs. And Bill Clinton demonstrated similar skills when he first sought the presidency, offering his own life story as a paradigm for the American Dream. Striving to sustain that theme, with its potent appeal to the middle class, during his first year in the White House, Clinton repeated no fewer than seventy times his campaign promise to serve the interests of "of all those who do the work, pay the taxes, raise the kids, and play by the rules."

The good news about character and values is that their responsible use can help politicians forge coalitions to break the gridlock that at times seems to paralyze the political process—and can also help the media to enlighten readers and viewers. The bad news is that the misuse of character and values drowns out substantive arguments, distorts reality, and undermines the public confidence in politics and the press.

At any rate, what is clear is that for better and also for worse, the impact of character and values is pervasive and growing, principally on the presidency but also on nearly every other national public office and institution.

One reason for this is the decline of ideological distinctions and partisan allegiances. The cleavages between the Republicans and Democrats produced by the Great Depression, which Franklin Roosevelt brilliantly dramatized, have been eroded by the spread of economic well-being. But the Republicans—President Reagan in the eighties, Speaker of the House Newt Gingrich in the nineties, or any of their lesser voices—have not yet been able to provide a satisfactory substitute. As a consequence, American politics is drifting, without any philosophical moorings. Many of the problems of government and society seem intractable, while debate centered on policy issues appears fruitless.

Just as significant is the turbulence in the moral arena. In the closing decades of the twentieth century, the nation has been shaken by a series of jolts challenging standards of behavior: the AIDS epidemic that mocked the sexual permissiveness dominant in the 1960s, the Wall Street scandals that stained the glorified image of the acquisitive entrepreneur established in the Reagan era, the revelations of sordid self-indulgence by the electronic clerics who had set themselves up as guardians of the public's mores, and, most recently, the scandal-stained record of the Clinton White House.

Another contributing factor is the increasing openness of the political system. As political parties have declined and presidential primaries proliferated, the media have become power brokers of a sort, partly replacing the old-time bosses who held sway in smoke-filled rooms and guarded the channels of political discourse.

"This is a different political system," Hugh Heclo, a George Mason University political scientist, argues. "There is no establishment which controls information. The whole range of candidate behavior has been opened up and it's ridiculous to think you can recreate those days."

In this environment, politicians, particularly presidents, have tended to personalize their office and, taking advantage of the new channels of communication provided by the explosion of communications technology, reach out through the media to exploit the emotions of the electorate. And the media, grappling with some of the same problems, have found it hard to resist their tactics.

Presidents have always enjoyed prestige, but in the past, they were regarded from a distance, as abstract representations of their office and their actions. The modern media, particularly television, have thrust them into our family rooms and have inflated their personas out of all proportion.

Yet not all this attention is welcome. If the personalized presidency has created cultural heroes, it has also produced political villains.

Just as the Cold War, establishing the permanent threat of nuclear destruction throughout the second half of this century, fastened attention on the president, upon whom our chances of survival seemed to depend, two great national traumas, Vietnam and Watergate, vividly demonstrated the connection between character defects and disastrous policies. Lyndon Johnson and Richard Nixon, two very different men, each from a different party, were seen as mendacious and deceitful, driven to self-destructive actions by forces they could not control.

The dramatic public reaction paved the way for the presidency of Jimmy Carter, the last Democrat to win the White House prior to Clinton. Carter made great capital of his background as a born-again Christian; his promise to never tell a lie and his sterling character traits, underlined by the contrast between him and Johnson and Nixon, helped him win the presidency. Of course, if uprightness were the sole criterion for presidential leadership, Jimmy Carter's visage would by now have been carved on Mount Rushmore.

But presidential character is complex. Carter's strong moral foundation could not offset another character trait—his rigidity, one of the major reasons his presidency failed.

Carter was defeated by Ronald Reagan, whose signal success in communication was making his personality the embodiment of his beliefs. He did this so well that his opponents joined his admirers in calling him the Great Communicator, an appellation that allowed them to suggest that Reagan's early success in the White House was founded on gimmickry. But Reagan's talent in communicating his political beliefs and values was not the result of any trick. Rather, it was his ability to bond his personality with his convictions. His message was persuasive because it was consistent with the messenger. Of course, Reagan's consistency did not entirely make up for a certain laziness, a tendency not to understand things he did not want to understand. This allowed Reagan to become ensnared in the notorious arms-for-hostages transaction with Iran, which cast a pall over the conclusion of his presidency.

George Bush had neither Ronald Reagan's gifts as a campaigner nor his strong convictions. But he broke new ground on the character issue in his race against Democratic standard-bearer Michael Dukakis. Instead of attacking Dukakis's character directly, Bush attacked his values, which he implied were evidence of the hapless Dukakis's character defects. Pounding away at a series of episodes in

Dukakis's record as Massachusetts governor, he depicted Dukakis as a figure outside the middle-class mainstream. Democrats accused Bush of cheap shots and distortion. But they recognized that his thrusts struck home with the voters.

In the wake of Dukakis's defeat, pollster Stanley Greenberg concluded that Dukakis's inarticulateness had left Bush's "savage caricature" as the dominant image of the Democratic Party—short on patriotism and indifferent to the values of work and family. Yet at the same time that the country was supposedly caught up in a pervasive conservative mood, Greenberg noted, polling data showed that voters favored an activist agenda for government.

What was needed to take advantage of these liberal impulses, Greenberg argued, was a Democratic model that could replace the New Deal and the Great Society and reach the middle-class voters who had left the party. This diagnosis set the stage for the New Democrat paradigm, which carried Bill Clinton to the White House. Along with a bundle of policy proposals, the model relied heavily on values and character, as embodied by Clinton, to touch the emotions and win the hearts of the voters. The problem with this strategy is that Clinton has fallen woefully short of living up to his part of it. Early in his 1992 candidacy, when he was dogged by allegations of infidelity and draft avoidance, he dismissed the issue of character. "The people whose character and patriotism is really an issue in this election are those who would divert the attention of the people, who destroy the reputations of their opponents and divide the country we love," he declared.

But once he escaped fatal damage from the first barrage of character attacks, Clinton appeared to change his mind about the relevance of character and values, as he tried to play out the role Greenberg had sketched for him. "My life is a testament to the fact that the American Dream works," he declared as he stumped the country on the way to the White House. "Leadership, rules, responsibility, and love . . . I got to live by the rules that work in America and I wound up here today running for president of the United States of America."

And as this book will show, the questions of character that have hung over his presidency like a cloud since its inception have been framed by this same contradiction. On the one hand, as he defends himself against the myriad allegations about his behavior, Clinton denies the relevance of character to his presidency. On the other hand, he makes every effort to convince the middle-class electorate that he does indeed embody those traits and values that make up the New Democrat model.

Yet for all the distortions and confusions surrounding the character issue during the Clinton presidency, the constant controversy serves only to underline the reality that presidential character remains a powerful element in the political system and, given the limitations of that system, a potentially constructive force. Moreover, given the highly personalized nature of the U.S. political system, politicians and scholars alike argue that there is no better way of choosing a candidate for president than by evaluating what kind of human being he—or she—really is. "Voters know that the issues a president will have to face will change in time," Robert Teeter, a GOP pollster and senior Bush campaign strategist, once told me. "But his character will always be there." And these words from a contemporary political operative reflect thinking that has prevailed in the Republic since its founders met two centuries ago in Constitution Hall.

2

FATHER FIGURE

THE HEAT AND HUMIDITY HUNG OVER the city like a curse. It was still only late spring in this year of 1787, which was, as the writ composed by the Massachusetts legislature for its delegation to the Constitutional Convention proudly observed, "the 11th year of independence of the United States of America." But already, as the delegates from the thirteen newly independent colonies could attest, this season was well on its way to becoming what Philadelphians would come to remember as the worst summer in nearly half a century.

At first glance, the Pennsylvania statehouse where the delegates gathered, with its darkened hallways, appeared cool, at least by comparison with the sweltering town outside. But this proved to be a temporary illusion. Despite the slatted blinds on the windows, by midday the delegates were mopping away the sweat, particularly since the windows were closed to preserve the privacy of their deliberations.

No one objected to this discomfort because everyone present felt the need for secrecy, for the delegates were all too well aware that they were engaged in what the eighth president of the United States, Martin Van Buren, would later call "an heroic and lawless act."

The lawlessness of their conduct was obvious from the start. The convention's mandate had been strictly and narrowly drawn by the Congress that had convoked their meeting. As phrased by the authorizing resolution, in words echoed by resolutions passed by most of the states, the delegates had been called together "for the sole and express purpose of revising the Articles of Confederation." But they had hardly begun their main business when it became clear that some of the gentlemen in attendance had far more in mind.

Appropriately enough, it was Virginia, the state whose sons, notably George Washington, Thomas Jefferson, and Patrick Henry, had provided the rebellious colonies with much of their military and intellectual direction, that took the lead in breaking new ground for the future of the infant republic. Edmund Randolph, Virginia's governor, early on confronted the delegates with fifteen resolves that painted a bold vision of the future, a future made up of an entirely new national government. The Virginians contemplated a structure made up of a judiciary, a legislature, and, most controversial of all for a country that had just shed itself of a monarch, an executive.

The Virginia plan was more rough draft than detailed blueprint. And the convention would spend three months wrangling over the mechanics. But everyone understood from the onset of the debate that what Randolph proposed was no mere refurbishment of the Articles of Confederation.

Instead, he called for the creation of a entirely new entity. And to those who insisted that they had no authority beyond amending the existing structure, James Wilson of Pennsylvania responded by recounting an anecdote about Alexander Pope, the eighteenth-century poet, who was barely able to walk because of a childhood affliction. When he occasionally stumbled on his way, it was Pope's custom to mutter, "God mend me."

Overhearing him, a street urchin is supposed to have remarked: "God mend you, indeed! He would sooner make half a dozen new ones."

Uninhibited by latter-day notions of political correctness, Wilson drove his point home: "This would apply to the present confederation, for it would be easier to make another than amend this."

Still, abundant reason remained for the delegates to feel trepidation, a reality underlined when near the end of one day's deliberation, Washington rose from his chair to address them. Washington would certainly have commanded their attention in any case because of who he was, because of the authority he wielded as president of the convention, and because he spoke out only rarely. But, in addition, on this occasion the glower smoldering in his eyes made his auditors stir with unease.

In his hand, Washington held a copy of the very resolutions that they had been debating in absolute privacy, the first state secret of the new nation. And yet this document, Washington informed the delegates, had been as carelessly set aside as if it were a particle of refuse and left unguarded in the precincts of the statehouse. Only by good fortune had it been discovered by a functionary of the convention, who had turned it over to Washington.

In this company, Washington hardly needed to dwell on the consequences of an early disclosure of their deliberations. "I must entreat Gentlemen to be more careful, lest our transactions get into the News Papers, and disturb the public repose by premature speculations." He paused to let his words sink in, then looked around the room. "I know not whose Paper it is, but there it is, let him who owns it take it," and with that, he threw the document down on the table, picked up his hat, and stalked from the room.

"Every person seemed alarmed," recalled William Pierce, delegate from Georgia, he not least of all. "Putting my hand in my pocket I missed my copy of the same paper." Not until he got back in his room and found his copy could Pierce shake off the anxiety. Not surprisingly, no one ever came forward to claim the document.

The delegates to that convention were all in their own right men of distinction and prominence who had proven their merit by force of arms or acts of statesmanship during the long struggle for independence. Yet for all of their own achievements, the respect in which they held Washington approached reverence. And that admiration for Washington's character would weigh heavily on the delegates as they went about creating the office that all there knew he would be the first to hold.

Washington's decision to attend the convention had been reached only after surmounting the considerable reluctance that attended all his exposures to public life. Although in December of 1786 the Virginia legislature had selected him as one of its delegates, this opportunity, instead of pleasing him, created a problem, which illustrates the complexities of Washington's approach to public affairs.

He had written the governor explaining that "Circumstances" would almost certainly keep him from accepting the position offered to him. The "circumstances," as he explained to his fellow Virginian James Madison, were that he had already declined to attend the annual meeting of the Society of Cincinnati, the group of veteran officers that had chosen him as president, to take place in May, also in Philadelphia. The excuse he had offered was bad health and the burdens of private business.

In fact, Washington had other reasons. Ever conscious of his prominence and the power that went with it, he wanted to steer clear of the controversy stirred by the suspicion that the Society of Cincinnati, in which membership was hereditary, saw itself as the forerunner of an American aristocracy.

Another, more substantive obstacle was the dubious legality of the convention. At the time Washington was chosen as a delegate, the only basis for its coming together was a call issued by the five states attending a convention in Annapolis in 1786 to deal with the problems of carrying on business across each other's borders under the jerry-built structure of the confederacy and to discuss "the situation of the United States." No one knew what that portended, but the potential for legal objections seemed boundless. "In strict propriety a Convention so holden may not be legal," Washington wrote John Jay, in March 1787.

Of course, the sponsors of the conclave were well aware of the legal shadow cast over their enterprise—which was one of the main reasons they wanted Washington there to participate. But if Washington's reputation was a valuable resource that might aid the convention, that reputation could suffer a blow, which apart from its effect on Washington himself would damage the cause of nationhood if the session turned out to miscarry. Fortunately for all concerned, Congress in March voted to recommend that states participate in the Philadelphia convention, thus lending the gathering a semblance of legitimacy and easing Washington's path to Philadelphia. "Secure as he was in his fame," Henry Knox, his old commander of artillery, wrote to the Marquis de Lafayette after Washington decided to attend the convention, "he has again committed it to the mercy of events."

It could hardly have surprised him that when the convention finally achieved a quorum and began its official business, he was nominated to be its president. There being no doubt about this decision, there was no debate and Washington was chosen unanimously. Thanking the delegates for the honor, Washington asked their indulgence for any mistakes that might arise from his "want of experience." Pierce of Georgia wrote: "Having conducted these states to independence and peace, he now appears to assist in framing a Government to make the People happy." Pierce added:

Like Gustavus Vasa he may be said to be the deliverer of his Country; like Peter the Great he appears as the politician and the States-man, and like Cincinnatus he returned to the farm perfectly contented with being only a plain citizen while enjoying the highest honor of the Confederacy—and now only seeks for the approbation of his country-men by being virtuous and useful.

Washington's greatness, his ability to exert his personal influence on the shaping of the United States, stemmed from his self-discipline and his self-confidence, shaped by the rigorous code he imposed on himself. Because he knew who he was and felt no need to prove himself to others, Washington avoided much folly. The mistakes he made were the honest errors made by a realistic and practical man, rather than the blunders weak men commit when, sometimes without fully realizing the consequences of their actions, they try to deceive others and themselves.

The most obvious basis for his self-assurance was his physical appearance. As Richard Brookhiser writes in his illuminating "rediscovery" of Washington's life, "The body is the basic unit of all human intercourse," including political communication. Washington's sheer presence helped him command attention, eliminating the need for him to rely on the superficial appurtenances of power. At six feet three inches tall, he towered half a foot above most of his contemporaries, an advantage that some thought unfair. With typical acerbity, John Adams once likened Washington to "the Hebrew sovereign chosen because he was taller by the head than other Jews." But Adams's wife, Abigail, took a different view. "You had prepared me to entertain a favorable opinion of him," she wrote her husband after her first meeting with Washington, "but I thought the one half was not told me." She was reminded of a John Dryden quatrain:

> Mark his majestic fabrick!
> he's a temple Sacred by birth,
> and built by hands divine.
> His Soul's the deity that lodges there.
> Nor is the pile unworthy of the God.

This "majestic fabrick" was stretched over the muscular and well-proportioned frame that Washington maintained throughout his life. He weighed 175 pounds in his late twenties and by the time he was fifty years old barely topped 200 pounds. An aide during his service in the Virginia militia described his head as "well shaped . . .

gracefully poised on a superb neck," to go with "a large and straight" nose, "blue grey penetrating eyes," high cheek bones, and a large mouth. His demeanor was said to be "at all times composed and dignified. . . . His movements and gestures are graceful, his walk majestic, and he is a splendid horseman."

The power of Washington's physical presence made less conse-quential his meager gifts as an orator. "This great man was agitated and embarrassed more than ever he was by the leveled cannon or pointed musket," the notably caustic Senator William Maclay of Pennsylvania said of Washington's delivery of his first Inaugural Ad-dress in 1789. "He trembled, and several times could scarce make out to read, though it must be supposed he had often read it before."

But Washington's woodenness at the podium was offset not only by his natural physical attributes but also by the military dignity that cloaked his demeanor. "Be easy and condescending in your deport-ment to your officers, but not too familiar lest you subject yourself to a want of that respect which is necessary to support a proper command," Washington counseled a young officer under his com-mand, and he himself exemplified that advice. As the prominent physician Benjamin Rush said, "There is not a king in Europe that would not look like a *valet de chambre* by his side."

The temperament that helped Washington carry on his seven-year war against Great Britain had been forged by the struggle he had fought all his life to battle both the limitations of his upbringing as a widow's eldest son and a notoriously short temper. Important assets in this struggle were "the Rules of Civility and Decent Behavior," which he culled from an English work on manners. Among the max-ims that he addressed to himself and pored over frequently: "Con-tradict not at every turn what others say" and "Labour to keep alive in your breast that Little spark of Celestial Fire called Conscience."

Some of these precepts, such as "In writing or Speaking, give to every Person his due title According to his Degree and the Custom of the Place," took on an additional dimension in the more egalitarian society that emerged with the revolution because they expressed the conviction that courtesy in human affairs was not to be limited to re-lationships between aristocrats.

But at first the main importance of these guidelines was in helping Washington get through a difficult adolescence. The death of Wash-ington's father, Augustine, left the rearing of eleven-year-old George in the hands of his mother, Mary Ball Washington, Augustine's second wife, a woman with a formidable will. A playmate of Washington's recalled being "ten times more afraid" of Washington's mother than of his own parents, adding: "Whoever has seen the awe-inspiring air and manner so characteristic of the Father of his Country, will remember the mother as she appeared when the presiding genius of her well-ordered household, commanding and being obeyed."

However highly she valued discipline, Mary Ball Washington clearly placed less importance on the need for a formal education. Unlike his half brothers, whom their father sent abroad to England for schooling, George was kept at his father's homestead, Ferry Farm, where he had only cursory schooling, even more limited than that received by two of his famously underprivileged successors, Andrew Jackson and Abraham Lincoln.

Young George learned enough about math and science so that he could pursue the surveying trade that became his first vocation, and he developed an impressive handwriting. But he knew little of the classics, and his spelling left much to be desired. Even as he matured and broadened his horizons, Washington remained conscious of the shortcomings of his boyhood education. When he returned to Mount Vernon after leading the colonies to victory in the revolution, he immediately retrieved his childhood notebooks and set about correcting his spelling and grammar. More important, his anxieties about his education may have contributed to his reticence to enter into formal political discourse, a limitation that in the eyes of some of his admirers became a virtue. When he remained silent after being profusely praised by the Virginia assembly for his military exploits, the Speaker of the House graciously told him: "Sit down, Mr. Washington, your modesty equals your valor, and that surpassed the power of any language that I possess."

Commending Washington's eagerness to enhance his education, Lord Fairfax, a neighbor, who gave the sixteen-year-old Washington his first surveying job, reported to his mother that "he will go to school all his life." But he added less sanguinely, "I wish I could say he governs his temper," touching on a fault of Washington's that would be evident throughout his career.

Early on, Washington showed a tendency to flare up at unjust criticism. And there was not much criticism that he did not regard as unjust. After serving four years on Washington's staff, Alexander Hamilton wrote that his commander was remarkable neither "for delicacy nor for good temper."

"I think he feels those things more than any person I ever yet met with," Jefferson wrote of Washington's reaction to the abuse inflicted upon him by Philip Freneau and other Republican journalists during his presidency. But the same hotheadedness that took and gave offense too readily was linked to the physical courage and forcefulness that contributed to his greatness. While Washington never completely conquered the fierce side of his nature, he controlled it enough so that it helped him in leading other men. During one skirmish in the French and Indian Wars, when troops under his command had by mistake begun volleying at each other, the young officer stepped between their weapons and parried them aside with his sword. Word of that episode swept through the colonies and became part of the growing Washington legend.

It was that reputation that made the choice of Washington as commander in chief of the colonial armies in 1775 all but inevitable. More than his skill as a tactician, which he really had only limited opportunity to demonstrate, that reputation rested on qualities of character—his bravery, as when he halted the "friendly fire" of his own troops against each other, and his forceful leadership. As one of his officers later wrote him: "You took us under your tuition and trained us up in the practice of that discipline which alone can constitute good troops."

When he accepted his commission as commander in chief, Washington declared that if "some unlucky event should happen unfavorable to my reputation, I beg it may be remembered by every gentleman in the room, that I this day declare . . . that I do not think myself equal to the command I am honored with." While such modesty was one of the hallmarks of Washington's character, in this case he had much to be modest about. His battlefield experience was confined to relatively minor skirmishes, a background that gave him little sense of the overall strategy of war. His limitations showed up early in the war. At Brooklyn Heights, he left his flank unprotected, then rushed reinforcements he could ill afford to spare into an already lost cause. But fortunately for him, and for the cause of independence, he was up against a British officer, in the person of General William Howe, who lacked the skill to exploit Washington's weaknesses.

"Any other General in the world other than General Howe would have beaten General Washington," a British strategist later remarked, adding, "And any other General in the world than General

Washington would have beaten General Howe." It took most of the war for Washington to gain the battlefield experience commensurate with the responsibilities he bore as commander in chief.

In the face of adversity, a sardonic wit flashed. Told that Robert Morris, who labored long and hard to raise money to finance the revolution, had his hands full, Washington retorted: "I wish he had his pockets full." When Washington moved away from a flaring fireplace blaze at his headquarters, one of his generals remarked that a general should be able to stand fire. Washington shot back that it did not seem appropriate for a general to receive it from behind.

When confronting the early setbacks to the colonial cause, Washington's self-confidence stood him in good stead, giving him the strength to gamble. On Christmas night of 1776, with the specter of defeat eroding the morale of his troops and slowing the arrival of the new recruits he desperately needed, he stormed across the Delaware River and routed the besotted Hessian garrison at Trenton. A week later, when the British sent a superior force to retake Trenton, the Americans retreated and then struck at the British rear at Princeton with Washington mounted on his horse, leading the way. "Parade with me, my brave fellows," he called. And then, as the British lines broke, leading his charging men forward to claim their victory, he shouted triumphantly, "It is a fine fox chase, my boys!"

Many other battles followed before the final decisive action at Yorktown in 1783, and not all were victories for the American cause. In fact, during the course of the conflict, Washington lost more battles than he won—achieving victory in only three major engagements while suffering defeat in six.

One of his darkest moments came in 1778, when, having finally caught up with the retreating British at Monmouth Courthouse in New Jersey, he dispatched the immodest Charles Lee to head the first wave. But Lee, a far better talker than fighter, withdrew in the face of an enemy he claimed to be superior in numbers. That was not Washington's estimate of the situation. Bearing down on Lee, he swore at him by the account of one of the American troops "till the leaves shook the trees." Then, dismissing the hapless Lee, who was subsequently court-martialed and removed from active command, Washington channeled the energy generated by his outburst to good use. Taking command himself, turned a dismal rout into a respectable draw. He "seemed to arrest fortune with one glance," Lafayette claimed. "By his own presence he brought order out of confusion, animated his troops and led them to success," Hamilton reported.

But more important than any individual skirmish was that Washington had developed a blueprint for victory—the only strategy that could possibly win for the Americans. He summed up this concept himself in 1778, when he realized that he had fought the British to a stalemate. His army had been forced out of its supposed stronghold in New York by the British. But the British, having taken over the city, found themselves unable to seize and hold the initiative or to cause serious damage to Washington's army.

"It is not a little pleasing nor less wonderful to contemplate," he wrote one of his generals, "that after two years maneuvering both armies are brought back to the very point they set out from. And that which was the offending party in the beginning is now reduced to the use of the spade and pickaxe for defense."

This insight was not easy to come by, nor was the strategy derived from it easy to execute. For Washington, this meant that he had to set aside the dreams of conquest natural to any general and, instead, content himself with survival. Given the material advantages possessed by the British, there was no other course. Not for Washington was there the possibility of winning a major clash that would crush the enemy—not until the war's climax, when he had the French support that made victory inevitable. But to gain that support Washington had to set aside the pride and conceit natural to his profession and wage the guerrilla combat of the underdog. Only in this fashion could he take advantage of the British deficits—the high cost and rising unpopularity of a war waged thousands of miles from their home over a treacherous and unfamiliar terrain.

It was the sort of war Washington's successors in command of the U.S. military would wage nearly two full centuries later in Indochina from the opposite side of the fence. Washington's strategy meant setting aside the chances of short-term successes for the sake of a long-range victory. Once again, it was a course made possible by his own strength and confidence—the same qualities that he would summon to aid him in his next assignment as president.

But before shouldering those responsibilities, Washington would play a vital part in the creation of that office and the constitution as leader of the Philadelphia convention.

As much reluctance as he felt about leaving the comforts of Mount Vernon, where he had retired only three years before, wreathed with the laurels of the victory over the British, the condition of the new country he had helped create made Washington's participation in the convention all but inevitable.

"The crisis is arrived," the preamble to the credentials of the Virginia delegates asserted. The time had come for "the good people of America" to decide whether they would "reap the just fruits of that Independence which they have so gloriously acquired . . . or whether by giving way to unmanly jealousies and prejudices . . . they will . . . furnish our Enemies with cause to triumph." The evidence to support this jeremiad abounded on all sides. With the burden of the war debt still pressing heavily, the economic and political chaos that prevailed under the Articles of Confederation mocked attempts at recovery.

As it had during the war, Congress attempted to solicit money from the states, in effect, begging for assistance. But in response to a request for $3 million, the Congress received a pittance of $100,000. A brief notice in the *New York Packet* on October 1, 1787, illustrated the miserly response of the states to the congressional pleas for help: "The subscriber has received nothing on account of the quota of this State for the present year."

If the delegates needed any further reminder of the impoverishment of the present regime, it came when Benjamin Franklin proposed that a chaplain be invited to open the convention every morning with prayers. "God governs in the affairs of men," Franklin argued. "And if a sparrow cannot fall to the ground without his notice, is it possible than an empire can rise without his aid?" This appeal to religion was particularly striking coming from Franklin, the famous skeptic. But what made it more depressing was that as Franklin was then informed, the convention had no money to pay a chaplain to conduct the prayer.

As congressional prestige shrank, John Hancock, of the famously bold signature on the Declaration of Independence, who had been elected president of Congress in 1785, did not trouble himself to come to New York to attend its sessions. And some states abandoned the idea of sending delegates to the convention Congress had called.

The governments of the states, for all their jealousy of each other and their insistence on the sovereign powers granted them in the confederation, found their own credit failing. They issued paper money, but outside their own borders, it was scarcely worth the paper it was printed on. Despite their poverty, nine states maintained their own navies, each seeking to guard its own interests against threats from its neighbors. Squeezed between Philadelphia and New York, New Jersey was like "a cask tapped at both ends," James Madison of the Virginia delegation wrote. North Carolina, pressured by Virginia at one border and South Carolina at the other, resembled "a patient bleeding at both arms." And Massachusetts, cradle of continental liberty, had to raise a special army to put down an armed band of debtors, led by Daniel Shays, rebelling against the state's tax collectors.

Particularly ominous was the threat from foreign powers, well aware of the enfeeblement of the nascent government in the New World. France, which still controlled Louisiana, denied navigation of the Mississippi River to the Americans. As for the rejected mother country, Great Britain, her troops still held vantage points in the West, from which they harassed American traders and settlers. And all this in four short years since the colonies had won their freedom and independence.

No wonder that in November 1786, Washington wrote to Madison: "No morn ever dawned more favorably than ours did, and no day was ever more clouded than the present." The root cause of the country's difficulties, Washington had come to believe, lay with the system of government. "That the Federal government is nearly if not quite at a stand, none will deny," he wrote to another Revolutionary comrade. "The first question then is, shall it be annihilated or supported?"

It was to help find an answer to that question that Washington had come to Philadelphia this hot summer. At the convention, Washington had little to say. His duties as presiding officer did not involve him in significant controversy. But his simple presence was to exercise a powerful impact on the proceedings as the delegates sought to confront a fundamental dilemma that was linked to the past and clouded the future of the young country.

On the one hand, it was plain to everyone that the Articles of Confederation were a feeble structure for dealing with America's needs and challenges both at home and abroad. On the other hand, Americans feared that by creating a strong governing structure, they would run the risk of suffering the same sort of oppression they had just waged a long and bloody war to overturn. This conflict dominated both the secret discussions at the convention and the prolonged public debate that preceded and followed ratification and colored the drafting of nearly every aspect of the proposed constitution.

But as wide-ranging as this controversy was, there was one particular feature of the new country's charter that inevitably aroused the greatest heat and intensity in this dispute, and this of course was the nature of the executive. As bold as the Virginians had been in propounding their fifteen resolves for the new government, there were some risks they were not prepared to take. Thus, Resolve 7 simply proposed "that a national executive be instituted," leaving open for the time the critical question of whether this office would be filled by a single person, awakening fears of a return to monarchy, or by a committee, which stirred anxiety about a continuation of the present chaos.

It was this point that soon became the focus of debate. Roger Sherman of Connecticut, making the case against the single executive, argued that in reality the executive was "nothing more than an institution for carrying the will of the legislature into effect." To create a sole executive would contravene that role and serve—here he used a term repeated time and again by the foes of a single executive—as "the foetus of monarchy."

But Pennsylvania's Charles Wilson, his patriotism attested to by his signature on the Declaration of Independence, his intellect trained at Edinburgh and Saint Andrew's Universities in his native Scotland and honed by the practice of law in his adopted land, counterattacked with great force and effectiveness. Far from leading to monarchy, Wilson argued, a single executive, because of its strength, would be the best bulwark against royal domination or any form of tyranny. And striking at the foundation of his opponents' case—the worry that the British system would be replicated in America simply because Britain was the mother country—he pointed to the differences between the two countries. It was true, Wilson conceded, that the size of the new land would require "the vigor of a monarchy." But it was safe to believe that a single executive would not drift into that royal path because in this new country "the manners are against a king and are purely Republican."

And so the argument raged. In the end, the single executive won out for two reasons. One was Madison's plan for pitting the branches of the new government against each other to ward off tyranny, thus imposing restrictions upon the government whose full significance would only become apparent in generations to come. The other reassurance was more concrete. It was provided by the knowledge that Washington himself would be the first to exercise whatever authority would be granted to the executive and the expectation that he could be counted on to establish a tradition of restraint that his successors would be hard-pressed not to follow.

If this point needed underlining, this was accomplished by Benjamin Franklin, who introduced a lengthy paper arguing that the executive not be paid. "There are two passions which have a powerful influence on the affairs of men," Franklin argued. "These are ambition and avarice, the love of power and the love of money." Salaries, no matter how modest to start, would soon be increased. And the fat salaries would bring about that dreaded consequence—a monarchy. And here Franklin made what he hoped to be his strongest case by referring to a figure who was very much present in the proceedings as president of the convention and very much on the minds of the delegates. If anyone thought, Franklin argued, that it was unrealistic to believe qualified men would take on the responsibilities of the executive without pay, let him remember that the country had seen "the greatest and most important of our offices, that of General of our armies, executed for eight years together without the smallest salary, by a patriot whom I will not now offend by any other praise."

As for Franklin's proposal, it was, as Madison dryly observed, "treated with great respect, but rather for the author of it than from any apparent conviction of its expedience or practicality" and duly tabled. But even if he lost the ostensible purpose of his resolution, by introducing it Franklin had accomplished a far more important objective—he had reminded the delegates that no matter what the executive was paid, the job would be carried out by the one man in the new nation whom they completely trusted.

By the time the convention adjourned, it had laid the basis for the personal presidency by not only creating a single executive but also by establishing a direct link between that executive and the citizenry who would elect the president—for the President would be chosen not by the Congress, as the Virginia resolves initially recommended, but by electors, who, as it turned out, would be chosen by popular vote. So it was that Washington's prestige made possible the first demonstration of the power of a president's character—even before he became president. As Pierce Butler of South Carolina wrote, the delegates were inspired to grant "full great" powers to the nation's chief executive by the reputation of the man who would take over that office.

That reputation, of course, also assured Washington election to the office that had been designed with him in mind, despite his deep-seated resistance to taking on that responsibility. "You must be president, no other man can fill that office," Gouverneur Morris wrote him in urging him to accept the presidency. "No other man can draw forth the abilities of our country into the various departments of civil life. You and you alone can awe the insolence of opposing factions." Colonel Henry Lee joined the chorus of prodders. "Without you the government can have but little chance of success and the people of that happiness which its prosperity must yield." And Hamilton argued in effect that Washington needed to accept the presidency to keep faith with the revolutionary cause that had led to the creation of the new government. "You will permit me to say that it is indispensable you should lend yourself to its first operations," he told his once and future chief. "It is to little purpose to have introduced a system if the weightiest influence is not given to its firm establishment in the outset."

Unanimously selected to be the nation's first president, Washington's prime objective goal was much the same as it had been as its first commander in chief—to endure. Washington won the Revolutionary War by outlasting the British, gambling successfully on the belief that time was on the side of the colonists. Similarly, his objective as president was to outlast the range of perils and pitfalls that confronted the young country that might have destroyed it in infancy. It was Thomas Jefferson who summed up the goal. "If the President can be preserved for few more years, till habits of authority and obedience can be established," he wrote, "we have nothing to fear." When Washington left office after eight years, it could hardly be said that there was "nothing to fear." But during his tenure, he had provided the time for physical and psychological growth that allowed the nation the chance to compete in a dangerous world.

His temper continued to plague him at times, particularly when he had to contend with the Madisonian limitations on his authority. Taking to heart the constitutional rule that the president's treaty-making power required "the advise and consent" of the Senate, prior to negotiating an accord with the Creek Indians, Washington paid a call on the Senate. The resultant episode, as described by Senator Maclay of Pennsylvania, would have been suitable for a Marx brothers film.

As Vice President John Adams read the proposals the government intended to make to the Creeks, his words were all but drowned out by the rumble of carriage wheels from the street outside. "Such a noise!" Maclay complained. "I could tell it was something about Indians, but was not the master of one sentence of it."

Closing the windows made the chamber quieter, but other problems arose. The senators fell into a rambling palaver about the proposal, during which one of their number asked to see documentation. That was about all Washington could take.

"This defeats every purpose of my coming here," he thundered and stormed out of the room in a "violent fret."

He returned subsequently, "placid and serene," to finish up. But left muttering that he would "be damned if he ever went there again."

He never did. And his predecessors have all concluded that they would receive the Senate's advice from a distance or on their own home ground in the White House.

As Washington's first term drew to a close, Hamilton and Jefferson, the men who had been his two chief lieutenants and who had led a bitter dispute over the course of the nation's future, were at each other's throats. It seemed that they could agree on only one thing—the necessity for Washington's staying in office.

Hamilton told Washington there were some figures of such "eminence" that society had a right to "control" their destinies by insisting on their serving the public interest. Jefferson put the situation more trenchantly: "North and South will hang together if they have you to hang on."

But it was Eliza Powell, wife of a prominent Philadelphia merchant and politician, who argued the case more fervently—and personally—than either of them. She warned Washington that it was wrong for him to consider "quitting a trust upon the proper execution of which the repose of millions might be eventually depending." Washington, Powell declared, "was the only man in America that dares to do right on public occasions. You have shown that you are not to be intoxicated by power or misled by flattery." In an elegant tribute to Washington's self-control, she told him: "You have frequently demonstrated that you possess an empire over yourself. For God's sake, do not yield that empire to a love of ease."

So far as is known, Washington made no direct response about his intentions to Eliza Powell or to anyone else. And as Richard Norton Smith notes in his absorbing biography, and as Washington certainly realized would happen, "The country took his silence for consent."

Washington's second term severely tested his firmness and restraint. At home, Pennsylvania farmers rose in armed rebellion against the federal tax on whiskey that Treasury Secretary Hamilton had pushed through Congress. To save themselves the trouble and expense of shipping the corn and rye they raised long distances, the farmers instead distilled much of the grain they raised into liquor, and the tax hit them hard.

When 7,000 rebels massed in protest under their own banner, hard-liner Hamilton urged a call-up of the militia to quell the so-called Whiskey Rebellion. "The very existence of Government demands this course," he told Washington. Edmund Randolph, who had replaced Jefferson as Washington's secretary of state in his second term, recommended that all-purpose political cure—creation of a commission to study the problem.

Washington, the old war horse, was surely tempted to crush the rebellion out of hand. But given the widespread resentment of the whiskey tax, Pennsylvania's governor doubted that the state's militia would follow orders to suppress the rebels. And even if they did, Washington had to ponder the consequences of American troops shooting down their own citizens engaged in a tax protest little more than a decade after the successful conclusion of a war largely inspired by that same grievance. However, Randolph's proposal smacked of temporizing and buck-passing—and would be taken a sign of weakness that would only inflame the challenge to federal authority.

Washington took a middle course. He mobilized an army of 12,000 from states bordering on the rebellious area and sent three emissaries to the scene, including his attorney general, William Bradford, to negotiate a settlement. Washington, Bradford explained, intended to convince these people and the world of the "moderation and the firmness" of the government he headed. The rebels took the point, the more so since Washington was in no hurry to deploy his force against them, giving them time to ponder their own predicament, invariably a potent weapon against political discontent.

Although united in their opposition to the tax, the farmers were divided over how to respond to Washington and Bradford. A meeting of their leaders concluded with a majority vote for submitting to the federal will. Washington dispatched his troops to sweep up the dissenting minority. About 150 were arrested, and twenty were indicted. Two were convicted of treason but pardoned by Washington. Instead of rending the Republic, the Whiskey Rebellion came to a conclusion that affirmed the new country's existence.

The tensions of international affairs created the final crisis of Washington's presidency and demonstrated once again the potency of Madison's checks and balances. Dispatched by Washington to negotiate America's postwar differences with Britain, John Jay returned early in 1795 with a treaty in which Britain agreed to give up its forts in the Northwest Territory but maintained the right to restrict U.S. trade during Britain's war with France. To rub this humiliation in deeper, the treaty prohibited American ships from carrying such staples as cotton, coffee, and molasses to any foreign port. Washington got the agreement through the Senate by the barest of margins but then ran into trouble in the House of Representatives, dominated by leaders of Jefferson's newly founded party, first called the Republicans but later the Democrats, who were bitter foes of Washington's Federalist regime. Asked to appropriate funds to implement the pact, the House rebelled, demanding to see all the documents related to Jay's mission.

Washington declared this to be a usurpation of powers under the Constitution, which gives the Senate, not the House, sole authority to ratify treaties. Nevertheless, he moderated his response to suit the realities of the partisan predicament he had helped to create. "I trust that no part of my conduct has ever indicated a disposition to withhold any information which the Constitution has enjoined upon the President as a duty to give," he told the House. Still, he reminded the lawmakers, diplomacy required confidentiality and prudence; giving in to the demand for documents would set a dangerous precedent. Besides, he argued artfully, it was hard to see what the point of such a disclosure as that sought for by the House would be, except to undertake impeachment, a step not mentioned in the resolution seeking the documents.

Washington of course knew that just the very mention of that drastic remedy would be enough to throw into confusion the opposition leaders in the House, who had feared the wrath of the public if the idea got across that they were intending to move against the Father of the Country.* Finally, Washington assumed his favorite and most potent stance—that of a dutiful and conscientious public servant. "A Just regard to the Constitution and to the duty of my Office, under all the circumstances of this case, forbids a compliance with your request," he said.

---

*This timidity about impeaching the first president exhibited by the 4th Congress was also displayed by the 105th Congress, 203 years later when it faced the possibility of impeaching the 42nd president.

Even so, the Republicans seemed to hold the upper hand, and Madison himself predicted victory by twenty votes. It took heroic efforts to turn the tide in favor of the treaty. The Federalists organized a grassroots campaign of support, exploiting their chief asset, Washington's popularity. Their great orator, Fisher Ames, made an impassioned argument for the treaty, leaving his supposed deathbed to do so and somehow managing to survive for a dozen more years. Finally, on the day of the vote, the Republicans' own Speaker of the House, Frederick Muhlenberg, cast his vote for the treaty and helped it to carry by a 51-48 vote, a deed for which his brother-in-law subsequently stabbed him in the chest.

Afterward, Jefferson acknowledged that, given his prestige, Washington was an immovable political force. As long as he remained as president, "Republicanism must lie on its oars, resign the vessel to its pilot and themselves hew to the course he thinks best."

Washington drew his own lesson from the experience, on evaluating the weight of public opinion. He would always try to go along with public sentiment, he said, though he added that "it is on great occasions only and after time has been given for cool and deliberate reflection that the real voice of the people can be known." The problem, he later wrote Jay, voicing a discontent that his predecessors would echo time and again over the next two centuries, was with the seeds of dissension sowed by the opposition press. "To this source all our discontents may be traced and from it our embarrassments proceed."

Probably, Washington's most enduring contributions to his country were also demonstrations of his self-discipline—his willingness to accept a second term at a time when every fiber of his being ached to return to Mount Vernon and his insistence on leaving office after that term concluded, at a moment when a grateful citizenry would have kept him in the presidency for the rest of his life. By staying on for his second tour of duty, Washington managed to hold the country together at a time when its political leadership was bitterly divided by conflicts at home and abroad. By leaving as he did, Washington prevented the damage that might have resulted from his staying on—the rise of monarchical sentiment or the spread of the belief that he or anyone else was an indispensable man.

Washington made up his mind to call it quits with as little fanfare as when he had decided to stay on for a second term. He made clear his intentions in May 1796 when he asked Hamilton to revise the speech announcing his intention not to seek a second term that

Madison had drafted four years before. The finished work was published four months later in September.

Not surprisingly, the speech touched on what had been the central purpose of his presidency—the determination to endure and thus assure the survival of the country. "Time and habit are at least as necessary to fix the true character of government as of other human institutions," Washington declared. That was no casual thought. It was a belief that had impelled him to give the his country eight more years of himself.

The preservation of the nationhood so dearly won required, Washington stressed, maintaining a healthy distance from the snares of the Old World. "Our true policy must be to steer clear of permanent alliances," Washington warned, in the best-remembered and most misquoted and misunderstood phrase of his speech. The more graphic expression, "entangling alliances," regularly attributed to him was actually used by Jefferson in his Inaugural Address in 1801. And generally overlooked in the zeal of latter-day isolationists to justify their own uncompromising beliefs was Washington's willingness to accept "temporary alliances for extraordinary emergencies."

The peroration of Washington's most celebrated public utterance included a characteristically modest point. "Though in reviewing the incidents of my Administration I am unconscious of intentional error, I am nevertheless too sensible of my defects not to think it probable that I may have committed many errors. Whatever they may be I fervently beseech the Almighty to avert or mitigate the evils to which they may tend."

But to many minds, the chief danger for the Republic was not in whatever harm Washington might have done but in what damage might be committed by his successors in an office that had been created in his unique image. Fearful that the bestowal of power on the president, because it had been made with Washington in mind, had been overly generous, Pierce Butler worried "that the Man, who by his Patriotism and Virtue Contributed largely to the Emancipation of his Country, may be the Innocent means of its being, when He is lay'd low, oppress'd."

3

"A VAPOR OF DUPLICITY"

SOME SLEPT SPRAWLED ON THE FLOOR, wrapped in their greatcoats. Others slouched in their chairs, waiting for the next roll call. The balloting had gone on for four days, and no one present could say the end was in sight. What they shared besides exhaustion was bewilderment at their being there.

The calendar showed the month to be February, the year 1801. The setting was the House of Representatives of the United States of America. And these bedraggled figures were lame-duck legislators, most of them of the Federalist persuasion, who had been turned out of office the preceding November in a great victory for Thomas Jefferson and his new Republican Party.

The conflict between the Federalists, led by Hamilton, and Jefferson's Republicans, the first great political argument in American history, was shaped by two disparate visions of the nation's future. Hamilton's view rested on the imperative of economic development. He believed in a powerful central government whose main purpose should be to foster the growth of commercial and industry with a structure of banking and credit along the lines of what had been established in Great Britain. Hamilton had little faith in democratic institutions or in the wisdom of the masses. "The people," he once said, "is a great beast." The key to Hamilton's hopes for the country was the nation's economic elite, whom he counted on to bolster the national government in order to advance their own interest.

Jefferson, by contrast, believed that the best hope for development lay with the farms, not the factories. He considered the "immensity of land" to be the country's chief resource. And he thought that through their productivity, the nation's yeoman farmers could create national well-being by shipping their crops abroad in exchange "for finer manufactures than they are able to execute themselves." In further stark contrast to Hamilton, Jefferson professed faith in the judgment of the citizenry to guide the ship of state. Proclaiming his trust in the people, he demanded strict adherence to the Constitution, a government framework that he called "the wisest ever presented," to protect individual liberties, and he supported the rights of the states against the rising power of the national government. To Thomas Jefferson, the greatest threat to the national welfare was posed by the privileged class striving to promote its own selfish interests, just the force that Alexander Hamilton relied on to achieve his dream for the country.

The tensions between these two factions had been sharpened and institutionalized during Washington's second term by the war between Britain and revolutionary France, leading to the emergence of the first political parties, the Federalists and the Republicans. The Federalists urged stronger ties with the mother country, whose institutions they regarded as a model for the economic pattern they envisaged for their own country. The Republicans sympathized with the new government in France, whose avowed principles they saw as consonant with their own ideals.

Aided by Washington's prestige, the Federalist candidate John Adams won the election of 1796, with Republican Jefferson as his vice president. A man of great energy and integrity, Adams had been one of the champions of independence, but he lacked grounding in politics, and his abrasive, introspective personality was totally unsuited for that profession. Adams quarreled not only with others but also with himself, forever subjecting his decisions to self-scrutiny. "Oh that I could wear out of my mind every mean and base affectation, conquer my natural Pride and Self Conceit ... acquire that meekness and humility which are the sure marks and characters of a generous soul," he lamented. With his troubled and troublesome nature, Adams was no match for the deep divisions within the country or for the guile of Hamilton within his own party. And in the election of 1800, the country turned to Jefferson and his Republicans.

But now it appeared that as a result of a quirk in the Constitution, that triumph might be snatched from Jefferson's grasp with disastrous consequences for the republic that had just chosen him as its leader. With all the debate over the manner of election of the president, the framers of the Constitution had neglected to separate the balloting for that office from the voting for vice president. As a consequence, a deadlock had developed, not between Jefferson and John Adams, the incumbent president and bitter Federalist foe, who had finished well behind Jefferson, with only sixty-five votes to the victor's total of seventy-three, but rather between Jefferson and his running mate, Aaron Burr.

As far as the apparently triumphant Republicans were concerned, there was little doubt that between those two, Jefferson and Burr, their first choice was Thomas Jefferson. Indeed, for many, Burr would not even be first choice for vice president. He had been selected for the ticket, not without reluctance, in the forerunner of many such arrangements for the vice presidency because of his influence in his native New York.

Nevertheless, to avoid the possibility of a deadlock, the Republicans had tried to arrange with their electors in two or three states to give one vote less to Burr than to Jefferson. But these plans had fallen through. It was clear, nevertheless, that Burr had no intention himself of making any move that would ease Jefferson's path to power. He was content to allow the deadlock to remain, hoping for the best for himself. And finally and most important, it was equally clear that the Federalists, bitter and intransigent in defeat and in control of the lame-duck House where the deadlock would be broken, were determined to undo the work of the electorate and deny the presidency to Jefferson.

"We do not see what is to be the end of the present difficulty," Jefferson wrote in the midst of the deadlock. He feared the Federalists would sidestep the prescribed election in the House and instead pass a statute installing one of their leaders, either the chief justice, John Jay, or the secretary of state and future chief justice, John Marshall, at the head of the government. Their objective, Jefferson calculated, was to hold another election in a year or so, meanwhile retaining control over the federal government. The government, as Jefferson analogized, would be "in the situation of a clock or watch run

down." And for this, the only solution was for the Republican leaders to play the part of political watchmakers, convene a brand new
convention, and repair the defects of the Constitution.

Fortunately for Jefferson, and for the country, he and his cohorts
did not have to follow such a risky and controversial course. The
man who saved Jefferson and the country from the spiteful wrath of
the Federalists was none other than Jefferson's own most dedicated
enemy, Alexander Hamilton. He acted not out of friendship or even
admiration for Jefferson but out of contempt for Jefferson's rival,
Burr, and probably out of concern for the welfare of the country.
Whatever his motives, Hamilton acted decisively. He wrote a letter
to Federal Representative James Bayard, in which he said of Jefferson, "His politics are tinctured with fanaticism . . . that he is crafty
and persevering in his objects . . . that he is not scrupulous about the
means of success nor very mindful of truth and that he is a con-
temptible hypocrite."

That hardly sounded like a recommendation for any position, certainly not the presidency. But it came to seem glowing praise by contrast with what Hamilton had to say to Bayard and others about
Burr. "He is in every sense a profligate; a voluptuary in the extreme
with uncommon habits of expense artful and intriguing to an incon-
ceivable degree . . . bankrupt beyond redemption except by the plun-
der of his country . . . as unprincipled and dangerous a man as any
country can boast."

In view of that indictment, Bayard was glad enough to abstain
from voting for Adams, thus allowing Maryland to cast its one vote
for Jefferson, breaking the deadlock and sending him to the President's House, as it was then called.

As Jefferson's election demonstrated, the significance of character
for the presidency did not diminish with Washington's tenure in that
office. To the contrary, just as the character issue dominated the
making of the president in 1800, presidential character continued to
guide presidential performance. Moreover, character has been a major force not only in influencing the course of individual presidencies
but also in shaping and reshaping the nature of the presidency itself.
These consequences were most evident during the presidencies of the
five chief executives who, from Washington's time to the creation of
the modern presidency by Franklin D. Roosevelt, had the greatest
impact on the destiny of the Republic—Jefferson, Jackson, Lincoln,
the Republican Roosevelt, and Woodrow Wilson.

Jefferson's character established the political style of presidential leadership. By bolstering his appeal to the mass electorate, Jackson's character reshaped the presidency into a far more democratic design than the Founding Fathers had imagined. Lincoln's character, dominated by his commitment to reason, helped him to save the union and give a new dimension to the political creed born with independence. As the nation entered the twentieth century, Theodore Roosevelt's gift for self-dramatization laid the foundation for the media presidency, and for America's new imperial role as a great power. Woodrow Wilson, the moralist who led the country into the Great War, sought to give that power a conscience and a global mission, the nature of which would divide his countrymen for generations to come. Moreover, these premodern chief executives demonstrated not only the potency of character but its potential for becoming a double-edged sword. For in all these presidencies, the greatest strengths of each man's character also turned out to be the source of his greatest vulnerability.

In the case of Jefferson, his character was to remain a riddle that hung over his presidency, as it does over history. If Jefferson deceived others, as Hamilton contended, it was because his personality led him to deceive himself. This duplicity stemmed from fundamental personal conflicts, between his yearning for privacy and his urge for power and recognition.

The death of Jefferson's father, a planter of comfortable circumstances, left the young man at the tender age of fourteen the head of a family that included, besides his mother, seven other children. This gave Jefferson responsibility without benefit of the maturity to exercise it, a predicament that his psychobiographer Fawn Brodie suggests may have contributed to his lifelong ambivalence toward power, "seeking it out and embracing it and then abandoning it for reasons his friends found inexplicable."

His contradictory nature was illustrated by his first important decisions as an adult. Yearning for privacy, he built a home, appropriately titled at first the Hermitage, and then Monticello, on a remote mountaintop, a site well-designed to shelter Jefferson's private self against the outside world. Nevertheless, the very next year, Jefferson entered the House of Burgesses, where he quickly gained a reputation as a wily and resourceful political operative. The conflict continued all his life. Even as he ascended in the turbulent political world of prerevolutionary America, he expressed his urge to separate himself from the harsh give-and-take of the political arena. "There may be people to whose tempers and dispositions Contention may be pleasing, but to me it is of all states but one, the most horrid," he wrote to John Randolph. His desire, Jefferson wrote in 1775, just as he was emerging as a major political figure, was "to withdraw myself totally from the public stage and pass the rest of my days in domestic ease and tranquility, banishing every desire of afterwards even hearing what passes in the world."

In the same vein, when resigning as Washington's secretary of state after nearly four years, Jefferson wrote the president: "Multitudes can fill the office in which you have been pleased to place me. *I* therefore have no motive to consult but my own inclination, which is bent irresistibly on the tranquil enjoyment of my family, my farm and my books."

Yet despite such protestations of political disinterest, Jefferson connived with his fellow Virginian Madison to create the nation's first political party, the forerunner of today's Democratic Party, much of his activity going on while Jefferson was serving in the cabinet of Washington, to whose policies the new party was unalterably opposed. And after leaving the cabinet, he schemed continually, and ultimately successfully, to pave the way for himself and his allies to take the reins of power.

The impression of himself that Jefferson presented to the public was of a man whose motives and methods transcended the gritty reality of political strife. But some of his contemporaries saw contradictions that made them uneasy. "He did not always speak exactly as he felt," wrote the nineteenth-century statesman Charles Francis Adams. "As a consequence he has left hanging over a part of his public life a vapor of duplicity."

Jefferson's conflicted view of slavery highlighted the complexities of his nature. Although at times he seemed to take the position that slavery was morally incompatible with the goals of the American Revolution, all his life, like most of his Virginia compatriots, including Washington, he owned slaves and worked them on his plantation. In drafting the Declaration of Independence, Jefferson included one passage condemning King George for waging "cruel war against human nature itself" by establishing slavery in North America but also denounced the king for "exciting those very people [slaves] to rise in arms against us." In other words, he attacked the king both for fostering slavery and for trying to end it. No wonder Congress deleted the passage.

Of far broader impact in raising questions not only about Jefferson's attitude toward slavery but about other aspects of his character was the Sally Hemings scandal, which erupted in his second term as president. Jefferson's nemesis in this affair was James Thompson Callender, a journalistic hatchet man who began his career as a Jefferson acolyte, turning his venom against Jefferson's enemies, sometimes apparently with Jefferson's encouragement. After victimizing Alexander Hamilton by exposing his adulterous affair with a Philadelphia housewife whose husband was blackmailing Hamilton, Callender had then gone on to smear another Jefferson foe, President John Adams, as "the corrupt and despotic monarch of Braintree," in a pamphlet that Jefferson had helped subsidize.

But when Jefferson himself reached the White House and rejected Callender's demands for a postmaster's job, the infuriated scrivener subjected Jefferson to the same treatment he had meted out to Jefferson's foes. At first, Callender's attack was relatively restrained, though he made a point of claiming that Jefferson had praised his work and subsidized his efforts against Hamilton, Adams, and other Federalist targets, even Washington. Among those shocked and outraged by these disclosures was former first lady Abigail Adams, who had been a friend of Jefferson's despite the Virginian's political differences with her husband. "This, sir, I considered a personal injury," she wrote to Jefferson. "This was the Sword that cut asunder the Gordian knot, which could not be untied by all the efforts of party Spirit, by rivalship, by Jealousy or any other malignant fiend."

But Abigail Adams's attack was minor compared to the barrage of abuse Jefferson would face when Callender exploded the bombshell allegation that Jefferson had fathered several children by one of his slaves, a young woman named Sally Hemings. After noting that Hemings had traveled to France with Jefferson while he served as ambassador there, Callender asserted that Hemings's eldest son, a boy of ten or twelve, had features that were reputed "to bear a striking though sable resemblance to those of the president himself."

Jefferson's friends maintained that he had been celibate since his wife, Martha, had died twenty years before and denounced Callender. But numerous federal publications reported Callender's allegations, and some even resurrected a timeworn account of Jefferson's attempted seduction of a neighbor's wife, Betsey Walker. Jefferson maintained a stony silence that his foes seized upon as an admission of guilt. They took particular zest in their attacks because of the image Jefferson had fostered of himself as a man given to platonic feelings rather than physical passions. "It does appear somewhat odd," ventured the *Frederic-Town Herald*, that the "solemn, the grave and the didactic Mr. Jefferson, a philosopher and metaphysician whom the world might take to be a man whose blood is very snow-broth . . . that such a man should have lived in the habitual violation of the seventh commandment with one of his own slaves."

The abuse from both sides reached a crescendo when Chief Justice John Marshall, a bitter Jefferson adversary, told Callender how much he admired his paper, the *Richmond Recorder,* praise that Callender predictably reported. That led a pro-Jefferson editor to warn the slave-owning Marshall that his appreciation of the Sally Hemings story should be tempered by the supposed fact that "upon this point his character is not invulnerable."

With this in the background, the 1802 midterm election campaign between Jefferson's Republican Party, as it was still called, and the Federalist Party, which had backed Washington and then John Adams, earned the distinction of being the most slanderous in history. As Fawn Brodie points out, "The country had the spectacle of the Federalists accusing Jefferson of exposing Hamilton's affair with Mrs. Reynolds, the Republicans accusing Hamilton of exposing Jefferson's affair with Betsey Walker, and both parties respectively accusing Jefferson and John Marshall of having slave mistresses."

But the political damage from the fallout was diminished by the political weakness of the Federalists, who, as John Quincy Adams noted, had been "completely and irrevocably abandoned and rejected by the popular voice," and by the limited reach and credibility of the newspapers of the day.

Like a lot of other politicians targeted for character attacks, Jefferson's view of the press soured. In his Inaugural Address, he had proclaimed that the media should "stand undisturbed as monuments of the safety which error of opinion may be tolerated where reason is left free to combat it." But in the wake of the Callender attacks, he wrote: "Our newspapers for the most part, present only the caricatures of disaffected minds." The nation's third president, he was not the first to complain about the press—and he certainly would not be the last.

The most enduring impact of Jefferson's character on the presidency was in establishing a paradigm for deviousness and dissembling that most of his successors have been only too glad to follow. Jefferson helped to create a uniquely American approach to leadership, biographer Joseph Ellis writes sympathetically in *American Sphinx,* "based on the capacity to rest comfortably with contradictions."

"If you begin with the conviction that government is at best a necessary evil," Ellis argues, "then effective political leadership must be undirect and threatening." Certainly that is the way Jefferson played out his political hand. He came to office with a reputation, founded in the Declaration of Independence and sundry other artifacts of his pen, for suspicion and mistrust of government. Yet once inaugurated, he did not hesitate to exploit the full potential of government and political power in ways that even his Federalist foes, whose support for a strong central government he had often denounced, had never attempted.

Jefferson's character allowed him to rationalize his betrayal of his previously deeply held beliefs by claiming that his expediencies served some greater good. Brushing aside the need for a debate on the constitutional issues that would have explored such vital questions as the status of slavery in the new territory, he pushed through the Louisiana Purchase. This departure from his own convictions he justified on the grounds that this expansion would allow the country to fulfill what Jefferson believed to be its future—westward expansion.

In 1807, when Britain and Napoleonic France were fighting for survival, Jefferson prodded Congress to close all American ports to trade with either of the European powers, on the theory that this would ultimately teach Europe's two warring giants a lesson—an illusion that was harmful to the economic and political well-being of his country and his presidency. Moreover, the enforcement of the embargo, which Jefferson prodded Congress into enacting, required the sort of coercive role by the federal government that contravened Jefferson's own convictions about individual freedom. But the embargo was based on another of Jefferson's visions—the moralist belief that America could remain true to its destiny only by breaking all ties with the intrinsically evil nations of the Old World.

Other biographers attribute Jefferson's inconsistencies to a "disjunction" in his thinking, which inclined him to separate generalizations from the specific, the long range from the short, broad principles from their concrete realization. Thus, even though he had railed against the economic infrastructure Hamilton had established during the Federalist presidencies, once in power, Jefferson concluded that they could not be readily overturned.

Americans have always feared and resented the idea of a government strong and efficient enough to intervene in their lives and at the
same time have valued the benefits government brings to them. The
tension between these two widely held attitudes—aversion to government and dependence on it—is the fundamental challenge that
faces every president. Jefferson's response to this dilemma was to
contradict his own beliefs when the need arose. And while Jefferson
may have been able to "rest comfortably" with this tension, the "vapor of duplicity" that he generated and that his successors mimicked
made it hard to enforce the claims of accountability inherent in the
political system Jefferson helped to design.

The tenures of Jefferson's immediate successors in the presidency reflected the combined impact of character and circumstance on presidential performance. James Madison had been a brilliant collaborator
with Jefferson while operating in his shadow. At five feet six inches
tall, he was small enough, as one chronicler of the times put it, "so as
not to excite the suspicion of men that he would be in competition
with them for anything." But his shyness and diffidence handicapped
him in the spotlight of the presidency, particularly so in contending
with the divisive impact of the War of 1812. Owing his presidency to
Jefferson's patronage and the backing of the powerful Republican
caucus in Congress, Madison lacked the personal dynamism required
to win him public support and establish his own political identity.

Madison's presidency also demonstrated how his own plan for pitting the branches of the government against each other would challenge the intellect and character of every chief executive through the
centuries. Hamstrung by the clash of authority and ambition he himself had ordained, indignant that a rebellious Congress would not let
him shape his own cabinet, he complained to his old collaborator,
Jefferson, that the Congress had become "unhinged."

Although he possessed neither Madison's intellectual energy nor
Jefferson's imagination, James Monroe nevertheless got by in outwardly tranquil times by relying on his stolid nature and statesmanlike demeanor to promote the impression of stability. Despite the
friction created by having three cabinet secretaries serving throughout his terms, all of whom wanted to succeed him, Monroe kept his
balance, trying equally hard neither to speak evil nor even to see it.
"He rather turns his eyes from misconduct," one of the three rivals,
secretary of state John Quincy Adams, observed. "And betrays a
sensation of pain when it is presented to him."

Monroe left the doctrine bearing his name, designed to shelter the young country from European intrusion, as a legacy to U.S. foreign policy. But the "era of good feeling" he had generated concluded abruptly with his presidency. As voting barriers toppled for white males and political parties sharpened their partisan claws, the electorate was swept by a tide of social and economic ferment. Riding its crest was the cantankerous figure who would become seventh president of the United States, Andrew Jackson.

Just as Jefferson's personality defined his leadership style, Andrew Jackson's character helped him forge a political base among the masses of voters drawn to his populist vision. Jackson's character was shaped by a series of personal tragedies from birth to maturity that would have been enough to shatter most individuals. But Jackson drew energy from these traumas, which gave his life a dual purpose. Seeing both himself and his reputation as always threatened, an embattled Jackson set out to destroy his enemies before they destroyed him. Moreover, he viewed every conflict, public or private, as an opportunity to vindicate himself. The consequence was to personalize the presidency more profoundly than had ever occurred even under Washington.

This personalization reached its apotheosis in the greatest battle of Jackson's presidency, against the Bank of the United States. With his health wrecked by the struggle, Jackson nevertheless told his closest adviser and future vice president, Martin Van Buren: "The bank, Mr. Van Buren is trying to kill me. But I will kill it."

The wounds that scarred Andrew Jackson began with his childhood in the isolation of Carolinas backcountry, where an Indian attack always threatened. His father died two months before Jackson was born in 1767, "fighting an uphill battle against poverty and adversity as no one in our generation would comprehend," or so Jackson claimed years later. Whatever the evidence for this dramatic assertion, it certainly reflected the son's view of life.

Jackson's mother, Elizabeth, was then forced to take up residence in the home of her sister, where Jackson grew up a rebellious youth who spurned formal education and devoted himself to the rigors of outdoor sports. A militiaman in the colonial army at fourteen, Jackson was taken prisoner by the British along with his older brother, Robert. The young men were released, but Robert died almost immediately of smallpox, contracted in the British prison where Andrew was also stricken. His mother, though, left his side to minister to two of her sister's children, who were also ill and in a British prison, a mission that claimed her life. Andrew had to confront his sense of loss at the death of his mother, who had been the sole beacon of stability and morality in his disordered existence.

Setting out to make his way in the world, Jackson tried his hand at the law, rising to a judgeship; in politics, where he won election to the U.S. Senate; and in the military, where he made himself a national hero as the victor of the Battle of New Orleans against the British. But as important to him as these tangible rewards of success was his unrelenting battle to defend his honor and reputation against slurs real and imagined, a struggle often waged with dueling pistols against those he believed had slandered him.

To Jackson's mind, slander was a worse offense than murder. "The murderer only takes the life of the parent and leaves his character as a goodly heritage to his children," he once wrote, "whilst the slanderer takes away his good reputation and leaves him a living monument to his children's disgrace."

The worst slander of all that Jackson had to endure resulted from his romance with Rachel Donelson, whom he married twice, the second time after the couple learned that Rachel's divorce from her first husband had not been final when she and Jackson were originally wed. In marrying Rachel Donelson, Jackson took a mate he was devoted to all his life, but he also assumed a burden that would add to the self-doubt and bitterness that had marked his life since childhood and would come to a head in his presidency.

Jackson's election to the White House in 1828 was preceded by his defeat in 1824, another of the wounds that fueled his drive for revenge and vindication. In that campaign, Jackson, spearheading the populist revolt against "King Caucus," the elitist coterie of congressional leaders who then dominated national politics, won one-third more popular votes than his nearest rival, John Quincy Adams, son of Washington's successor in the White House. But the presence of two other candidates in the race, the Speaker of the House, Henry Clay, and William Crawford, who was President Monroe's treasury secretary, denied Jackson a majority, and the election was thrown into the House of Representatives. There, Clay settled matters by throwing his support to Adams, who, after ascending to the presidency, made Clay his secretary of state.

Jackson's rage was scarcely greater than his delight at having what he took as dramatic evidence of the correctness of his oft-stated conviction that politics was essentially corrupt. And the outcome of the election provided him with a ready-made platform in 1828, when he campaigned on the promise of ending corruption and unseating King Caucus, while his supporters took pains to remind the citizenry of his victory at New Orleans. They were also forced to organize a "whitewash committee" to defend their candidate against innumerable charges made against his character. Not only was the legitimacy of his marriage attacked but so was the reputation of his long-dead mother, who was accused of being "a prostitute who had intermarried with a Negro."

But the voters shrugged off such charges and swept the hero of New Orleans into office with a landslide. But Jackson scarcely had time to savor his victory before his good fortune was overtaken by another tragedy—the death of his wife Rachel of a heart attack. In his grief at losing her, Jackson lashed out at the scandalmongers who had tormented her during the campaign, in what turned out to be the closing months of her life. "She was murdered—murdered by slanders that pierced her heart," he cried out, standing by her grave soon after the funeral. "May God Almighty forgive her murderers as I know she forgave them. I never can."

For the public, Jackson's loss was overshadowed a few months after Rachel's death, when he took the oath of office and thousands of his partisans thronged the White House grounds, forcing Jackson to exit by a back door and take refuge in a hotel. The revelers remained, enjoying the food and drink and staining the furniture and rugs. One observer called it "the reign of King Mob." It was the inauguration not only of a new president but of a new era in the American presidency, making the holder of the office a creature of mass appeal.

Once the celebration had ended, though, Jackson's anguish over Rachel's death remained. Suffering from a variety of physical afflictions, he soon allowed himself and his presidency to become all but submerged in what would come to be known as the Peggy Eaton affair. The central figure was Peggy O'Neale, the twenty-nine-year-old daughter of a Washington tavern keeper, a woman of uncommon vivacity and questionable virtue. Peggy had only recently become the wife of John Eaton, Jackson's presidential campaign manager and his secretary of war. Their wedding prompted snide comparisons between Peggy and Rachel until Rachel died, when it was then speculated that the newly wed Peggy Eaton would take over as sort of acting first lady.

All this was too much for a number of the wives of administration officials, notably Vice President John Calhoun's wife, Floride, who cut Peggy dead and led the way in ostracizing her. Meanwhile, her husband, who not so secretly coveted the presidency, urged his wife on, seeing the furor as a way to force Eaton out of the cabinet, embarrass Jackson, and clear the way for his own succession.

He failed to take Jackson into account. Feeling a natural kinship for the Eatons, given the treatment accorded his own late wife by the Mrs. Grundys of the political world, Jackson immediately personalized what he regarded as the persecution of Peggy Eaton, allowing it to dominate his presidency. He set out not only to gather evidence to disprove the charges of looseness directed against the woman but also to punish Calhoun for his wife's behavior and what Jackson viewed as Calhoun's role in spurring his wife on.

Over time, Jackson came to regard Calhoun as one of the leaders of "a corrupt and profligate community" and the author of all of Jackson's "troubles, vexations and difficulties." And he found an occasion for venting his wrath against Calhoun when Calhoun's home state of South Carolina, resentful of a new tariff passed by Congress and fearing the rise of abolitionist sentiment in Washington, adopted a tract, written by Calhoun, that claimed that the states had the right to "nullify" laws passed by Congress.

Jackson was furious—even though the support for state's rights had been one of the main themes of his own party when it chose him as its presidential candidate. But such considerations were outweighed by Jackson's rage at Calhoun for what he regarded as a threat to what Jackson held most dearly—his reputation and character.

At a dinner in 1830 honoring Jefferson's birthday, when it came Jackson's turn to offer a toast, he stared Calhoun straight in the eye and declared, "Our Federal Union it must and shall be preserved."

He might as well have slapped Calhoun in the face. Grimly, the vice president responded with a toast of his own: "Our union—next to our liberty the most dear." But this was no mere battle of wits. It was a struggle for control of the country's future, shaped on Jackson's part by visceral feelings over his good name and the true meaning of morality. In this competition, Calhoun did not have a chance against the president. By the end of Jackson's first term, nullification was a dead issue, Jackson having smothered the South Carolina revolt with congressional backing. And equally dead was Calhoun's political future, Jackson having driven him out of the vice presidency, replacing him with Martin Van Buren.

Just as he had in the battle over Calhoun's doctrine of nullification, Jackson also personalized the other great struggle of his presidency against the Bank of the United States, whose supporters were seeking to get its twenty-year charter extended before it expired in 1836 at the end of Jackson's first term.

Jackson had been resentful of the bank since its manipulations triggered the financial panic of 1819, in which Jackson's own economic fortunes suffered severely. Following the panic, he began to view the bank as a threat to his financial standing, which was to his mind equivalent to an attack on his reputation. "I cannot sleep indebted," he once remarked to a friend, and as his financial resources dwindled, he brooded increasingly about his predicament. "For the last two years I have had not control over my expenses and it has exceeded my means," he wrote, shortly before the voters in 1828 sent him to the White House.

Jackson's vague resentment of the bank was intensified partly as a result of the Eaton affair, which polarized Jackson's view of the political world and led him to suspect that the bank had tried to intervene in the 1828 election in cahoots with those who had assailed his reputation. The aggressiveness of the bank's president, Nicholas Biddle, in pushing for the charter extension in league with lawmakers who were already opposing Jackson on other issues, only served to confirm Jackson's fears of the bank and heighten his anxieties.

He struck back, first openly questioning the constitutionality of the bank. And then in 1832, after Congress approved the rechartering, Jackson sent the bill back to Capitol Hill with a veto message that sounded the Klaxon for American populism and nationalism louder than it had ever been heard. Condemning the bank as a dangerous monopoly whose profits were drained "out of the earnings of the American people," Jackson charged that its stock was held only by members "of the richest class" and foreigners. He would not allow, Jackson said, the "prostitution of our government to the advancement of the few at the expense of the many." The message gave the mass of voters a new and emotional reason for backing Jackson—his opposition to the despised and threatening bank—and helped carry him to a another landslide victory in 1832.

Jackson's character, which made him view himself as the enemy of the political and economic establishment, expanded the constituency of presidential politics from a relatively small elite into a broad-based mass. It was a change that had been signaled by the revelry at his inaugural and that was confirmed by the veto message that reinforced the faith of those who had celebrated Old Hickory's ascension to power.

Although Jackson had crushed Calhoun and his doctrine of nullification, the spirit of Southern secession never died. It thrived amidst the festering morass of the slavery debate, while a nearly unbroken parade of political mediocrities presided in the White House. Character made a significant contribution to the record of presidential failure.

Jackson's handpicked successor, Van Buren, sought to follow in Old Hickory's footsteps. But in contrast to Jackson's boldness and passion, Van Buren had the soul of a trimmer. He fussed over his appearance, giving rise to stories that he wore a corset. Caution governed his every move, and disappointed Jacksonians complained that the only belief to which he was committed was the "creed of non-commitalism." When a severe depression struck, Van Buren could not hold Jackson's base, smashing Democratic dreams of a populist dynasty.

The Democratic debacle paved the way for the emergence of the Whig Party, which displayed an early flair for marketing its candidates on the basis of personality traits, even if it had to manufacture them. The first Whig president, General William Henry Harrison, hero of the famous 1811 victory over the Shawnee at Tippecanoe Creek, was presented as a simple and nonpolitical old soldier, in contrast to the slick Democratic incumbent Van Buren. This, despite Harrison's descent from a line of Virginia aristocrats and his decade-long record as an Ohio politician. But Harrison, at sixty-seven the oldest president yet elected, had the poor judgment to deliver his one-hour-and-forty-minute Inaugural Address in a driving rainstorm, after which he caught pneumonia and died within a month. His successor, John Tyler, an ex-Democrat, could not rally his new party behind him, opening the door for return of the Democrats and the election of John Polk of Tennessee in 1848. Although he was the most forceful character of all the chief executives in this dismal era, Polk's sanctimonious and suspicious personality alienated political leaders and the public alike. Thus, despite the expansion of the nation's borders to take in California, New Mexico, and Oregon during his tenure, a development that would ordinarily be expected to win acclaim for the nation's leader, the abrasive Polk achieved a remarkable level of unpopularity.

Back to power in 1848 came the Whigs, on the shoulders of another old general, Mexican War hero Zachary Taylor, whom they dubbed Old Rough and Ready. Taylor lasted longer than his Whig predecessor Harrison, but only by a year. His death at age sixty-five and the undistinguished stewardship of his vice presidential successor Millard Filmore finished the Whig Party, setting the stage for the birth of the Republican Party in 1856.

The Democrats took back the White House in 1852, but the best they could offer to confront the worsening crisis of slavery was the irresolute leadership of Franklin Pierce and James Buchanan. Pierce, the last-gasp choice of a deadlocked convention, was an obscure and weak-willed New Hampshire politician who had been forced to quit the Senate because of his heavy drinking and whose response to the challenges of his office was to return to the bottle. His successor, Buchanan, a plodding hack, sought to compensate for his inability to make large decisions by his obsession with minutiae—he once rejected a $15,000 check because it was short 10 cents. "I am the last president of the United States," he lamented, as he watched the country drift toward civil war, while the Republicans elected their first president, Abraham Lincoln. He was, like Jackson, a man of lowly origins but of very different character.

In the turbulent days between Lincoln's election and his inauguration, one of Honest Abe's ardent supporters pledged to prevent any interference with his taking the oath as president, even if it cost his last drop of blood. But Lincoln demurred, telling the story of the young soldier leaving for battle whose sisters presented him with a belt embroidered with the motto: "Victory or death."

"No, no," the youth protested, as Lincoln told the story. "Don't put it quite that strong. Put it: 'Victory or get hurt pretty bad.'"

Lincoln's humor, which he relied on so much that it irritated some of his pompous associates in government, was his way of keeping in touch with reality in the midst of the immense tensions he faced as president and commander in chief.

More fundamentally, humor was another aspect of reason and rationality. And it was Abe Lincoln's reliance on reason that was the key to his character and to his political leadership. Unlike the tempestuous Jackson, who vented his outrage whenever he felt himself threatened or scorned, Lincoln depended on reason to govern his sometimes chaotic emotions and to keep in check his seemingly un-quenchable ambition. Again, it was reason that he relied on to con-fuse his enemies and hold his friends together.

Asked to furnish material about his early life for a presidential campaign biography, Lincoln replied that it all could be summed up in a single sentence from Gray's *Elegy*—"The short and simple an-nals of the poor."

Lincoln's father, Thomas, struggled for survival as a farmer, first in the backwoods of Kentucky, where Lincoln was born, then in Indiana. Lincoln's mother, Nancy, died before he was ten, leaving a burden of grief that Lincoln would bear all his life. Although the boy was an adept student and an omnivorous reader, he lacked direction. "A piece of floating drift wood," was the way he described himself when he left his father's house and made his way to New Salem, Illinois. As it hap-pened, he drifted into politics, winning election to the state legislature on his second effort when he was only twenty-five, and that success seemed to give focus to his life and crystallize his ambition.

Lincoln himself underlined the intensity of that ambition, and his faith in reason, in a talk he gave in 1838 to the Young Men's Lyceum in Springfield, Illinois, an opportunity for the young legislator, who was also now an up-and-coming lawyer, to boost both careers. Cit-ing recent episodes of racial violence, Lincoln warned against the "mobocratic spirit" that was spreading over the fast-growing coun-try. In a sense, Lincoln contended, this threat was an outgrowth of the success of the nation that Washington and Jefferson had founded. In the country's early days, "the struggle to demonstrate the capability of a people to govern themselves" was enough to in-spire and assure the loyalty of all. But now that experiment had be-come a proven success, it had lost some of its magic to those who dreamed of leadership. "This field of glory is harvested, and the crop is already appropriated," said Lincoln. "But new reapers will arise, and *they* too, will seek a field."

To be sure, Lincoln conceded, many good men could be found whose ambitions could be satisfied by what the existing order had to offer—a seat in Congress, or perhaps even the presidency. "But such belong not to the family of the lion or the tribe of the eagle," and mentioning Alexander, Caesar, and Napoleon as examples, Lincoln warned: "Towering genius disdains a beaten path. . . . It thirsts and burns for distinction and, if possible, it will have it whether at the expense of emancipating slaves or enslaving freemen."

Although probably few in his audience realized it, Lincoln, many biographers agree, was pointing the warning finger at himself. His ambition knew no bounds. His law partner and biographer William Herndon called it "a little engine that knew no rest." Lincoln wanted "to link his name with something what would redound to the interest of his fellow man." And he brooded that he "had done nothing to make any human being remember that he had lived." What gave this ambition extra urgency and made it all the harder for Lincoln to control was the great obstacles facing its fulfillment as a result of the hardships he had faced in early life—the grinding poverty and the emotional impoverishment resulting from his mother's death.

To scale the heights of distinction that Lincoln sought to reach, in the face of such handicaps, meant an ambition that could not afford to recognize the restraints that might check other men. Such drive could only be held in check by extraordinary efforts, as Lincoln told the Lyceum audience.

This would mean that emotion must be suppressed by the force of rationality, as Lincoln explained:

> Passion has helped us; it can do so no more. It will in future be our enemy. Reason, cold calculating unimpassioned reason, must furnish all the materials for our future support and defense. Let those materials be molded into general intelligence, sound morality and in particular a reverence for the constitution and laws; Upon these let the proud fabric of freedom rest as the rock of its basis, and as truly as has been said of the only greater institution, "the gates of hell shall not prevail against it."

Lincoln's formula was designed not just for the stewardship of the nation but also for governance of his own complex personality. For Lincoln, reason was more than a tool of the intellect. His devotion to it was an inherent part of his personality, and he spoke of it with an intense fervor that resembled the passion he decried. Rejecting attempts to coerce alcoholics into sobriety in an address on temperance delivered in 1842, he praised instead methods that depended on "persuasion, kind unassuming persuasion." With drunkenness, as with social and political disorder, only through faith in reason could society reach the "happy day when, all appetites controlled, all passions subdued, all conquering mind, shall live and move the monarch of the world. Glorious consummation! Hail fall of Fury! Reign of Reason, all hail."

In politics and government, Lincoln blended his rationality with a strong dose of fatalism. Realizing that like most humans he had little control or influence over many of the events that controlled his fate and the country's destiny, Lincoln was able to resign himself to events. In this way, he was able to conserve his energy for circumstances he could alter and also to rationalize defeats and setbacks to his supporters.

In 1864, after having served in the White House during the most tumultuous period in the nation's history, he explained why he had finally proposed the abolition of slavery after promising only to oppose its extension: "I claim not to have controlled events but confess plainly that events have controlled me." Later, in justifying his moderate approach to Reconstruction, he remarked: "The pilots on our Western rivers steer from point to point as they call it—setting the course of the boat no farther than they can see; and that is all I propose to myself in this great problem."

Fatalism also helped him to make the best of a bad situation, such as in the Confederate threat to Fort Sumter during the early weeks of his presidency. If Lincoln acted forcefully, he might prod some states that were still dubious about their course into seceding from the Union. Yet, as Lincoln knew, his indecision might produce the same damaging result. Facing this dilemma, he set as his objective making the rebellious states appear to be the aggressors against the federal government.

Lincoln decided not to evacuate Sumter, since such a retreat would have made the North seem weak. But he also did not attempt to reinforce the fort's garrison, which the South would have construed as a warlike act. Instead, he tried to bolster the garrison with food only—promising not to send in men or munitions without warning. No sooner did the Union ships show up than the Southern batteries opened fire—blocking the effort to resupply and at the same time bombarding the troops within, who were forced to surrender within thirty-four hours. The Union lost the fort, but Lincoln gained a powerful symbol to help him rally the North for war.

But ultimately, it was the issue of slavery that provided the severest and most significant test of Lincoln's rule of reason. At first, reason seemed to lead him on a moderate course. Although he was inherently opposed to slavery, Lincoln was disturbed by the tactics of the abolitionists, whom he regarded as driven by the very sort of passions that he had deplored in his Lyceum speech as threatening the institutions of the Republic. And all through his campaign for the presidency, while deploring slavery and warning that its continued existence threatened the nation's survival, he could not bring himself to endorse its abolition—contenting himself with opposing its extension beyond the states in which it already existed.

During the first year of the war, he still held back from any action that might seem to inflame the passions that he had warned against or that would put him too far ahead of public opinion. Implored to issue a proclamation of emancipation by a multidenominational delegation of clerics, he fell back on fatalism. "It is my earnest desire to know the will of providence in this matter," he declared. "And if I can find out what it is, I will do it." Taking General McClellan's limited victory at Antietam as the sign he awaited, Lincoln finally issued the long-sought Emancipation Proclamation, freeing the slaves in the states warring against the Union. Even so, it was drawn in narrow, legalistic language, what one impatient official called "the meanest and the most dry routine style." But by the time the proclamation became effective on New Year's Day of 1863, Lincoln had invoked "the considerate judgment of mankind and the gracious favor of Almighty God" and declared: "I never, in my life, felt more certain that I was doing right, than I do in signing this paper."

Eventually, though, the faith in reason that undergirded Lincoln's character served him well, helping him find the intellectual and moral foundation for his action, which not only endowed his proclamation with suitable dignity but helped to broaden and strengthen the public's faith in what Lincoln had called the American experiment. As he pondered his actions after the fact, it became clear that the Constitution itself was not sufficient basis for what he had done since the Constitution, as drafted—as the South and its sympathizers never tired of pointing out—gave tacit endorsement to slavery.

Searching for broader ground than the Constitution to justify emancipation, Lincoln found it in the Declaration of Independence and annunciated it in the Gettysburg Address, in which he proclaimed the "the new birth of freedom" that would redefine American democracy. In the speech, he made clear that the United States as a nation was older than its Constitution, that it had in fact been born "four score and seven years" before the battle of Gettysburg, in July 1776. And it was the Declaration of Independence, not the Constitution, that contained the proposition "all men are created equal" to which the new nation had been dedicated.

This was not the first time that Lincoln had given recognition to the importance of the declaration and the revolutionary ideology it embodied. In his address to the Lyceum in Springfield, warning against the peril of social disorder, he had declared: "Let every American, every lover of liberty, every well wisher to his posterity, swear by the blood of the Revolution, never to violate in the least particular, the laws of the country; and never to tolerate their violation by others." It had taken Lincoln a quarter of a century filled with strife and passion to progress from the idea of conserving the national birthright expressed at Springfield to the concept articulated at Gettysburg. On that battlefield he rededicated the nation he led "to the great task remaining before us" of assuring the survival and success of "the government of the people, by the people and for the people."

To a degree, this was, of course, a journey of the mind. But it also represented a development in character without which Lincoln's intellect could not have made the leap from defense of the past to staking out a new vision for the Republic, which would become the legacy of his character to his country and his successors.

4

IN SEARCH
OF CRISIS

UNLIKE LINCOLN, WHO RODE his inner conflicts to greatness, Theodore Roosevelt fought a losing battle to control the forces that shaped his character. Although he gained great fame and influence, he ultimately fell short of fulfilling his ambitions and his promise. While he did demonstrate the potential for what would become the media presidency, the development of this potential would await a new technology and a new President Roosevelt. And strive as he might, TR could not transform realities at home and abroad to match his grandiose view of America's destiny in the world.

Roosevelt assumed the presidency at the dawn of a new century, on the heels of one-third of a century of untrammeled economic growth that had been presided over by lackluster political leadership in the White House. Indeed, it was Andrew Johnson, Lincoln's vice president and successor, whose pigheadedness brought on his impeachment, setting the tone for the era. While Lincoln fought the Civil War to preserve the Union and end slavery, the achievement of those objectives had another profound consequence—the unleashing of the energies of capitalism on the continent that the United States now dominated, leading to the creation of unprecedented wealth and political power. In this environment, tycoons were in the saddle, tugging the reins to which political leaders responded.

The swift growth of industry and of the cities presented vast opportunities for graft and corruption. Determined to promote their burgeoning enterprises no matter what, the great buccaneers of the Gilded Age were all too willing to reward the bosses of either party, whichever happened to be in charge, for special favors. This eminently pragmatic bipartisanship was typified by Jay Gould, who controlled, among other things, the Erie Railroad: "In a Republican district I was a Republican, in a Democratic district I was a Democrat," Gould recalled of his political dealings. "In a doubtful district I was doubtful. But I was always Erie."

At the national level, from the late nineteenth century through the opening decades of the twentieth, the Republican Party aggressively linked itself to the interests of business while espousing restraint in government. As Eugene Roseboom points out, with the Civil War, the Republican Party had become not just a partisan grouping but a national institution, its reputation defined by the "great humanitarian crusade" it had waged. But Republicanism had another more practical side that was chiefly concerned with tending to the great business interests. And now, with the great crusade completed, it was this face that the Grand Old Party turned to the world. As for the Democrats, for the most part they concentrated on maintaining their Southern base, sheltered by white supremacy, assuring themselves of seniority on Capitol Hill and even an infrequent stay in the White House.

With a few exceptions—the Republicans championed the protective tariff and the gold standard while the Democrats advocated free trade and, for a while, free coinage of silver—party differences were manifested more in rhetoric than in specific proposals that divided the electorate. Conflicts between the parties were frequently overshadowed by clashes between presidents and their own parties and the Congress. Despite brief flurries of reforming zeal, when in control of the presidency, neither party was able to muster consistent support for programs to deal with the inequities of industrialization and the power of the economic oligarchs.

Party bosses dominated the nominating process, insisting on candidates who they believed would not cause undue controversy and whom they could control. The most tragic case was that of Ulysses S. Grant, savior of the Union, the nation's greatest military hero since Washington, whom the Republicans rushed to nominate to restore the prestige that had been tarnished by the Johnson impeachment. But the decisiveness and self-confidence that accounted for Grant's mastery of the battlefield deserted him in political life.

There, it was supplanted by an overpowering inferiority complex, born of the long years of obscurity and disappointment that had marked his earlier career. He was an easy mark for the gang of unscrupulous political operatives and greedy financial manipulators who plunged his administration into a cesspool of corruption unmatched at that time in the nation's history.

The stench from the Grant scandals forced the kingmakers to pay more attention to character, though in doing so they were generally content to settle for the lowest common denominator—a candidate who did not overtly offend decency and the law, even if he lacked any suspicion of excellence. "Hayes has never stolen. Good God, has it come to that?" complained Joseph Pulitzer of the *New York World*, about the GOP's choice of Rutherford B. Hayes, a seemingly honest man of pedestrian gifts as its nominee in 1876. As it turned out, Hayes soon belied his favorable reputation by going along with a backroom deal in which the GOP stole the presidency from Samuel Tilden, a Democrat who had gotten the most votes in the 1876 election in return for pulling federal troops out of the South, where they had been the only bastion of defense for the rights of the newly freed slaves.

All this contributed to mounting public cynicism, which forced the character issue to the forefront in the 1884 contest between Democrat Grover Cleveland, governor of New York, and Republican James Blaine, Speaker of the House of Representatives. Blaine was heralded by his supporters as "the plumed knight from the state of Maine." But that sobriquet was called into question by the revelation that he had used his congressional office to help carry off a railroad bond swindle at great profit to himself. Democrats rushed to the attack, but Republicans struck back with the revelation that Cleveland, a bachelor, had ten years before fathered a child out of wedlock, a charge that Cleveland, hitherto regarded as among the dullest and least daring of men, stunned the political world by freely admitting. While the public pondered the choice between the two tarnished warriors, one shrewd backer of Cleveland suggested a solution: Let Blaine, whose private life was unstained, be retired to private life, while retaining Cleveland, whose public record was clean, in public life. In any event, this was the formula the electorate adopted, sending a Democrat to the White House for the first time since the Civil War.

When political parties were in opposition, rather than offering significant policy alternatives for public debate, each party depended upon the presidential party being overwhelmed by calamities or its own blunders. Thus, the financial panic of 1893 during the administration of Democrat Grover Cleveland and his party's nomination of William Jennings Bryan in 1896 led to the presidency of William McKinley and sixteen years of Republican rule. Candidates of independent bent had difficulty, and when such a candidate did get nominated and elected, as the experience of Theodore Roosevelt illustrated, the limitations of the system ultimately pitted him against his own party.

Indeed, Roosevelt gained the presidency in the first place only by accident, in the fulfillment of a mistaken whim by Tom Platt, Republican boss of New York state, where Roosevelt had managed to get himself elected governor on the strengths of his exploits as organizer and leader of the Rough Riders in the Spanish-American War. Fed up with Roosevelt's freewheeling reformism in the governor's chair, Platt arranged for the hero of the charge up San Juan Hill to become McKinley's running mate in 1900. In doing so, he disregarded the misgivings of the party's national chairman, Mark Hanna, who presciently warned that Roosevelt's elevation to the vice presidency would mean "that there's only one life between that madman and the White House."

When he took the oath of office in 1901 after McKinley's assassination, Roosevelt had already been a national celebrity for two decades. Born into wealth and privilege in New York City in 1858, young Roosevelt, as his doctor observed, was "a bright, precocious boy" and an avid reader who lacked only one gift—good health—and this was to prove the bane of his early existence. His eyesight was poor, asthma made the simple act of breathing a threat to his heart, and his puny physique became an increasing embarrassment as he grew older.

The embarrassment was intensified because of the contrast with his father, one of New York's business and civic leaders, the only man the future president said that he ever feared. Theodore Roosevelt Sr.'s whole being seemed infused, one relative observed, "with a sense of abundant strength and power." "You have the mind but not the body," the elder Roosevelt told his son, when he was not yet twelve. "And without the help of the body the mind cannot go as far as it should. "You must *make* your body. It is hard drudgery to make one's body, but I know you will do it."

"I'll make my body," the son replied through gritted teeth.

But even with the weight lifting that young Theodore threw himself into, this was easier said than done. This reality was driven home to him in the most humiliating fashion two years later, when he encountered a couple of aggressive youngsters his own age. "They found that I was a foreordained and predestined victim and industriously proceeded to make life miserable for me," Roosevelt later recalled. "The worst feature was that when I finally tried to fight them I discovered that either one could not only handle me with easy contempt, but handle me so as not to hurt me much, and yet prevent my doing any damage whatever in return."

Convinced now that as hard as he had been laboring to "make" his body, he needed to work harder, Roosevelt took up boxing lessons, a sport he continued to pursue at the White House more than thirty years later. And he spent more time than ever in the private gym his father had set up in their home, lifting dumbbells and swinging on the horizontal bars.

Roosevelt's struggle to overcome his physical inadequacies and his sense of inferiority had important consequences. It generated a relentless impulse to demonstrate his strength and forcefulness by imposing his will on others and, along with that, making himself the cynosure of all eyes. "Father always wanted to be the bride at every wedding and the corpse at every funeral," one of his sons remarked.

As a political leader, his impulse was reflected in his devotion to creating an American empire and in his belligerent stance toward the rest of the world. "No triumph of peace is quite so great as the supreme triumphs of war," he declared in 1897 when he was assistant secretary of the navy, a post that he soon resigned to fight against Spain. While paying his respects to those who had labored in peace to achieve America's "wonderful material prosperity," Roosevelt added that "the men who have dared greatly in war, or the work which is akin to war, are those who deserve the best of the country."

Yet all the while, lurking beneath Roosevelt's braggadocio and bluster was the fear he would scarcely admit, even to himself, that he might not measure up to his own rigorous standards. He asked and sought no quarter in fulfilling his commitment to running his life in high gear and full speed. "Don't fritter away your time; create, act, take a place where you are and be somebody," he urged. When he was engaged to Alice Lee, his first wife, he became so obsessed with the fear that someone would run off with her that he acquired a set of French dueling pistols to drive off the abductors who never showed up. "There were all kind of things of which I was afraid at first," he admitted late in life. "But by acting as if I was not afraid I gradually ceased to be afraid." Or so he chose to believe.

Roosevelt's obsession for the vigorous life and the hope of finding relief for his chronic asthma led him in his early twenties to investing in a cattle ranch in the still unsettled West, where he found a way of life that lent itself to his romantic instincts. "Every man who has in him any real power of joy in battle knows that he feels it when the wolf begins to rise in his heart," Roosevelt cried. "He does not then shrink from blood or sweat or dream that they mar the fight; He revels in them, in the toil, the pain and the danger, as but setting off the triumph." Dismissing criticism of the white man's conquest of the prairies as reflective of "a warped, perverse and silly morality," he saw it instead as the first stage in creating the American Empire and part of "the spread of the English speaking peoples over the world's waste space."

Searching for a vocation in which he could make his mark, Roosevelt was naturally attracted to politics. Holding office was one laurel that even the dazzling Theodore Roosevelt Sr. had never worn. Moreover, politics was a way for his son to exercise the "masterfulness"—one of his favorite words—and vigor he exalted.

When his elitist friends sneered at him for signing up with the local Republican organization in New York, Roosevelt dismissed them as people caught up in "social pretension" and "the easy life." Warned that he would meet no gentlemen in politics, only grooms and saloon keepers, Roosevelt, by his own account, replied: "If that is so, the groom and the saloon-keeper are the governing class. . . . You have all the chances, the education, the position, and you let them rule you."

Choosing to make himself part of the "governing class," he followed a path that took him from the New York state legislature to the governor's mansion and ultimately to the White House. While disdaining the materialism and self-indulgence of the upper crust, whom he accused of "timid and short-sighted selfishness," he made no bones about his mistrust of the masses, as represented by the forces of organized labor and social protest. Following the Haymarket riots in Chicago in 1886, Roosevelt, then enjoying the rugged life on his Western ranch, wrote that his cowboys "would like a chance with rifles at one of the mobs. . . . I wish I had them with me and a fair show at ten times our number of rioters; my men shoot well and fear very little."

As police commissioner of New York City, one of his stepping stones to the governorship, Roosevelt made clear his iron-fisted convictions about industrial unrest. "We shall guard as zealously the rights of the striker as those of the employer," he said. "But when riot is menaced it is different. ... Order will be kept at whatever cost. If it comes to shooting, we shall shoot to hit. No blank cartridges or firing over the head of anybody."

In the presidency, Roosevelt's personality and his rhetoric won him support among the middle class, made anxious and fractious by the growing power of industrial capitalism on one hand and the increased militancy of the trade union and Populist movement on the other. His flair for showmanship bolstered his appeal. A cross between Saint Vitus and Saint Paul was the way the visiting British statesman John Morley described him. The "two most wonderful things" he had seen during his travels in America, Morley said, were "Niagara Falls and the President of the United States."

The White House gave Theodore Roosevelt an unparalleled opportunity to enlarge the image of himself that he had vigorously promoted for twenty years, and he took full advantage of it. Grateful reporters noticed how well tuned he was to their deadlines and the special interests of their readers. Determined to control the public's perception of himself, he was happy to have the press cover his hikes and hunting forays, which lent support to his preachments about the strenuous life. But no photo was ever taken of TR on the tennis courts. And he advised William Howard Taft, his successor, not to allow coverage of himself on the golf links, which, like tennis, he believed had an effete image.

With his relentless exuberance and boundless confidence, Roosevelt served both as a distraction and as reassurance that the forces that had made life satisfying for middle-class Americans still existed. He proselytized the faith that hard work was a good thing, that the world was making progress, that change was for the better, as long it was gradual change.

But he preferred to sidestep the fundamental economic problems that confronted the country while focusing on his enduring need to prove himself. He presented himself as a progressive reformer and his bellicose rhetoric in that role was enough to disturb some conservatives. But as president, he avoided directly challenging the Republican hierarchy and the business community, remaining a creature of the huge corporations that controlled his party and funded his election campaign.

"Go slow," Mark Hanna advised him when dealing with economic policy.

"I shall go slow," Roosevelt replied, and he was as good as his word.

To be sure, the tycoons of that era were so accustomed to getting everything their own way that inevitably some complained when Roosevelt filed an occasional antitrust suit or showed some vestige of independence. "He got down on his knees before us," Henry Clay Frick, the steel baron, complained, recalling Roosevelt's pleas for financial support. "We bought the son of a bitch and then he didn't stay bought."

But in reality, Roosevelt's reputation as a trust buster was ill deserved. Because of his own overriding need for "mastery," he could not allow the trusts to be stronger than the federal government he headed. But mastery could be best attained by regulating the big corporations rather than wrecking them. Any effort to destroy the giant corporations "would work the utmost mischief to the entire body politic," Roosevelt told Congress in 1902. "We draw the line against misconduct, not against wealth."

The Square Deal was more bombast than substance, points out biographer John Milton Cooper. And it is questionable whether what Roosevelt did was much tougher on the trusts than what McKinley himself would have done had he lived to serve out his second term. Soon after Roosevelt was sworn in, he confided to his brother-in-law that McKinley himself was planning some form of antitrust action along the lines of the celebrated Northern Securities suit Roosevelt himself filed and which so angered big business.

Stymied at home, Roosevelt sought an outlet for his frustration by extending American influence abroad. Indeed, he had laid the groundwork for an aggressive foreign policy in his first term, when he made the phrase "Speak softly and carry a big stick," first used to apply to the New York Republican hierarchy, the motto for his foreign policy. The most enduring and outrageous demonstration of Roosevelt's ambition was the creation of the Panama Canal. A disciple of Admiral Alfred Thayer Mahan, prophet of sea power, Roosevelt was convinced from the start of his presidency that swift deployment of the great fleet he envisaged for the United States required carving out a passageway across Central America to link the two oceans.

The ideal site, he soon decided, was Panama. To be sure, Panama was then a province of Colombia, which balked at the terms offered by the United States, contending it was being shortchanged by the United States. But TR refused to let the pretensions of the Bogotá regime stand in the way of his country's destiny. And he found ready-made allies among advocates of Panamanian independence who were already prepared to mount a revolution. They received his assurances that the revolution would succeed. That was all it took. The Panamanians rebelled, Roosevelt sent the USS *Nashville* to hamstring the Colombian army, and the yoke of Bogotá was cast aside. With the blessings of newly independent Panama, work on the canal began in 1903.

Roosevelt's high-handedness came under fire: "A rough riding assault upon another republic over the shattered wreckage of international law and diplomatic usage," complained William Randolph Hearst's *Chicago American,* normally no great respecter of the rights of other nations. His feelings bruised but his ego as enormous as ever, Roosevelt likened the attacks on him to the abuse poured upon Lincoln during the dark moments of the Civil War. "I get an idea of what he had to stand after Bull Run," he wrote his son, Ted.

But he got little comfort from his own cabinet. Asked to provide a legal rationale for his handling of the canal at a cabinet meeting, Attorney General Philander Knox replied wryly: "Mr. President, if I were you I would not have any taint of legality about it."

Nonplussed, Roosevelt demanded: "Have I answered the charges?"

"You certainly have, Mr. President," replied War Secretary Orrin Root. "You have shown that you were accused of seduction and you have conclusively proved that you were guilty of rape."

Another "big-stick" exercise followed a rebellion in Venezuela, which led to Germany and Britain pressuring the new revolutionary government to pay off money owed to their investors.

At first glance, it might seem that Roosevelt would let this pass. He had scant sympathy for the revolutionary regime in Caracas, whose leader, Cipriano Castro, he subsequently referred to as "an unspeakably villainous little monkey." Moreover, until this moment in history in 1901, no one, certainly not Roosevelt, had pretended that the Monroe Doctrine, the supposed cornerstone of American foreign policy, forbade such debt collection by foreign governments in the hemisphere. Indeed, Roosevelt himself had declared, when he was still vice president: "If any South American country misbehaves toward any European country, let the European country spank it." In addition, the United States itself had violated its own doctrine, or at least the section pledging that it would not interfere with the existing colonies of any European nation, a few years earlier when, with Roosevelt's enthusiastic support, it had annexed the Philippines, seized from Spain in 1898.

Nevertheless, when German and British warships blockaded Venezuela's coast, seized its ships, and bombarded its fortifications, Roosevelt professed to view this as a sign of territorial ambitions by the two powers in the hemisphere. Exactly what he did still remains unclear. His later claim that he had threatened the kaiser's government by vowing to dispatch Admiral Dewey and the U.S. fleet to Venezuela's troubled waters unless Germany backed off is hard to document. But whatever his precise response, Roosevelt appeared to have brought enough pressure to prod both Germany and England to agree to arbitration of their claims.

Continued political upheavals in the region raised in Roosevelt's mind new threats of European intervention, leading to his proclaiming in 1904 of what amounted to a corollary to the Monroe Doctrine. In the case of "chronic wrongdoing," he claimed for the United States the right to serve as self-appointed policeman for the area, punishing miscreant nations whenever and however it saw fit. This extravagant assertion of authority over other nations' sovereignty opened the way for three decades of gunboat diplomacy, which, despite the Good Neighbor Policy and the Alliance for Progress, the United States is still trying to live down.

Despite his oft-expressed admiration for warfare, it was as a peacemaker that he achieved his greatest distinction abroad, by helping to bring an end to the war between Russia and Japan that broke out in 1904. Roosevelt agreed to take on the tasks of mediator, in part because of his concern that continued Japanese victories in the war might increase the threat of the "yellow peril" to the United States. And for his role at the peace conference in Portsmouth, New Hampshire, he was awarded the Nobel Peace Prize.

But even such recognition could not allay the deep-rooted insecurities that lurked behind Roosevelt's brassy facade. His anxieties had reared their head as the 1904 election approached. Fearful that his bellicose language and style had alarmed the business community, which might turn to the Democrats, who had chosen the ultraconservative Alton B. Parker as their standard-bearer, Roosevelt sought to placate the robber barons as the 1904 election approached.

He need not have worried. Even with Parker heading the Democratic ticket, business knew on which side its bread was buttered and stuck with the GOP and Roosevelt. So did the middle-class voters who enjoyed the show TR put on.

Even the huge victory he won in 1904 by gaining the presidency in his own right did not allay Roosevelt's doubts. No president before or since has been given such a rich opportunity. Not only did he have a landslide and a full term to exploit it but he had the option of running again in 1908, when he could have claimed an exception from the third-term tradition, since he had only been elected once to the presidency. But at this zenith of his career, Roosevelt's character did him in. Instead of taking confidence from his victory, he dreaded the task of matching it four years hence. To avoid that challenge and still preserve his place in the limelight, Roosevelt committed the only act that would have overshadowed his own victory. He announced he would not succeed himself in 1908.

Roosevelt had trumped his own ace and paid a price by making himself a lame duck. All through the frustrating closing years of his second term, he privately complained that he would give all he possessed for the chance to take back his renunciation: "I would cut my hand off right here," he reputedly told a friend, pointing to his wrist, "if I could recall that written statement." But that opportunity never came. And his frustration grew after he had left the White House, because his own handpicked heir, William Howard Taft, failed to measure up to Roosevelt's expectations. And so Roosevelt did run for president again, though under circumstances he would hardly have imagined when he was at the height of his power and prestige. Rejected by his own GOP, he formed a third-party insurgency that had the effect of assuring Taft's defeat and the victory of Democratic standard-bearer Woodrow Wilson.

In the closing years of his career, as he vainly sought to regain the presidency and the attention he had relinquished, Roosevelt was reduced to blaming his frustration on fate. "If during the lifetime of a generation, no crisis occurs sufficient to call out in marked manner the energies of the strongest leader," Roosevelt complained, "then of course the world does not and cannot know of the existence of such a leader." By "crisis" Roosevelt meant war, which was the only kind of crisis he understood.

In fact, there were challenges enough in America affecting the welfare of millions of citizens ground under the heel of business. But this was the kind of conflict Roosevelt's character was not suited for dealing with.

"When I left college I had no strong governmental convictions beyond the very strong and vital conviction that we were a nation and must act nationally," Roosevelt once said of his early political career. "I had not thought out or been given the opportunity to think out, a great many questions which I have since recognized as vital." But in reality, what was true at the beginning of TR's career was equally true at its conclusion. Although Roosevelt may have recognized the great questions that faced the country, he offered no clear answers. He had no coherent intellectual framework, only a series of personal convictions and prejudices, energized by his ambition and anxiety.

Just as Roosevelt infused the presidency with the energy and dynamism that marked the twentieth century, Wilson sought to instill in the office a moral vision that the new age desperately needed. Wilson's belief in his own destiny and his devotion to morality propelled him into the White House, making possible his greatest achievements. But the same character traits wrecked his presidency and his hopes and left his admirers and supporters, indeed much of the citizenry, disillusioned and embittered.

The most powerful influences on Wilson's early life were the Calvinist faith of his forebears and the imposing presence of his father, Joseph Ruggles Wilson, a Presbyterian minister of considerable distinction in the community in Staunton, Virginia, where Thomas Woodrow Wilson was born in 1856. Since Calvinism holds that a human being's sole chance for salvation lies in being elected by God to a state of grace, those who manage to persuade themselves that they have achieved this exalted condition become convinced that they are doing the Lord's work on earth, while the views of others tend to be of little consequence. The impact of this creed on young Wilson was vastly heightened by the demanding nature of his father in setting goals for the boy, particularly for scholastic achievement. "His idea was," Woodrow Wilson's daughter, Margaret, said later in describing her grandfather's approach to teaching, "that if a lad was of fine tempered steel, the more he was beaten the better he was."

The combination of the Calvinist faith and Dr. Wilson's rigorous rearing produced a man whose strengths included idealism, ambition, and self-discipline but who would also be painfully rigid and self-righteous to the point of sanctimoniousness and who, no matter what he achieved, would always be driven to reach for more, thus creating for himself a permanent state of discontent.

As Wilson reached adulthood, he fell into a pattern of behavior, as his biographers Alexander and Juliette George have pointed out, that reflected his drive for power and his unwillingness to yield on matters that he considered important and sanctified by morality. In the first stage of this pattern, when Wilson was seeking power, first as president of Princeton, then in New Jersey politics, and ultimately as president, he controlled his tendency to impose his will and instead cooperated with others to achieve common objectives. But in the second stage, once he had achieved power and found himself defending an objective linked to his self-interest, he abandoned such restraint and threw all his considerable energies into overwhelming his opponents, often hurting himself in the process.

Although setting his eye on a political career early on, Wilson pursued this goal in a roundabout way. Seeking to make his mark in the world before risking his pride in the hurly-burly of politics, he entered law school after graduating from Princeton. As he later explained, "The profession I chose was politics; the profession I entered was law."

But this strategy misfired. Wilson found the law boring and after a brief stint in practice, he returned to academe, teaching at Bryn Mawr and Johns Hopkins, before joining the faculty at his alma mater in 1890. As a lecturer in constitutional law and international law, his performance won the plaudits both of his Princeton colleagues and his students. Meanwhile, Wilson had already attained distinction with the publication of *Congressional Government* in 1885, in which he argued, at least by implication, that Americans would be better off with a parliamentary government along the lines of Great Britain's than with the Madisonian model of separated powers. A subsequent flood of other books and articles, along with widespread public speaking, enhanced Wilson's reputation and won him national attention. With scores of other institutions bidding for his services, it was only inevitable that in 1902 when Princeton's presidency became vacant, the post was offered to Wilson.

On taking that office, he insisted on being given full power of appointment and removal of faculty members. At first he worked in harmony with the faculty in carrying out a sweeping revision of the curriculum and installed a tutorial system, changes that revitalized the university. Yet amid these triumphs, signs of trouble loomed as Wilson, now having consolidated his position, sought to expand his power. To add to the unlimited authority he had been granted over the faculty, he demanded that he have a say in appointments to the Board of Trustees. Then, when a dispute developed over the location of some of the new laboratories that Wilson's efforts had helped bring to campus, he remarked: "As long as I am President of Princeton I propose to dictate the architectural policy of the university."

Ultimately, Wilson's ambitions clashed with those of another prominent leader of the university, Dean Andrew Fleming West, who had been chosen to direct the development of Princeton's new graduate school. In fact, West had been persuaded to stay at Princeton, instead of accepting an offer from the Massachusetts Institute of Technology, with the promise that his plans for the graduate school would be carried out. Despite this pledge, Wilson unveiled an ambitious plan for yet another reform that would group the students in residential quadrangles. If carried out, Wilson's scheme would have sidetracked West's long-dreamed-of graduate school. Wilson's quadrangle plan was rejected. But it touched off a prolonged series of battles between Wilson and West that threw the university into turmoil and tarnished Wilson's achievements.

After refusing to compromise and facing likely defeat, Wilson decided rather to quit than to fight on. But his decision to leave was in large part facilitated by an attractive opening in another field, which offered Wilson an even greater opportunity for influence and power and which had always been the first choice of his heart—politics, in particular the chance to run for the governorship of New Jersey.

Wilson's entrance into politics reflected the combination of idealism and ambition that defined his nature. He was recruited for the governor's race by conservative politicos and businessmen, who saw in Wilson, with his lofty moral tone and intellectual accomplishments, a man who could help them develop a safe alternative to the reform fervor that then dominated the debate in both parties and threatened their interests. For his part, Wilson did all he could to encourage this notion. At a time when the excesses of big business were under broad attack, he defended the giant trusts as symbols of stability, condemned the trade unions, and denounced William Jennings Bryan, the prime engine of reform, as a "holder of foolish and dangerous beliefs."

With his eye on the New Jersey governorship, Wilson promised Jim Smith, New Jersey's Democratic boss, that if elected, he would do nothing to challenge the machine Smith dominated. But Wilson, whose ambitions extended beyond Trenton to the White House, realized that given the national mood, he had little hope of a political future as a tool of the bosses and the trusts. No sooner had he won the nomination, with the help of all Smith's power and resources, than Wilson began to sing a different tune.

Now he proclaimed himself independent of the bosses and backed up that claim by endorsing the sort of reforms that were the dream of the Progressive movement and the nightmare of the conservatives who were his sponsors. And once Wilson had gained office in the election of 1910, he kept his promise, defying the bosses by backing the reform candidate for U.S. Senate and then pushing through the legislature a broad program of reforms that made his state, hitherto a symbol of backwardness and corruption, a symbol of progress and turned him into one of the brightest stars in the Democrats' national political firmament.

To accomplish this, he demonstrated an ability to compromise that had been markedly absent from his style during his feuds at Princeton. Convening a bipartisan conference on reforms to develop his legislative program, he drew on the suggestions made there to revise his own ideas. To enact them, he had to win the backing not only of the Democrats who controlled the Assembly but of the Republicans who ruled the upper house. At one point, attending a gathering of state senators, he even joined a key Republican lawmaker in a cakewalk around the room. "I am on easy and delightful terms with all the senators," he bragged later. "They know me for something else than an ambitious dictator"—the epithet leveled against him by his foes at Princeton.

Some reformers remained skeptical, notably William Jennings Bryan, who still remembered Wilson's undisguised scorn for the Great Commoner's own populist beliefs. But Wilson solved that problem with an oration at the Democratic Party's Jackson Day dinner in 1912, in which he hailed "the steadfast vision . . . the character and the devotion and preachings of William Jennings Bryan."

"That was splendid," Bryan remarked and clambered aboard Wilson's presidential bandwagon.

But soon a contretemps developed, reminiscent of the bitter battles that had darkened Wilson's final service to Princeton. In the state legislature, Republicans weary of bending to Wilson's will on reforms showed their independence by adopting a program of their own. When Wilson used his veto pen with a heavy hand, the Republicans replied by accusing Wilson of neglecting his responsibilities to pursue his presidential ambitions. Wilson once again saw his foes as the agents of darkness. He privately described the leader of the Republicans in the legislature, who also taught at Columbia University, as "without a single moral principle to his name," adding: "I have never despised any other man quite so heartily."

Yet, summoning all his self-control, Wilson kept his bitterest feelings to himself and avoided the sort of prolonged battle that he had waged against West at Princeton. He had something else on his mind—winning the presidency.

In this regard, he had great help, first from Bryan, still the inspirational force behind the Democratic Party, whose backing cleared the way for Wilson's nomination as president on the forty-sixth ballot. But he had another important if unwitting ally in Theodore Roosevelt, whose break with President Taft divided the Republican Party and made Wilson's victory all but inevitable. But to make sure, Wilson offered his own program of reforms, countering TR's New Nationalism with the New Freedom, redolent of Wilson's moralism and bolstered by his evangelical zeal.

In the White House, Wilson retraced the patterns of behavior he had established at Princeton and reinforced in Trenton. No longer forced to seek after power, he now wielded it in the highest office in the land. Freed from the necessity of compromise, he sought to impose his own will. Once again, as he had at Princeton and Trenton, he pushed through a series of wide-ranging reforms—tariff reduction on a scale not undertaken in half a century, currency reform reordering the structure of the nation's financial system, and antitrust legislation breathing new life into federal efforts to regulate business and the Federal Trade Commission, the most significant action taken by the government to protect consumers against the excesses of corporate giants.

Wilson had top-heavy Democratic majorities in both the House and the Senate to help him. But because he would accept almost no modification of his proposals, he had to exert heavy pressure to get even the legislators of his own party to bend to his will. "We must act now, at whatever sacrifice to ourselves," the president declared in urging Congress to adopt his currency reform plan without any significant change. And as the *New York Times* noted, "he emphasized the 'now' with a snap of the jaw."

In the councils of his own party, he denounced dissidents therein as "rebels and no Democrats." In all these conflicts, he was armed with the conviction that the right, intellectually and morally, was on his side, and so was the public. "Nothing has to be explained to me in America, least of all the sentiment of the American people," he once declared with awesome arrogance. "And the advantage of not having to have anything explained to you is that you recognize a wrong explanation when you hear it."

Wilson's determination gained him landmark legislative accomplishments and reelection, though by a narrow margin in 1916. But his steam-roller tactics earned him ill will on Capitol Hill, particularly among Republicans. "There is to be no real debate upon the banking and currency bill," protested Republican senator Albert Cummins of Iowa. "The real legislation of this body is now taking place in a Democratic caucus."

Wilson had the votes and the iron will to override such resentment in his first term, which was devoted almost exclusively to domestic issues. But in his second term, he faced a different and more formidable challenge, as his plans for domestic reform were overshadowed by the Great War raging abroad.

At first, Wilson tried desperately to resist American involvement in the war in the face of demands from the war hawks led by Roosevelt that the national interest required a forceful response to German aggression. He found it difficult to adjust his ideology, which relied on moral absolutes, to the harsh realpolitik that defined the clash between the Western Allies and the kaiser. Always searching for the high ground, Wilson found his chosen terrain in preserving neutrality in the face of admitted provocation, an idea consonant not only with his idealism but with his stress on self-discipline. "There is something so much greater to do than fight," he declared in 1915. "There is a distinction waiting for this nation that no nation has ever yet got. That is the distinction of absolute self- control and self-mastery."

"There is such a thing as a man being too proud to fight," he declared three days after the torpedoing of the *Lusitania* outraged the public. "There is such a thing as a nation being so right that it does not need to convince others by force that it is right." Finally, when

Wilson could no longer help himself in the face of German intransigence, notably the resumption of unrestricted submarine warfare and the hatching of Foreign Minister Zimmerman's hare-brained scheme to persuade Mexico to make war on the United States, he led the country into the battle. But he idealized the nature and purpose of the war to suit his own psyche.

In order for Wilson to accept the terrible responsibility of sacrificing the lives of young Americans on a wholesale basis, the moralist president had to believe that the cause was just. Dissatisfied with the war aims of the Western powers, he promulgated his own moral vision of the war, spelled out in his Fourteen Points and then in his plan for the League of Nations. This would be a war to end all war. And it would be war to make the world safe for democracy. Thus, like Roosevelt, Wilson's character drove him to war. Roosevelt sought war for its own sake, so he could conquer by force of arms. Wilson entered the war seeking conquest by another means—so that he could design the peace and shape the postwar world.

The idealism Wilson espoused had great appeal not only for him but also for the American public. But Wilson betrayed the public, not because he did not mean what he said about the war's purposes but rather because, as he should have known, few American political leaders and almost no one in power abroad shared his vision. Moreover, Wilson himself was unwilling to do what had to be done to change their minds.

Instead, he waged the war and fought for the peace in the grip of the same self-certitude and rigidity that had clouded his accomplishments at Princeton and in Trenton. But this time, his defeat was tragic, not only for his career but for the nation he led. Although the challenge he faced would have been formidable in any case, Wilson made matters worse by the way he treated the Congress, particularly the Republicans. He had already angered GOP lawmakers, notably the influential Henry Cabot Lodge of Massachusetts, by disregarding them as he pushed his domestic program through. He exacerbated that tension by seeking total control of the war effort, backing measures that many lawmakers felt pointed the way toward absolutism.

He heaped insult upon injury when, on the eve of the 1918 midterm elections, he appealed to the voters to return a Democratic-controlled Congress, in words that could not fail to outrage the GOP. A Republican victory would be viewed abroad "as a repudiation of my leadership," Wilson claimed. "It is well understood there as well as here that the Republican leaders desire not so much to support the President as to control him." Not only did this rhetoric infuriate the Republicans, who pointed out that they had loyally backed Wilson's conduct of the war, but it fell flat with the American people, who rejected Wilson's logic and his party, giving the Republicans control of both houses of Congress. This made Lodge, whom Wilson had turned into his arch-enemy, chairman of the Senate Foreign Relations Committee, assuring him of an important role in the ratification of whatever treaty was negotiated to put a formal end to the war.

Even more remarkable, having contributed to this debacle, Wilson, determined to prove himself right, proceeded to behave as if it had not taken place. In the climactic stage of his syndrome of self-righteousness, Wilson disdained taking any step to consult the critics of his plan for a new international organization. He not only made himself head of the American delegation to the peace talks but he totally ignored Congress, omitting any member, either Republican or Democrat, from the delegation. The only Republican he picked—retired diplomat Henry White—had never held office or taken any part in the leadership of the GOP.

It soon became clear from his behavior abroad, where the other Allied leaders found him remote and unrealistic, that as much as Wilson was devoted to winning a lasting peace, his tactics were really designed mainly to vindicate himself and humiliate the Senate. The stupendous welcome that Wilson received in Paris when he arrived to attend the treaty talks rivaled the reception given Napoleon. Two million grateful French lined the Champs Elysées to cheer. But their enthusiasm did more harm than good—only hardening Wilson's conviction that he alone was in the right.

In fact, the treaty that Wilson negotiated, including the League of Nations covenant, was popular with the public, and his foes faced a difficult task in defeating it. The tactics shrewdly chosen by Lodge to exploit Wilson's rigid self-righteousness included a series of "reservations" to Wilson's plan, intended to clarify and protect American interests. Republican supporters of the League urged Wilson to accept a compromise, approving some minor changes that they pointed out would not significantly diminish the power of the League or the U.S. role in the new organization.

Any such concession by Wilson would have undercut Lodge's opposition and gained him the support he needed to make the League a reality. But Wilson would not hear of it. When Wilson's spokesman in the Senate, Senator T. S. Martin of Virginia, told him that without a compromise the treaty could not be saved, Wilson rejected the advice. "Anyone who opposes me in that, I'll crush." In the end, it was the treaty and its supporters who were crushed, when, because of Lodge's opposition and Wilson's refusal to bargain, the treaty failed to gain even a simple majority.

Years later, it was Lodge who offered the best explanation for this debacle, based on his careful study of Wilson's behavior under pressure. "Mr. Wilson in dealing with every great question thought first of himself," Lodge wrote. "He may have thought of the country next, but there was a long interval. . . . Mr. Wilson was devoured by the desire for power."

As it turned out, Wilson's worst enemy was not Lodge but his own unyielding character. His stubborn ambition helped keep his party out of the White House for twelve years until the Great Depression shattered the nation's economic and social structure. And it left Americans so estranged from world affairs that awakening them to the next threat from abroad would turn into a Herculean task and a severe test of the character of the next Democratic president.

5

"PSYCHOANALYZED BY GOD"

SLOWLY HE MADE HIS WAY down the aisle to the back of the speaker's platform, leaning on his son James and on a single crutch, while the thousands who packed Madison Square Garden for the Democratic National Convention of 1924 held their collective breath. He waited until it was time for him to be introduced, then took the other crutch from James and headed for the podium.

Step by step, Franklin Roosevelt struggled, his eyes riveted on the floor, sweat running down his forehead. The delegates and galleries watched in silence, remembering the dashing figure Roosevelt had cut four years earlier, when he had been the party's vice presidential candidate. At last he reached the lectern, set down the crutches, threw back his leonine head and flashed a smile of triumph, and the crowd thundered a welcome fit for a hero.

The address that followed this electrifying overture, nominating Al Smith for president and memorable chiefly for Roosevelt's dubbing Smith "the happy warrior of the political battlefield," was almost an anticlimax. And the presidential campaign that ensued was a disaster for the Democrats. But Roosevelt's appearance at the podium, the silent eloquence of his conquest of the damage fate had worked on his body, had elevated him to a prominence that few in his party could match.

The iron will that Roosevelt publicly exhibited at the 1924 Democratic convention and that he called upon in private in his long struggle against polio was one of the mainsprings of his character. But FDR's battle against the disease that struck him at the height of young manhood illustrated another and equally important aspect of his character—his deviousness. The dramatic scene at Madison Square Garden would become an almost unique vignette in American political history because Roosevelt rarely, if ever, allowed himself to be seen in public on crutches again.

Before his first-term inauguration in 1933, his longtime political operative, Louis Howe, inspected the hallways and doorways of the White House, with an eye for locations where the president in his wheelchair might be exposed to view and to photographs by visitors. He sent Roosevelt's press secretary, Steve Early, to consult with the chief of secret service, Colonel Ed Starling, a veteran of the last months of Woodrow Wilson's presidency, when Wilson, a stroke victim, also had been in a wheelchair. Howe's arrangements helped to insure that most Americans had no more than a dim idea of the severity of the president's condition, that he actually spent most of his life in a wheelchair, that even with his braces he could not stand erect without support, and that even with assistance he could walk only a few yards usually along a well-planned route.

A complaisant press corps submitted to the White House ban on pictures of the president in a wheelchair, being lifted out of an auto, or being carried up stairs. When Roosevelt fell in the mud at Philadelphia's Franklin Field as he was about to deliver his address accepting his party's renomination to the presidency in 1936, Secret Service agents and aides quickly surrounded him, shielding his sprawling figure from the 100,000 onlookers. Pool reporters knew about the incident, but never reported it.

The pairing of deception with determination made for an unbeatable political combination and allowed Roosevelt to reshape the nation's highest office in his own image, lending it a scope and grandeur that would present an enduring challenge for his successors. It may have been mainly his resolve that impelled him to the podium in 1924 to herald his comeback to national politics. But it was his skill at camouflage and misdirection that was at least as important in carrying him to the presidency and through thirteen momentous years in the White House.

Entering office in the midst of the worst economic crisis in the nation's history and later faced with a total war against forces that threatened the country's very existence, he exploited the powers of the presidency in ways unimagined by any of his predecessors, transforming the relationship between Americans and their government. In doing so, he was armed not only with self-certitude but with an elusiveness that helped him to escape the normal penalties for inconsistency and self-contradiction, to appease and assuage his friends, and to befuddle and frustrate his foes. "His mind does not follow easily a consecutive chain of thought," his secretary of war, Henry Stimson, once complained to his diary, "but he is full of stories and incidents and hops about in his discussions from suggestion to suggestion and it is very much like chasing a vagrant beam of sunshine around a vacant room."

After vainly trying to get a straight answer out of the president on a key appointment, his interior secretary, Harold Ickes, exploded. "You won't talk frankly even with people who are loyal to you and of whose loyalty you are fully convinced," Ickes told Roosevelt. "You keep your cards close up against your belly. You never put them on the table." Rex Tugwell, one of the charter members of the New Deal "Brains Trust" and later Roosevelt's biographer, summed up his frustration with this task when he wrote: "The serious student is forced to conclude that this man deliberately concealed the processes of his mind."

It was this sinuous personality, more than an set of ideological beliefs, that held together the New Deal during the Great Depression and then served as the linchpin for the Grand Alliance against the Axis powers in World War II. And what made it possible for Roosevelt to carry off his leadership role, to combine his dogged pursuit of certain objectives with his inherent evasiveness, was his monumental aplomb, reflected in his regal bearing and his strong, resonant voice. "A second class intellect, but a first class temperament," was the famous judgment rendered by Oliver Wendell Holmes when he first encountered FDR as president elect in 1933. In his years in the White House, Roosevelt had adjusted his personality to his office and at the same time had tailored his office to match his personality, until it became difficult for most Americans to tell where one left off and the other began. "He must have been psychoanalyzed by God," a spellbound aide once remarked.

But FDR's self-confidence stemmed not from therapy but rather from breeding. It was rooted in a privileged upbringing as the only child of an indulgent father and a doting and domineering mother. His father, James, who was fifty-three when Franklin was born in

1882, rode to hounds, and hosted afternoon teas and formal dinner parties at Springwood, his Hyde Park estate. Franklin's mother, Sara Delano Roosevelt, a tall and stately beauty, was proud of her Huguenot Delano forebears, who had set foot in the New World even before the Dutch Roosevelts.

"In the past—on both sides of your ancestry—they have a good record and have borne a good name," Franklin was reminded by his father. James Roosevelt was worth about $300,000, hardly more than petty cash when compared to the holdings of some of his Hyde Park neighbors. These included Frederick W. Vanderbilt, who had inherited from his grandfather, Commodore Vanderbilt, the shipping and rail tycoon, an estate of more than $70 million, including a lavish Italian Renaissance mansion that dwarfed the seventeen-room home of the Roosevelts.

With the exquisite snobbery that comes with old money, the Roosevelts looked down on such nouveau ostentation. When he turned down an invitation to the Vanderbilts, James had only to tell Sara: "If we accept we shall have to have them at our house."

Still, the Roosevelt family's own lifestyle was scarcely austere; Franklin had governesses and tutors to polish his manners and drill him on his lessons, and yachts and ponies to enliven the carefree hours at Springwood. By the time he was fifteen, he had been to Europe eight times and had been introduced to Mark Twain and President Grover Cleveland, not to mention his frequent visits with his fifth cousin, Theodore, who was already en route to the White House.

At Groton, Endicott Peabody, the headmaster, sought to instill a social conscience in his privileged young charges. Franklin heard from speakers such as reformer Jacob Riis and other advocates for the downtrodden, enlisted in Groton's Missionary Society, and signed up for a summer campaign for youngsters from the slums of New York and Boston. Intellectually, though, Groton was not challenging; its tutelage put more stress on manners and morals than on grades and knowledge. This was fine for FDR, who there, as later during his college days at Harvard, was more interested in sports and good fellows than grades.

But his early years were not without problems. His doting mother was reluctant to send her son away to school, so Franklin was admitted to Groton at fourteen, not twelve, which was the standard age. He was slow in developing, too. Still a soprano at fourteen, his willowy frame and unmarked features gave him a girlish appearance, and his speech seemed stilted, with a trace of an accent.

All this set him apart from his classmates. To a degree, he reacted by being driven in on himself, developing a shell that persisted all his life. But at times, he tried consciously to prove he was a regular fellow, once deliberately breaking the rules in class. "I have served off my first black mark today, and I am very glad I got it, as I was thought to have no school spirit before," he wrote his parents. In the same vein, he tried out for football, baseball, hockey, and boxing but never made the varsity.

At Harvard, he was the stereotypical Joe College. His big success, editing the *Crimson*, was focused on boosting school spirit and supporting the football team. He also faced his first political test, and suffered his first setback, losing an election for class marshal, from which he learned a valuable lesson. Taking the outcome for granted, he had not bothered to get himself endorsed by the campus political machine or to organize the independent voters. It was a mistake he would not make again.

But a far bigger impact on his life than his formal education was the career of his cousin Theodore Roosevelt. By his startling swift ascent of the political heights, TR, who was twenty-four the year Franklin was born and had already won a seat in the New York legislature, demonstrated to Franklin that for a Roosevelt, no political goal was unattainable. The trail TR blazed charted a course for his young cousin to follow—state legislature, assistant secretary of the navy, governor of New York.

In 1907, as a twenty-five-year-old law clerk in New York City, while his cousin was finishing his second term in the White House, Franklin confided to his colleagues that he did not intend to pursue the law as a career but instead had his eye on the presidency. "Any one who is Governor of New York has a good chance to be President with any luck," he remarked.

But when he ran for vice president in 1920 the thirty-eight-year-old FDR was still merely a jejune facsimile of his distinguished relative, who had passed away the year before. "Franklin is as much like Theodore as a clam is like a bear cat," jeered the *Chicago Tribune*. "If he is Theodore Roosevelt, Elihu Root is Gene Debs and Bryan is a brewer."

Franklin's energetic efforts to mimic the robust style of his celebrated relative sometimes backfired, most notably when he boasted of the influence he had wielded as assistant secretary of the navy. "You know I have had something to do with the running of a couple of little Republics," he claimed in arguing that if the United States joined Wilson's League of Nations, it could be assured of the backing of its small neighbors in the Caribbean. "The facts are that I wrote Haiti's Constitution myself and, if I do say it, I think it's a pretty good constitution." Besides being arrogant, the statement was blatantly untrue; Assistant Navy Secretary Roosevelt's involvement in Haiti was limited to a brief visit there during the U.S. occupation in 1917.

Republican Warren Harding, on his way to becoming the twenty-ninth president, called Roosevelt's statement "shocking," and an embarrassed FDR could think of no better response than to claim he was misquoted by the Associated Press. This only worsened matters when supporters of both parties who had been present signed a statement backing the AP's account.

But for the most part, Roosevelt cloaked such excesses of ego with a personal charm reputed to be so overpowering that some political foes were said to shrink from private encounters with him lest they succumb to his wiles. At Harvard, editor Roosevelt got along so well with other *Crimson* staffers that his coeditor recalled, "in his geniality was a kind of frictionless command." And his distant cousin, Anna Eleanor Roosevelt was so captivated by his gaiety and natural ease that she married him in 1905, soon after his graduation from Harvard.

Still, after a while some found his personality began to wear thin. Rex Tugwell thought that Roosevelt's charm ultimately became "part of a whole apparatus of defense" designed to conceal his true beliefs. Although he was the champion of multitudes, he avoided intimacy with individuals, even those closest to him. "He had a trick of seeming to listen, and to agree or to differ partly and pleasantly, which was flattering," Tugwell recalled in later years. "This was more highly developed as he progressed in his career and it was responsible for some misunderstanding. Finally no one could tell what he was *thinking*, to say nothing of what he was *feeling*."

Among those he effectively shut out of his life was his wife, whom he at times treated with condescension. While Franklin was serving as assistant secretary of the navy, Eleanor was asked by a reporter what she had done as a homemaker to be in tune with the wartime themes of sacrifice and austerity. "Making my ten servants help me do my saving has not only been possible but highly profitable," she said.

When Roosevelt saw that blunder in print, he paid his wife back with cutting sarcasm: "Please have a photo taken showing the family, the ten cooperating servants, the scraps saved from the table," he wrote. "You have leaped into fame, all Washington is talking of the Roosevelt plan."

A far more serious problem was Franklin's romance with Eleanor's part-time secretary, a woman named Lucy Mercer. When Eleanor found out and threatened divorce, her husband tried to minimize the problem. "Don't be a goose," he told his wife.

"I *was* a goose," the newly awakened Eleanor replied, and refused to back down.

To clinch matters, Roosevelt's mother, Sara, warned she would cut him off financially if he left his wife and children. Roosevelt ended the relationship, preserving his marriage and his political prospects. But decades later, after Roosevelt had become president, his old flame, since married and widowed and now known as Lucy Mercer Rutherfurd, came back into his life. The two began seeing each other again in 1941, without Eleanor Roosevelt's knowledge. And Lucy Rutherfurd was with FDR in Warm Springs, Georgia, when he died on April 12, 1945.

By the time FDR had become president, his wife "knew very little more what he was thinking than did any of the rest of us around him," Tugwell observed. To his children, he was like a fun-loving uncle, but he rarely disciplined them or took their problems seriously. He did insist that his offspring go to church on Sunday. But his wife could not help noting that he himself often headed for a golf course.

"At heart the president was a boy, sometimes a spoiled boy," Jim Farley, the Democratic Party warhorse who helped as much as anybody to make him president, believed. "Although he had tremendous charm and vitality, he had a few petty attributes which were continually getting him into trouble." One of these was that he was forever trying to get even with someone for some slight, real or fancied.

In the closing days of the 1932 campaign, Republican incumbent Herbert Hoover, embittered by the blame heaped upon his shoulders because of the depression, lashed out at FDR. Although Roosevelt was comfortably ahead of his opponent and nothing that Hoover had said seemed likely to erode his strength, an indignant Roosevelt wanted to strike back at Hoover: "I simply will not let Hoover question my Americanism," he said. It took all the efforts of his aides to persuade him to drop the idea.

FDR's intellect mirrored his temperament. "His mind, while it was capacious, and while its windows were open on all sides to new impressions, facts and knowledge, was neither exact nor orderly," observed Ray Moley, one of the early New Deal brain trusters. "Deep in his heart I think he knew this because he seldom trusted himself to say in public more than a few sentences extemporaneously."

But if he was no Jefferson or Wilson when it came to brain power, Roosevelt got along well with men of ideas, taking from them whatever was useful to him, while avoiding any commitment beyond that particular issue. Uppermost always was his psychological need to preserve utmost flexibility for himself. "It is a little bit like a football team that has a general plan of game against the other side," he told reporters of his blueprint for economic recovery in the midst of the New Deal's First Hundred Days. "Now the captain and the quarterback of the team know pretty well what the next play is going to be and they know the general strategy of the team, but they cannot tell you what the play after the next play is going to be until the next play is run off. If the play makes ten yards, the succeeding play will be different from what it would have been if they had been thrown for a loss. I think that is the easiest way to explain it."

Roosevelt's addiction to ad hocery helped attract advisers who saw an opportunity to shape history. "He was a progressive vessel yet to be filled with content," Tugwell said. "He was late in maturing all the way along, and he had to conceal this from others. He became, in consequence, a consummate actor."

But some brains trusters were flabbergasted by FDR's unwillingness or inability to draw distinctions. Early in his first term, when he was given two drafts of a speech on tariff policy, each presenting sharply divergent views, Roosevelt ordered Moley: "Weave the two together." And when Moley said this was impossible, FDR took on the job himself. When he was done, Moley, who was himself opposed to the more ardent tariff cutters, was nevertheless shocked that FDR's draft had substantially ignored their arguments in favor of the other side. "There, you see. It wasn't as hard as you thought it was going to be," FDR remarked.

Moley and his other aides put up with FDR's deceptions because they coveted the propinquity to power that their status gave them. And they basked in the aura of drama and excitement he generated around himself and the sheer pleasure he took in gaining and using power. He was never at a loss for the dashing gesture or the arresting word, and he loved the battle for its own sake.

"I am an old campaigner and I love a good fight," he declared during the 1940 campaign, on his way to a precedent-shattering third term.

If, as critics suggested, there was more form than substance to his leadership, it was form that had been shaped in Darwinian fashion during a lifetime committed to the political system. As a prospective candidate for the presidency, FDR had detractors, notable among them Walter Lippmann, then the nation's preeminent political columnist, who was particularly critical of the New York governor's tendency to play both ends against the middle. "Sooner or later some of Governor Roosevelt's supporters are going to feel badly let down, for it is impossible that he can continue to be such different things to such different men," Lippmann warned, as Roosevelt was preparing for his first presidential run. "He is an amiable man with many philanthropic impulses, but he is not the dangerous enemy of anything . . . a pleasant man who without any important qualifications for the office would very much like to be president."

Although Lippmann would later hedge that appraisal by saying it applied to Roosevelt in his pre–White House years, FDR displayed some of the same weaknesses Lippmann pointed to after he had gained the White House as well. Even Roosevelt's admirers, like Rex Tugwell, conceded his limitations as chief executive. "Vitality, charm, a sense of confidence in the midst of spreading fear, were what Franklin had to offer," Tugwell later recalled. "No one who voted for him did it because he presented himself as learned or competent in all the matters he talked about. They voted for the big easy smiling man who had no fear of failing at anything, who seemed capable even of saving sinners from themselves."

Perhaps the most glaring example of FDR's elasticity was his pledge during the 1932 campaign, made in a speech in Pittsburgh, to balance the budget. Scheduled to return to the Steel City four years later during his campaign for a second term, mindful that his administration was awash in red ink, Roosevelt asked speechwriter Sam Rosenman to devise an explanation for the vast gulf between promise and reality.

"Deny you were ever in Pittsburgh" was the best advice Rosenman could offer.

FDR's temperament helped him to actually enjoy the tensions and pressures he confronted when he first took office. During the historic tumult of the celebrated First Hundred Days, "confusion, haste, the dread of making mistakes . . . made mortal inroads on the health of some of us and left the rest of us ready to snap at our own images in the mirror," Moley recalled. "Only FDR preserved the air of a man who'd found a happy way of life."

Roosevelt slipped easily from one thing to another. A swim in the White House pool would be interrupted by a briefing on railroad legislation. An evening's discussion of bank deposit guarantees would shift into a night of leisure, as FDR worked on his stamp collection and told yarns of his days in the Wilson administration. If these transitions did not make for short-run efficiency, they were certainly a clue to his staying power.

The breakneck pace of his governance became part of American folklore. In the hit musical comedy *I'd Rather Be Right,* George M. Cohan, impersonating FDR, dictated new statutes to a secretary rather than wait for congressional approval. Cohan would turn to the actor playing FDR's aide, Marvin McIntyre, and say: "Mac, take a law." FDR never saw the play but had heard enough of it so that he would often commence dictation to his secretary, Grace Tully, by saying: "Grace, take a law."

Of all the aspects of Roosevelt's tenure, none was more pronounced or more profound in its consequences than the personalization of the presidency that reached new heights.

Discussing his reelection strategy for the 1936 campaign with Moley, Roosevelt brushed aside criticism of his tax policies. "That's a detail," he said. "There is one issue in this campaign. It's myself, and people must be either for me or against me."

The squire of Hyde Park's self-depiction as the tribune of the masses reached its climax in the closing hours of the campaign. After ticking off his enemies—financial monopoly, speculation, reckless banking, class antagonism, sectionalism, war profiteering—to a packed house at Madison Square Garden, Roosevelt cried: "Never before in all our history have these forces been so united against one candidate as they stand today. They are unanimous in their hatred of me—and I welcome their hatred," he said, as the crowed roared.

"I should like to have it said of my first Administration that in it the forces of selfishness and of lust for power met their match," Roosevelt asserted and then delivered his punch line. "I should like to have it said of my second Administration that in it these forces met their master."

Trouble set in after his 1936 landslide victory carried him to a second term. His overwhelming majority consisted of fundamentally incompatible cohorts held together by their common belief in Roosevelt's promise to bring them each happiness and prosperity, based, as Moley said, "on a score of contradictory specifications."

Moreover, the massive scope of his reelection victory—an unprecedented forty-eight-state landslide—brought out the hubris that always lurked beneath the congenial veneer of his personality. He now felt empowered to confront the Supreme Court, which had continually thrown judicial roadblocks in the path of his legislative program. That Roosevelt should challenge the court was not entirely unexpected. But no one, including his potential allies, was prepared for the way he went about it, which had more to do with the president's personality than with his policies. On display in Roosevelt's proposal to enlarge the court by appointing a new justice for every member of the court over seventy were two of the hallmarks of his character—his obsession with secrecy and his preference for artifice. Although he had been mulling over his strategy for two years, he kept it to himself until its abrupt unveiling. And he presented his plan as a prescription for remedying judicial inefficiency, when everyone knew what he really wanted to was to reverse the court's seemingly intractable conservatism.

The scheme was doomed by his own disingenuousness. Roosevelt's secrecy undermined his chances of mobilizing the broad coalition that had elected him in November to support the plan. Under these circumstances, the personal appeal that he had relied on in the election was no match for his foes on the Court and in the Congress, each defending their institutional prerogatives. The plan collapsed.

One defeat soon led to another: The court debacle was followed by a tide of misfortune that seemed to mock his reelection triumph. Having successfully defied the supposedly invincible FDR by rejecting his court-packing scheme, Congress balked more and more often at the New Deal agenda. Meanwhile, the economy dipped steeply, and by early 1938, the dismal statistics gave currency to an ominous new term: Roosevelt recession.

In June 1937, railing against congressional "Copperheads" all too willing to concede defeat in the struggle for his liberal reforms, FDR cut out for himself a bold new role in the forthcoming congressional primaries. He declared himself ready to campaign for one Democrat against another in cases where principle was at stake, thus in effect declaring war on his intraparty foes. FDR threw all his resources into the struggle in which he sought to enlist local party activists and officials in his cause.

But he had done nothing to lay the groundwork for such an effort. He had built his 1936 landslide around his own personal appeal, leaving the party faithful to fend for themselves. Rather than hurting his foes and aiding his allies, FDR's stumping in the hustings often seemed to have the opposite effect, as his targets benefited from complaints of White House meddling in local campaigns. By September, national party chairman Jim Farley summed up the end result this way: "It's a bust." Not only did FDR fail in nearly every case to recast his party but the internecine battle weakened the Democrats in the fall struggle against the Republicans, who took full advantage, making big gains in the Congress and leaving FDR more vulnerable than ever.

Midway through Roosevelt's second term, historian Walter Millis declared that the New Deal had been "reduced to a movement with no program, with no effective political organization, with no vast popular party strength behind it, and with no candidate"—a somber verdict few could dispute. As for Roosevelt himself, given the deeply ingrained custom of limiting a chief executive to two terms in office, he seemed nothing more than a lame-duck politician who had lost his grip, facing the dead end of his career.

Then, before the next year was out, the war in Europe erupted, slowly but steadily altering the American political landscape and presenting Roosevelt with a breathtaking opportunity. The cause of freedom, intertwined with patriotism, could serve as surrogate for the domestic goals of the early New Deal and kindle the intellectual and emotional spark needed to revitalize his presidency. And the threat of war and aggression could provide the strongest of all possible reasons to justify breaking the third-term tradition. But to carry this off, he would have to reconcile the conflicting demands of international affairs and domestic politics. And what made this even harder was that in all his years in the White House, Roosevelt had done little to prepare the country to deal with the dangers it now faced from abroad. His foreign policy had been defined by the same combination of determination and deviousness that had shaped his domestic policy.

All through his early years in the White House, FDR, who came of political age as a scion of Wilson internationalism, maintained a strange alliance with isolationists, whose votes helped pass many of the basic reforms of the New Deal. In his first term, he did little to prevent the rejection of U.S. membership in the World Court, cooperated with the probe into the munitions industry by the Senate, which bolstered opposition to U.S. preparedness and meekly accepted the arms embargo, and that tied his hands as the threat of German aggression heightened in Europe. As the storm clouds darkened, Roosevelt was caught in a conflict between the two poles of his character. As determined as he was to aid the Western Allies against the Axis powers, who he realized ultimately threatened the security of the United States, he was unwilling to risk his prestige by mustering his enormous powers of persuasion to mobilize public support against the danger. The result was that he charted a corkscrew path, marked by temporizing and dissembling.

Early in his second term, in the wake of Japan's invasion of China and facing the escalating threat from Hitler, Roosevelt accused a few unnamed countries of "threatening a breakdown of all international law and order." Likening this to "an epidemic of physical disaster," he seemed to call for "a quarantine" of aggressor nations.

The speech, given in October 1937, captured attention around the world. At the League of Nations in Geneva, where a response to the Japanese attack was under debate, "its effect was instantaneous and put an end to considerable shilly shally that was going on," a State Department observer recorded in his diary. The next day, the League's General Assembly voted to condemn the Japanese attack and issued a call for a multination conference on the Far East.

At home, the initial reaction was also favorable, as attested to by a flood of favorable letters and telegrams to the White House. And approbatory editorials from newspapers ranging from the *Los Angeles Times* and the *San Francisco Chronicle* to the *Christian Science Monitor* and the *New York Times* welcomed the speech as a sign of a stronger U.S. foreign policy.

But the Hearst papers and other isolationist organs attacked the speech, and even though they were in the minority, their criticism was enough to scare off Roosevelt, who, as soon became evident, had no clear idea of what he meant by "quarantine." Many people supposed that the least he had in mind was some form of economic sanctions against the Japanese, since anything less would render his statement meaningless. Roosevelt himself scotched that idea, though, during an off-the-record exchange with reporters the day after his speech.

"Look, 'sanctions' is a terrible word to use," he said. "They are out the window."

What about a peace conference? he was asked. But that idea, too, was "out of the window," the president said. "You never get anywhere with a conference." When pressed, he referred reporters to the concluding words of his speech: "America hates war. America hopes for peace. Therefore America actively engages in the search for peace." This of course explained nothing. But the president dropped the subject, disheartening his early supporters and leaving the field to the isolationists, who continued to denounce the speech.

With the outbreak of war in the fall of 1939 and the fall of France the following spring, Roosevelt's internal tensions magnified. His determination to find a way to stop Hitler increased with the worsening crisis—but he remained unwilling to put the issue to the American people directly. A desperate plea from Winston Churchill provided an alternative tailored to Roosevelt's character. With his country alone in facing the Axis scourge, Churchill asked FDR for the loan of fifty U.S. destroyers to help beat off the expected German invasion of Britain and curb the menace of the Nazi U-boats to Britain's supply lifeline to the United States.

That put Roosevelt on the spot. He feared that without all the help the United States could provide, Britain might collapse, leaving Hitler and his Japanese allies to concentrate on the United States, which, as a result of Roosevelt's unwillingness to face the Nazi peril, was unprepared for war. But Roosevelt knew that U.S. laws strictly forbade his offering the destroyers to Churchill. The president had a choice. He might have gone to the country and the Congress and argued that the U.S. needed to aid Britain for its own survival. By making such a public argument, Roosevelt could probably have pressured Congress into legalizing the destroyer deal and have provided impetus for the United States to bolster its defenses while remaining at peace.

But that sort of direct approach was contravened by Roosevelt's nature. If he had chosen to fight the isolationists, he would have had to expose his own hand to the public and reveal his assessment of the seriousness of the Nazi threat. Predictably, Roosevelt found another way. Negotiating in utmost secrecy, he cooked up a momentous swap with Churchill, giving the Briton the ships he wanted but getting in exchange naval bases for the U.S. fleet on a chain of British possessions in the Western Hemisphere.

The result was just what Roosevelt wanted. Even isolationists did not object because of their delight in getting the naval bases—which turned out to be of little use. And though legal scholars pointed out that what Roosevelt had done flouted the Constitution, the president likened the deal to the Louisiana Purchase.

The destroyers, like the island bases, were only of marginal consequence. What really mattered was that the United States was locked on a collision course with the Axis. Hitler's top naval commander, Grossadmiral Erich Raeder, underlined this reality in a meeting with the führer. The destroyer deal, Raeder said, "represents an openly hostile act against Germany" and the prelude to "the closest cooperation between Britain and the U.S.A." The situation required "an examination of the possibilities for *active* participation in the war on the part of the U.S.A." and of the German response to that event.

Moreover, the deal drove the Japanese closer to their ultimate alliance with Germany, in the Anti-Comintern Pact. The treaty was a dagger aimed at the United States. Fifteen months after it was signed, Hitler's new ally, Japan, drove the blade home at Pearl Harbor. Roosevelt's machinations with the British had made war all but inevitable, and he was convinced of that himself. "Things are coming to a head," Roosevelt told his confidant, Interior Secretary Harold Ickes, in March 1941. "Germany will blunder soon." Ickes had no doubt of Roosevelt's "scarcely concealed desire" for a submarine attack or some other incident that would allow the United States to declare war on Germany or at least to convoy the merchant ships on their way.

In the aftermath of the destroyer deal, emboldened by its approval and his own reelection, Roosevelt at times addressed the issue of aid to Britain directly. In one of his most memorable phrases, in December 1940, he proclaimed the United States to be "the arsenal of democracy" and declared that the country confronted "an emergency as serious as war itself." Responding to yet another desperate appeal from Churchill, this one for financial help, Roosevelt conceived of and pushed through Congress the lend-lease program, allowing Britain to get billions of dollars worth of arms without having to put up the cash it no longer had. To simplify the scheme, the president borrowed a metaphor Ickes had used on behalf of the destroyer deal, saying it amounted to nothing more than lending a garden hose to help put out a neighbor's fire before it spread. Lend-lease in effect repealed the Neutrality Act's requirement for cash payments, although the prohibition on U.S. ships carrying arms abroad remained in force. With its endorsement by Congress, it bore the stamp of legality, but the road to this landmark in U.S. foreign relations had been paved by Roosevelt's manipulations in bringing off the destroyer swap outside the law.

For the most part, though, the president continued to follow his long-established pattern of calculated ambiguity. Throughout the spring of 1941, he resisted pressure from the British and from the hawks in his own cabinet—Stimson and Knox—to have the U.S. Navy convoy the British merchant ships on their way across the submarine-ridden Atlantic, believing that Congress would reject any such proposal. Even when he had reason to be encouraged about public reaction to the danger, FDR backed off. In May 1941, after a powerful speech explaining his decision to extend the range of the navy's neutrality patrol to a point halfway across the Atlantic, pledging "every possible assistance to Britain," he added: "All additional measures necessary to deliver the goods will be taken." He declared "an unlimited national emergency," which required, he said, "the strengthening of our defense to the extreme limit of our national power and authority."

Afterward, Roosevelt invited Robert Sherwood, who had drafted the speech, and his guest Irving Berlin to the Monroe Room on the second floor where he insisted that Berlin play and sing "Alexander's Ragtime Band" and many other of his hits. Still later, when Sherwood went to Roosevelt's bedroom to bid him good night, he found him sitting in bed surrounded with what seemed Sherwood to be a thousand telegrams. "They're ninety-five per cent favorable!" Roosevelt exclaimed. "And I figured I'd be lucky to get an even break on this speech." Just as favorable, Sherwood noted, was the response of the press.

Yet at his press conference the next day, to Sherwood's astonishment and dismay, Roosevelt retreated. He dismissed any notion of ordering the navy to convoy merchant ships or of asking Congress to change the neutrality law.

Harry Hopkins, who supposedly knew Roosevelt as well as anyone, could not account "for this sudden reversal from a position of strength to one of apparently insouciant weakness." Sherwood blamed the backtracking on the "long and savage campaign" waged against the president by isolationists, even though their tactics "had failed to blind American public opinion." But the real reasons were locked up in FDR's psyche, particularly his resistance to commitment.

Meanwhile, Roosevelt's expectation that the United States would enter the war grew firmer. By late October 1941, according to Sam Rosenman, the president "was convinced that American entry into the war was almost unavoidable." Many Americans felt the same way, judging by some of the president's mail, which was turned over to Sam Rosenman for speechwriting fodder. Typical was the letter from a St. Louis banker, urging the president to tell Americans "the whole truth about the terribly dangerous situation we are in." The letter added: "Tell them now. Lead us. We will follow you as we always follow you." But Roosevelt was unwilling to act on that advice.

In an open letter to the president in late October 1941, Robert E. Wood, head of the America First Committee, which had emerged as the most important group battling aid to Britain, challenged him to ask Congress for a declaration of war. Wood candidly stated that America First would fight against the resolution and, he believed, help defeat it.

Wood's challenge was an attempt to end Roosevelt's policy of "subterfuge," as Wood called it, by forcing the president to draw the issue between war and peace so the Congress and the country could choose. If Congress voted to declare war, Wood pledged that America First "and all other patriotic Americans would respect that decision." Stimson, Ickes, and the other hawks in the administration wanted Roosevelt to meet Wood's challenge, believing that the president could rally the public on his side. Roosevelt thought otherwise. He chose not even to answer the letter. "The very fact that such a demand now came from an important spokesman for isolationism," Sherwood wrote later, "provided Roosevelt with sufficient confirmation of his conviction that, were he to do this, he would meet with certain and disastrous defeat."

This was a remarkable judgment from a man who had three times been elected to the presidency and who was considered to be one of the most effective molders of public opinion the nation had ever seen. Meanwhile, FDR waited for the other side to commit the "blunder" he had mentioned to Ickes, which would allow him to lead the country into war after the choice of peace had been eliminated.

The president was right in forecasting an overt act. But instead of the submarine attack he had predicted, it was the Japanese assault on Pearl Harbor that caused a national disaster. Nor did the cost of Roosevelt's unwillingness to deal with reality stop with the damage to the fleet at Pearl Harbor. The price also had to be measured in the terrible toll taken in lives and treasure during the first years of a war for which the United States had not been prepared. Roosevelt's gravest sin as a leader was not that he was too political but that he lacked the courage to use his political skills to promote his own convictions. As Ben Cohen, the legendary architect of many of the New Deal reforms, approvingly put it, Roosevelt "instinctively refrained from committing himself definitely or completely to a specific course of action, whether it was executive action, national legislation or international engagement until he had some idea of the support he might expect or the strength of the opposition he might encounter."

Henry Stimson saw this trait differently from Cohen. He could not help comparing Franklin Roosevelt with his cousin Theodore, who had first brought Stimson into public service. As McGeorge Bundy describes Stimson's thinking: "From what he knew of both men, he was forced to believe that in the crisis of 1941 T.R. would have done a better and more clean-cut job than was actually done. . . . Franklin Roosevelt was not made that way. With unequaled political skill he could pave the way for any given specific step, but in so doing he was likely to tie his own hands for the future, using honeyed and consoling words that would return to plague him later."

When Roosevelt died, soon after winning an unprecedented fourth term, he left a nation stricken with grief at the loss of his electrifying personality. But his legacy also ensured that the vapor of duplicity that Jefferson had generated at the start of the nineteenth century would dominate the modern presidency that FDR created.

Beyond that, FDR had so enlarged the presidency that the grandeur of the office transformed even outwardly drab personalities such as that of Roosevelt's successor, Harry Truman. "I'm not big enough, I'm not big enough for this job," Truman confided to an old Senate colleague on the day Roosevelt died, April 12, 1945. The contrast with the supremely self-assured FDR could hardly have been greater and became more evident with each day Truman spent in the office, where to many Americans it seemed he did not really belong.

The new chief executive's listless oratory, his rasping voice, his thick spectacles, his square face and doughy features, all served to

make more painful for the citizenry the remembrance's of Roosevelt's eloquence and his buoyancy. The provocative columnist and
radio commentator Drew Pearson summed up the difference as well
as anyone. "For twelve years we had the champion of the common
man in the White House," Pearson remarked of Roosevelt's tenure.
"And now," he lamented, "we have the common man."

But if Truman's manner and bearing seemed ordinary, he possessed uncommon virtues. And the comparisons with FDR that at
first seemed unfavorable to Truman would ultimately provide the
key to his character and to his remarkable strengths as a presidential
leader. Truman's great asset was that he understood his own shortcomings and was willing to come to terms with them. An honest
man, at peace with himself, relatively free from inner torments, he
was able to make the most of his abilities.

Above all else, Truman saw himself as an underdog, reveled in this
role, and exploited it to his personal and political advantage. This
self-image had a grounding in his childhood, in particular in his limited vision, a handicap that he at times referred to as a "deformity."
"Of course they called me four-eyes," he told one interviewer.
"That's hard on a boy. It makes him lonely and gives him an inferiority complex." Asked during a chat with visiting schoolchildren after he had left the presidency whether he was popular as a boy, Truman remarked with typical candor. "Why no, I was never popular.
The popular boys were the ones who were good at games and had
big, tight fists. I was never like that. Without my glasses I was blind
as a bat, and to tell the truth, I was kind of a sissy. If ever there was
any danger of getting into a fight, I always ran. I guess that's why
I'm here today."

Growing up, Truman shed much of his inferiority complex. But he
retained his childhood memories, and they helped to lay a foundation for his acceptance as an adult of the populist creed, which was
then pervasive among Democrats in the heartland and which Truman, providing his own embellishments, would make the hallmark
of his leadership.

Contributing to the shaping of his character and values, and rein-
forcing his underdog outlook, were the traumas of the farm economy in the early twentieth century. His father, John, lost everything
he had speculating in grain futures about the time young Harry finished high school in 1903. As a result, Truman never attended a university, the only twentieth-century president not to have graduated

from college, dropped out of business school, and gave up piano lessons.

Then, two decades later, after he had completed what had been the most successful experience of his life, as an artillery officer in World War I combat, the haberdashery business he started in Kansas City went belly up. Bankrupt, Truman blamed the disaster on the tight money policies of the new Republican president, Warren Harding, policies Truman complained "put farm prices down to an all-time low, raised interest rates and put labor in its place." Alonzo Hamby, Truman's most discerning biographer, says the failure was due more to Truman's poor business judgment.

Whatever Truman's limitations as an entrepreneur in his first political job as a district judge, which was really more of a managerial than a judicial post, he built a reputation for good management and honesty, working closely with the Kansas City Public Service Institute, a nonpartisan advocate of the managerial approach to local government, by promoting road improvements and zoning regulation, all administered efficiently and without regard to partisan advantage. Truman's commitment to this approach helped shield him from most of the less savory machinations practiced by the notorious Pendergast machine, the most powerful force in local Democratic politics. Truman liked to tell the story of being summoned to Pendergast's office in 1928, where he found a group of "crooked contractors." As Truman recalled the circumstances, Pendergast said: "These boys tell me that you won't give them contracts."

"They can get them," Truman replied evenly, "if they are low bidders."

Whereupon Pendergast supposedly turned to the contractors and remarked: "Didn't I tell you boys he's the contrariest cuss in Missouri?"

As self-serving as this anecdote may be, there is reason to believe that it was not merely apocryphal. As Jonathan Daniels points out, Pendergast regarded himself not as a crooked politician but as an ambitious businessman, skilled in the art of "honest graft." By promising the voters that he would award road contracts on a low-bid basis, Truman had overcome the resistance of voters to construction bond issues, the cost of which had often been inflated by corruption. As a businessman as well as a politician, Pendergast was shrewd enough to understand that low-bid road building was better for business and for politics than no building at all.

Truman's success in politics did not entirely erase the bitter memories of his business failure. That experience, along with his populist heritage, helped to make him one of the New Deal's most ardent loyalists when Missourians sent him to the Senate in 1934.

But the Senate was no bed of roses. As a presumed tool of the Pendergast machine, which then dominated Missouri politics, Truman had to suffer the scorn of his colleagues, who treated him, as he later complained, "as a sort of hick politician who did not know what he was supposed to do."

Roosevelt was certainly no comfort. Despite Truman's loyalty, FDR and his intimates viewed Truman with such ill-disguised disdain that Truman complained that he was tired of being treated "like an office boy." Of more practical concern, Truman got no help from FDR when he faced a major challenge for his party's renomination in 1940. Indeed, the president sought to ease Truman out of office by suggesting he take an appointment on the Interstate Commerce Commission. By the time he won reelection, the beleaguered Truman felt, he later wrote, like a battered old legal document that looked as if it "had been through hell three times with its hat off."

Even when he became FDR's choice for the office that would soon become the stepping-stone to the presidency, Truman got short shrift from the White House. Instead of telling Truman of his intentions directly, Roosevelt had the word passed to him by Democratic national chairman Bob Hannegan. "You tell him that if he wants to break up the Democratic Party in the middle of war, that's his responsibility," FDR bellowed at Hannegan over the phone, loud enough for Truman to hear. Then he hung up.

Reluctant to take the job, Truman wondered aloud: "Why the hell didn't he tell me in the first place?"

In the White House, Truman had a difficult time at first, and understandably so. He was following in the wake of the president who, with the possible exception of Lincoln, had had a greater impact on the lives of other Americans than any in history. And he was taking over the presidency under circumstances that could not have been more trying. He still had the war to win, which meant deciding to drop the atomic bomb on Japan and finding a way to deal with the Soviet Union under Stalin's iron hand. Finally, he had to supervise the transformation of America back to peacetime footing amid competing demands from labor and business to advance their own interests.

Among the most serious of the domestic difficulties was trouble with organized labor, a key component of the alliance that Roosevelt had constructed and one that Truman needed to preserve if he was to win the White House in his own right. Having been handcuffed by wage controls during the war, the unions now pressed for wage increases. Strikes and work stoppages in the auto plants and other major industries—steel, meatpacking, and electric appliances—drove up prices and fired public resentment. The labor unrest was closely tied to concern over inflation, which had supplanted recession as the most serious apparent danger to the economy. Truman was caught in a dilemma between the threat of rising prices and public resentment of price controls. He temporized, asking for extension of price controls but failed to put his full prestige behind the idea. In the spring of 1946, Congress stripped the wartime Office of Price Administration of nearly all its powers, and prices soared 15 percent in a single month.

No wonder Truman struggled, particularly after the voters handed control of both houses of Congress over to the Republicans in the 1946 elections. Yet this sea change turned out to be the making of the Truman presidency, the crucible that allowed Truman to transform his self-image as an underdog into a powerful political asset.

In the 1948 election, Truman converted his difficulties with the GOP Congress into a devestating weapon and staged the most dramatic political upset in modern history. After overcoming intraparty resistance to his nomination at the Democratic convention, Truman came out fighting in his acceptance speech. "I'm going to win this election and make those Republicans like it," he declared.

Actually, Truman had some solid reasons to back up that boast. In particular, there was the vigorous condition of the economy, which had recovered from its postwar convulsions and was generating jobs at a reassuring pace. It was true, though, that for many Americans, the perception of this reality was blurred by the still sharp recollections of the inflation and angst that had followed hard on the heels of V-J Day. Moreover, most politicians assumed that the dramatic Republican victory in the 1946 midterm election was a sure omen of GOP victory in the 1948 presidential election.

Hence, hardly anyone believed Truman's optimistic assessment of his chances. Politicians in his own party shunned him. Late in October, as Truman campaigned in New York City, an aide had to lock arms with Ed Flynn, Bronx Democratic boss and former party national chairman, and literally pull him out of the car and up onto the platform with the president. Flynn did not want to be seen with a loser. Journalists of every leaning regarded Truman's defeat as inevitable, and pollsters unanimously forecast his defeat. Barring a "major convulsion," one of the most prominent, Elmo Roper, announced soon after Labor Day, "Mr. Dewey is just as good as elected."

But Truman fought on. And by fighting at a time when most saw his cause as hopeless, he evoked not sympathy but admiration and respect. His attacks on the Republicans gave rise to the cries of "Give 'em hell, Harry," the phrase that became the hallmark of his candidacy and to which Truman responded: "I have never deliberately given anybody hell. I just tell the truth on the opposition."

The election was a great personal victory for Truman and an affirmation of the strength of his character. But the youthful anxieties that led to his underdog image, which he used so effectively as a campaigner, remained to plague him when his adversaries could not be confronted directly. As chief executive, Truman was often frustrated by forces he could not control, and his continued awareness of his own shortcomings led to occasional outbursts that lowered his standing with the public.

Public disapproval might have been even higher if citizens had been aware of the letters Truman wrote and then did not mail. In what Truman himself called "my spasms," he showed himself to harbor feelings about the press that if expressed publicly would have typed him as close to a paranoid. Considering himself the target of a conspiracy organized by the lords of the press, Truman reviled the "the sabotage press" and raged that the "prostitutes of the mind are much more dangerous than the prostitutes of the body."

Although Truman was prudent enough to trash these missives, he could not always suppress the evidence of his insecurity. To blunt the criticism of him as inexperienced and unstatesmanlike, Truman at times assumed a confidence that was not always justified and made brash statements that came back to haunt him. During the congressional investigation of spying charges against Alger Hiss, Truman dismissed the probe led by a young Republican congressman from California named Richard Nixon as a "red herring," a remark the Republicans would throw back into his teeth countless times after Hiss was ultimately convicted of perjury.

A far more serious example of hip shooting was Truman's decision to send U.S. troops into combat in Korea, without support of Congress, an action that would ultimately mean the ruination of his presidency. That commitment came in the context of constant attacks leveled against Truman by Republicans for allegedly losing China. When the North Koreans crossed the thirty-eighth parallel in June 1950, Truman knew his own reputation was at stake. As Truman historian Robert Donovan wrote, "Vicious domestic political repercussions, damaging to the President, would have been inevitable if the 'loss' of China were to be followed by the 'loss' of Korea."

But the threat was not just to Truman's political base, it was to his own self-esteem and to his ability to fulfill his assigned role as commander in chief. In committing the United States to the defense of South Korea, Truman claimed that he was fulfilling U.S. obligations under the U.N. charter. In fact, the United States was not legally obligated; the U.N. had only "recommended" that member states give help to the South Koreans.

Congress would probably have approved Truman's intervention, if consulted. But Truman had personal reasons for bypassing Congress. The unilateral action gave the appearance of strength in an area where he had been accused of weakness. Moreover, a Capitol Hill debate on the Korean issue certainly would have led to questions about Truman's ultimate goals in intervention and what price he would pay to achieve them, inquiries that Truman would much rather have avoided since he had not fully considered them himself.

Because he failed to set out U.S. objectives in Korea and rally the public behind them, Truman was forced to bear alone the political burden of fighting a frustrating conflict that stirred massive discontent at home and wrecked hopes for domestic reform and progress. He also ended a long period of Democratic dominance of the White House.

His tenure gave impetus to the increasing importance of character in the presidency. By his reelection victory in 1948, Truman affirmed that the new role for the presidency conceived during the depression and enhanced during World War II would become a permanent part of national life. Moreover, Truman's decision to drop the atom bomb, by giving future presidents the literal power of life and death over much of the planet's population, added a new dimension to the role of character in the presidency.

In a sense, the 1952 election of Dwight Eisenhower represented the purest triumph of the character issue since the creation of the Constitution and the election of Washington. That choice was dictated not by Eisenhower's political beliefs—about which little was known by anyone, including the man himself—but by the almost universal appeal of Eisenhower's personality, an attitude summed up by the unofficial slogan of his campaign: "I Like Ike."

Eisenhower's lack of interest in ideology was rooted in his childhood, and his family's fervent adherence to the Mennonite faith, which acknowledged no authority outside the Bible and the enlightened conscience of the individual. This creed filled the intellectual space that might have been occupied by some sort of political belief. Although the Kansas of Eisenhower's formative years seethed with agrarian discontent and radicalism, his family, sheltered by their faith that the rewards for the good life lay in some other world, ignored these sectarian fevers. Instead of resenting the powers that controlled his family's destiny, young Dwight accepted life as he found it and concentrated on improving his own lot.

Eisenhower's military career transformed his disinterest in politics into downright antipathy. As a soldier, he was cut off from most of the social and economic forces that dominated civil life and shaped American politics. Moreover, disdain for politics was part of the military tradition. As one of Eisenhower's West Point instructors wrote: "If any convictions . . . were acquired by the cadet they were generally of contempt for mere politicians and their dishonest principles of action."

Just as significant as this aversion to conventional politicians was the fact that Eisenhower's military career exposed him to a certain kind of political experience—a much narrower and limited part of the political world than if he had run for office. Rather than viewing himself as a novice who had much to learn from career politicians, Eisenhower felt that as president, he was simply extending his previous leadership experience. On his first day as president, he wrote in his diary that "this seems like a continuation of all I've been doing since July '41—even before that."

But in reality, what shaped Eisenhower's presidency was not his scant background in politics but rather the thrust of his character, dominated by his drive for success but also tempered by fear of failure if he set his goals too high. His response to this conflict was to get people to like him rather than to challenge them directly. This strategy, which Eisenhower liked to label as "teamwork," executed with what biographer Piers Brendon called "calculating dexterity," allowed him to promote himself while maintaining the protective coloration of good fellowship.

In part, his prudence stemmed from his humble origins. When his parents came to live in Abilene, Kansas, shortly after Dwight's birth, with three small children, they could afford little more than a shack, just south of the railroad tracks, with no indoor plumbing. In the seven years they lived there, three more sons were born. Cash was short—the Eisenhower boys had to wear hand-me-downs—and they peddled groceries door to door. "They made us feel like beggars," Dwight's brother Edgar later said.

Although confident of his abilities, Dwight early on learned that for a poor boy trying to make his way in the world, ingratiation was often the better part of valor. "I think his grin saved Ike a lot of trouble," one friend said of the nineteen-year-old Eisenhower.

At West Point, Ike put up a show of defying of authority, though this had mostly to do with minor rules of deportment, such as card playing or smuggling in food. Most of his aggressions he took out on the football field. But his genuine feelings were reflected in his decision to become a cheerleader after his knee injury sidelined him from football, an experience that was said to be one of the most devastating of his life. By his willingness to go out and root for the team in the face of his own bitter experience, he had made the code of West Point the rule of his own life.

And his ability to get along in difficult situations was far more important than his skimpy military experience in his rise to the pinnacle of the U.S. military machine during World War II, and this characteristic also made him immensely popular as a president. However, this same character trait contributed to his dismal failure in dealing with the two most critical domestic issues of his presidency: the scourge of McCarthyism and the civil rights revolution.

Eisenhower's response to McCarthyism as president was foreshadowed even before he took office during the 1952 presidential campaign. Infuriated by McCarthy's attacks on George C. Marshall, Eisenhower's old boss and patron, for allegedly helping to "lose China" to the Communists, Eisenhower decided to strike back by pointedly paying tribute to Marshall while stumping in Milwaukee—"right in McCarthy's backyard," as Eisenhower put it.

But when Wisconsin Republican leaders saw the prepared text of Eisenhower's speech, they protested, arguing that these words would give offense to McCarthy. That was all Eisenhower had to hear. He deleted the controversial paragraph from his speech—but only after reporters covering Eisenhower's campaign had read it in the advance text. The net result not only embarrassed Eisenhower but actually boosted the stature of McCarthy by demonstrating that even Eisenhower was unwilling to challenge him.

The drive to overturn nearly a century of racial segregation confronted Eisenhower directly after the Supreme Court's unanimous decision in *Brown vs. Board of Education*. This opinion, written by Earl Warren, the Republican chief justice whom Eisenhower had himself appointed, and joined in by Southerners like Hugo Black of Alabama and Stanley Reed of Kentucky gave Eisenhower a historic opportunity to rally the nation behind the court's ruling and to begin healing the nation's racial wounds. Instead, true to his nature, Eisenhower sought to maintain a sort of neutrality between the court and the opponents of the decision, a posture that inevitably fostered resistance to the ruling.

A month after the *Brown* ruling, the president asked about legislative proposals to ban segregation in interstate travel, saying he believed that progress could be better achieved "through the cooperation of people, more than law, when we can get it that way." Eisenhower's irresolution over civil rights was underlined when the crisis over court-ordered integration of Central High School in Little Rock, Arkansas, exploded in public. Eisenhower at first temporized in his dealings with Arkansas's archsegregationist governor, Orval Faubus, and when his indecision led to violence, Eisenhower sent in troops, inflaming resentment across the South.

This was a transforming event because it permanently sealed off certain avenues for leadership and locked American politics and society on a divisive and violent course that shaped the ensuing three decades. Later, Eisenhower speechwriter Emmet John Hughes summed up the episode as illustrating Eisenhower's "explicit resolve to try one's patient best—to leave things undone."

Paradoxically, Eisenhower was not unaware of the flaws of passive political behavior, as when he complained to his diary about the excessive caution of moderate Republican senators who did not "seem to realize when there arrives that moment at which soft speaking should be abandoned and a fight to the end undertaken." Ike added: "Any man who hopes to exercise this leadership must be ready to meet this requirement face to face when it arrives; unless he is ready to fight when necessary, people will finally begin to ignore him." Yet Eisenhower's character made it far easier for him to preach this principle in privacy than to practice it in public.

Still and all, in his eight years in office, Eisenhower demonstrated the power of passivity in the presidency. In that sense, he appeared to both reflect and reinforce what many people took to be the ambience of the times. But after a while, national moods tend to shift. And if Eisenhower's personality was a bulwark for stability, his successor would demonstrate what a powerful catalyst presidential character can be for change.

6

THE PRINCE
OF CHARISMA

AS THE EISENHOWER PRESIDENCY and the decade of the Fifties
drew to a close, most Americans had every outward reason for con-
tentment. Although the Cold War persisted, the end of the Korean
War in Ike's first term meant that no American troops stood in
harm's way. At home, the greatly enlarged middle class was absorbed with tapping into the new opportunities for affluence created
by the postwar boom. Under the circumstances, few political leaders
saw evidence of a groundswell for change.

Just the opposite. Lyndon Johnson, the highest-ranking elected
Democrat in the land, who had every intention of swapping his post
as his party's Senate leader for the desk in the Oval Office, complained about the zeal of some of his liberal Democratic colleagues
on Capitol Hill in pushing proposals to remedy social and economic
inequities. "The country doesn't want this," Johnson grumbled to
historian Arthur Schlesinger Jr. "The country wants to be comfortable; it doesn't want to be stirred up." Yet this was just what the
youthful junior senator from Massachusetts intended to do—get the
country "stirred up."

But to achieve his objective, this aspirant for the Democratic presidential nomination did not intend to use the sort of radical policy
proposals Johnson opposed. Rather, what John Fitzgerald Kennedy
chose to depend upon was the force of his own personality, and the
result would work a transformation on the presidency comparable
only to the impact of Franklin Roosevelt.

For Eisenhower, the national hero, often likened to George Washington, character had been a relatively simple and straightforward force, as he drew on his reputation as conqueror of the Axis and his innate congeniality. But Kennedy, mustering all his energy and imagination, made character the foundation of a complex and subtle manipulation. His vigorous style and his own war record, somewhat embellished, cast him as macho role model for males, while his movie star visage and sophisticated manners captured the hearts of their wives and his elegant rhetoric stirred the intelligentsia.

Yet Democratic party elders saw Kennedy as a threatening presence. "Senator, are you certain that you are quite ready for the country, or the country is ready for you?" demanded Harry Truman, eight years out of office, as Kennedy started his march for the nomination: "May I urge you to be patient."

But the old campaigner, like many of his generation, missed the point. Kennedy's timing was right on mark. Seeing through the veneer of complacency that masked the public mood, Kennedy realized that the time was ripe for the sort of change he had to offer. For a decade and half since the end of the war, Americans had been a nation in flux—economic, social, and political.

Between 1940 and 1960, the population increased by 47 million, from 132 million to 179 million. Nearly all of this gain was registered in the metropolitan areas, which showed a jump to 112 million from 70 million. During the same twenty-year period, the gross national product multiplied fivefold, from $100 billion to more than $500 billion. Also striking were the gains in family income from 1950 to 1960.

At the beginning of the decade, 10 percent of American families earned under $2,500, measured in 1978 dollars; by 1960, only 5 percent were below that level. And while in 1950, under 50 percent of American families had incomes in excess of $10,000, again measured in 1978 buying power, that figure had climbed to nearly 70 percent by 1960. Educational levels were improving, too. In 1940, only 35 percent of the population had completed four years of high school or more. By 1960, that figure had jumped above 40 percent, and college graduates in the population had increased from under 5 percent to nearly 8 percent.

The most important consequence of this dynamic from Kennedy's perspective was the erosion of traditional partisan allegiances and the undermining of the authority of the once-supreme party bosses.

As they confronted changing constituencies with increasingly complex interests, the party leaders found it harder to define and dominate political debate. Voters were more independent. Increasing income and leisure had fostered the emergence of an influential class of intellectuals—in the media, the foundations, and academia—who generated and managed political information and who found a growing audience for their output.

And then there was television. The magic box had become a pervasive and intrusive force, at once enlightening and confusing, informing and distracting. Between 1950 and 1960, the number of American families owning television sets had increased tenfold, to more than 45 million, or nearly 90 percent of the population. The medium's capacity for instant projection of ideas and personalities into living rooms everywhere created a voice that drowned out the traditional political chain of command.

With all this ferment underway, the way was clear for forging new loyalties, on the basis of personality. His background and circumstances all combined to shape Kennedy as the paradigm of the new politics of charisma, tailored for the television age. In his long march to the White House, Kennedy was driven by the ambition that had been bred into him since childhood as the scion of wealth and privilege. The overriding reality of his upbringing was the affluence and prestige of his father Joseph P. Kennedy Sr., a man consumed by ambition, mostly unrequited, a domineering yet thwarted patriarch figure, tycoon, diplomat, politician, philanderer, and, last but certainly not least, founder of what he hoped would be a political dynasty. Like many men of his ilk, Joseph Kennedy Sr. was often guilty of stretching the truth—but never further than when he wrote in his 1936 campaign book, *I'm for Roosevelt*, "I have no political ambitions for myself or for my children."

But it was not just political office that the senior Kennedy had in mind. From the start, he expected his offspring to get to the top of whatever field of endeavor they happened to be in. When his sons raced on Nantucket Sound he trailed them in a boat, tracking their errors for later coaching.

The death of his eldest son, Joseph Jr., for whose political stardom Kennedy senior had prepared, meant that the next son in line, John, would have to play that part. John Kennedy once said later that "wanted" was not strong enough to describe his father's feeling about his second-oldest son entering politics: "He demanded it."

Although this aggressiveness was inevitably part of John Kennedy's psychic legacy, it was cloaked with a restraint more in keeping with the son's own environment. Not having to battle as hard as his father had, young Kennedy could afford to respond to Joe Kennedy's heavy-handed striving with what one biographer has called "fastidious withdrawal." This contributed to the detachment that was one of John Kennedy's principal characteristics and that served as a governor on his own aggressive instincts, making them less conspicuous and less threatening than they might otherwise have seemed.

Kennedy's closest aide, Theodore Sorensen, was struck by Kennedy's ability "to look at his own strengths and weaknesses with utter detachment." His skepticism extended to his own religion. When a Catholic friend remarked that he was uncertain about the teachings the church presented as unquestionable truths, Kennedy responded that he shared that ambiguity.

While Eisenhower's drive to succeed was spurred by his family's mean economic circumstances, that was certainly not the case with Kennedy. Money was a subject his family did not need to think about and that the elder Kennedy would not even allow to be discussed at the dinner table, so the Kennedys grew up with a strange innocence of money. Hearing them talk about money, a friend once said, was "like listening to nuns talk about sex."

Instead of poverty, the problem that Kennedy and his family had to overcome was class snobbery, as practiced by the New England Brahmins. The Boston papers delivered to the Kennedy family doorstep had a separate social section for the Irish, apart from the section that covered the Yankee upper crust.

His father was refused membership in exclusive clubs, snubbed in his own state's resort towns, and the local papers in the city that his father-in-law Honey Fitz had governed as mayor would not list his daughters among the season's debutantes. Fed up with being called Irish, Joe Kennedy once said: "I was born here. My children were born here. What the hell do I have to do to be an American?" This consciousness of prejudice would drive the father, and his sons, harder to gain the success needed to overcome it.

Kennedy's ambition was served by a discipline that had also been drilled into him from his earliest days. "I grew up in a very strict house," the future president once said. "There were no free rides and everyone was expected to give their best to what they did. There was a constant drive for self-improvement."

Joe Kennedy did not hit his children. He did not need to. "His eyes would take you right out of the window," a family friend recalled. Even in his absence, his letters kept up the pressure. "Don't let me lose confidence in you again, because it will be pretty nearly an impossible task to restore it," he warned young Jack after the boy had fallen down in his grades at school.

Pushing to reach the goals his father set for him, the young man did not divert himself with ideology; he had little commitment to the doctrines of either the right or the left. As wealthy and powerful as his family was, because of his Irish Catholic heritage, Kennedy thought of himself as an outsider in a world dominated by the Protestant establishment. Moreover, his father's example as a buccaneering capitalist taught him the advantages of lone-wolf operation.

When John Kennedy entered Harvard in the fall of 1936, Hitler was already on the march in Europe, the New Deal at its peak, and the Harvard campus alive with intellectual energy and protest. But the young student remained remote from all this. His grades were poor in his freshman year, and he did not even join the Young Democrats. "The fact of the matter is," he later told Sorensen, "I fiddled around at Choate and really didn't become interested until the end of my sophomore year at Harvard."

But even as he became more serious about his studies, he remained ideologically neutral. At Harvard, one of his political science teachers, Arthur Holcombe observed: "He had no interest in causes, his approach was that of a young scientist in a laboratory." The most conspicuous evidence of young Kennedy's intellectual invigoration was his senior thesis at Harvard, *Why England Slept,* completed in 1940, which analyzed the reasons for England's failure to prepare itself against Hitler. The work reflected the twenty-three-year-old author's by now characteristic detachment; he criticized those who had been overemotional in reacting to Munich. With his father's encouragement, advice, and vigorous assistance, the thesis was transformed into a book that made the best-seller list, though critics complained that its author was so evenhanded in spreading the blame for Munich that it was hard to tell what the lesson was for Americans.

John Kennedy's political career traveled that same nonideological path from the beginning. At twenty-nine, now a war hero as a result of his surviving the sinking of the torpedo boat, PT-109, that he had captained in the South Pacific, he made his maiden run for Congress in 1946, a year in which voters seemingly had "had enough" with the New Deal. And the young candidate was taking no chances. While promising to bring his district the benefits of government activism—housing, social security, and medical care, he nevertheless termed himself "a fighting conservative." In that contest, ideology did not matter as much as Kennedy's own resources—his renown as a war hero, his family's myriad contacts in the Boston political world, his father's wealth, which he dispensed lavishly, and the energy of the friends and relatives who campaigned for him. Although he continued to run and win on the Democratic ticket, first as a congressman, then as a senator, he kept his distance from party regulars, whom he once described as "tarnished holdovers from another era."

He also detached himself from the party's traditional ideological moorings without establishing clearly defined ideas of his own. A Harvard *Crimson* reporter, noting Kennedy's failure to take specific positions, reported that the young lawmaker "feigns an ignorance of much in the affairs of government and tells you to look at his record in two years to see what he stands for." But far from hindering him, this lack of positioning gave Kennedy the flexibility he wanted on his climb up the political ladder.

When he challenged moderate Republican Henry Cabot Lodge for his Senate seat in 1952, Kennedy differed so little from the incumbent that his strategists argued about whether to attack Lodge from the left or the right. As it turned out, he did both. Meanwhile, he relied mainly on personality. His mother and sisters hosted a series of receptions designed to offset the "snob appeal" of Boston Brahmin Lodge and his clique. And Kennedy created a network of supporters who labored for his candidacy independent of the state's Democratic Party organization.

Once in the Senate, the way was clear for a run at the presidency. Styling himself as an outsider, Kennedy overcame the traditional party leaders and bosses, relying heavily on his Catholic faith. While some voters rejected him because of his religion, a good many others backed him mainly for that reason. But probably far more important was the impact on a broader segment of voters who were neither bigots nor ardent Catholics. In their minds, Kennedy's religion gave his candidacy a special identity, setting it apart from others and endowing it with a moral fervor it otherwise lacked.

No large policy questions informed Kennedy's quest for the nomination. He was running on his personality, and the so-called religious issue, defined by Kennedy as whether a Catholic could be elected president, was the only reason that his candidacy had for existence beyond its own success.

In the general election, Kennedy defeated Eisenhower's vice president, Richard Nixon, for the presidency much as he had conquered Lodge in their battle for the Senate. He attacked him from the left on domestic issues and from the right on foreign policy. But these differences were of little consequence, creating a blur around Kennedy's fundamental promise to "get this country moving again" and making it necessary for his ardent supporter and adviser Arthur Schlesinger Jr. to write a book revealingly titled: *Kennedy or Nixon: Does It Make Any Difference?* As it turned out, the historian was desperate for material to prove his point that there *was* indeed a great difference. Significantly, for two-thirds of the book, Schlesinger was forced to dwell on the contrasts of style between the two men, concluding: "The hard fact is that Nixon lacks taste."

In the White House, with the help of a worshipful press corps, Kennedy managed to entrance the public with his own carefully sculpted depiction of himself as the bold Galahad of the New Frontier. This image was a function of political necessity. His hairbreadth victory margin in the election—after the vote had been tallied, Mort Sahl, the popular satirist, wisecracked that "every time Kennedy sees two people walking down the street he knows one of them doesn't like him"—undermined his chances of fulfilling his vague campaign pledge of action.

In public, Kennedy discounted the limitations imposed by his razor-edge triumph, saying, "There may be difficulties with Congress but a margin of only one vote would still be a mandate." But in private, he conceded the wisdom of Thomas Jefferson's counsel: "Great innovations should not be forced on slender majorities."

But Kennedy was unwilling to have history grade him as nothing more than an obscure, transitional figure in the presidential pantheon. Seeking action, or at least the appearance of action, he turned his attention, and that of the public, from the domestic arena, where his options were limited, to the broader horizons overseas and also in outer space, where he had far greater freedom. In these domains, if his deeds were not always substantively significant, they were invariably infused with eye-catching symbolism.

Determined to fire the public's imagination, he set goals for himself and the nation that reached literally to the moon, and to hold the voter's attention, he orchestrated his presidency, like his candidacy, around his own personality.

The Kennedy presidency drew its life force from crises, some of which could not be avoided, others of which the president seemed to seek out. Sorensen, the aide closest to the president, devoted one chapter of *Kennedy*, his chronicle of the presidency, to discussing "The Early Crises—the Bay of Pigs," another to "The Berlin Crisis," and yet another to "The Continuing Crises"—the Congo, Laos, Vietnam, Red China, and India. In this environment of permanent danger, the mundane routines of government could be overlooked and the public's attention focused on the personality of the president.

His Inaugural Address, with Sorensen's contrapuntal cadences and biblical syntax and Kennedy's fervid delivery, set the tone. For his purposes, Kennedy abandoned the cool detachment and rational discipline on which he prided himself and instead seemed determined that if he could not get Americans moving again, as he had promised, he could at least get their adrenaline racing. He pledged his country "to pay any price, bear any burden, meet any hardship, support any friend, oppose any foe to assure the survival and success of liberty." For the future, he forecast "a long twilight struggle" and exulted in this prospect. "Only a few generations have been granted the role of defending freedom in its hour of maximum danger," he said. "I do not shrink from this responsibility, I welcome it."

This rhetoric led Kennedy on a search for challenges around the world and beyond. A few months after he entered the White House, he committed the nation to send a man to the moon by the end of the decade. Whatever the scientific value of this enterprise, it was symbolism on a galactic scale. If Americans could reach for the moon, then under Kennedy's leadership, nothing on earth should be beyond their grasp.

And so he set forth on a policy of adventurism around the globe. Within weeks of taking office, Kennedy gave the green light to the ill-fated landings at Cuba's Bay of Pigs, afterward lamenting not because the United States had violated its own standards of international conduct but because he had miscalculated the expedition's chances for success. "All my life I've known better than to depend on the experts," he said in the voice of the existential man. "How could I have been so stupid as to let them go ahead?"

Contributing to this folly was an element of macho pride ingrained in Kennedy's personality. "I know everybody is grabbing their nuts on this," he told Sorensen beforehand; but he himself, the president said, would not be "chicken."

Yet this fiasco did not deter him from further risks abroad, most notably in Vietnam, where he began the buildup of U.S. forces that would eventually tear the nation apart, but also in Berlin, then a flash point for the Cold War turning hot, where he once again indulged himself in rhetorical excesses. *"Ich bin ein Berliner,"* he told a cheering crowd that greeted him on his visit there, after he had undertaken a buildup of U.S. garrisons facing the Red Army, and the reaction was so frenzied that Kennedy himself was taken aback.

Nevertheless, he continued to engage in rhetorical excess, in part because the recollections of the Bay of Pigs fiasco gnawed at him. When the luckless prisoners of the invasion brigade were finally ransomed back to the United States, Kennedy greeted them in the Orange Bowl in Miami with the provocative pledge that their battle flag would be returned to them some day "in a free Havana."

Kennedy was never able to keep that promise. But it was the tension between Kennedy and Fidel Castro that led to the ultimate confrontation of his presidency, the October 1962 missile crisis. As Sorensen later acknowledged, the presence of the Soviet missiles in Cuba *"made no difference in fact"* in the balance of nuclear weaponry. "But the balance would have been substantially altered *in appearance*" (his emphasis).

On these grounds, Kennedy, whose presidency relied so much on appearances, led the nation and the world to the brink of nuclear destruction. But if the macho side of his character led him into trouble, the other side of his psyche, his rationality and discipline, saved him and the country from potential disaster. Kennedy learned from what he did wrong and what he did right in the Bay of Pigs, and the lessons reinforced his adherence to reason and logic when cataclysm threatened in the missile crisis.

"You're in a bad fix, Mr. President," Air Force Chief Curtis LeMay told Kennedy as he gathered his top advisers to plot a course through the nuclear thicket. Kennedy coolly shrugged off the remark with a joke. Facing the threat of a nuclear collision with the Soviet Union, he needed no one to remind him that he was in a monumental jam.

He had to contend against not only Soviet Premier Khrushchev, who had secretly lodged missiles in Cuba in the face of Kennedy's warnings against such action, but also the U.S. military leaders, who, like LeMay, argued for an air strike or an invasion of the island, as opposed to the blockade Kennedy decided to rely on.

Kennedy was willing to acknowledge the uncertainties he faced: "It's a goddamn mystery to me," he said of the Soviet action—and to try to understand his adversary's viewpoint: "Maybe our mistake was in not saying [to the Soviets], sometime before this summer, that if they do this we're going to act," he remarked early in the crisis. Later, when Khrushchev countered the U.S. demand that the Soviets withdraw their missiles from Cuba by insisting that the United States remove *its* missiles from Turkey, Kennedy observed: "He's got us in a pretty good spot here. Because most people would regard this as not an unreasonable proposal. I'll just tell you that."

Prudently, he sought the counsel of his Republican predecessor, Eisenhower, and asked if Ike thought the Soviets would respond to an invasion, for which some Kennedy aides were lobbying, by launching nuclear weapons against this country.

"Oh, I don't believe they will," Eisenhower replied.

"You would take that risk if the situation seems desirable?" Kennedy pressed him.

"What can you do?" Eisenhower responded. "I'll say this: I'd want to keep my own people very alert."

But Kennedy did not share Eisenhower's equanimity about a nuclear holocaust risk taking and resisted the pressure for invasion.

On the final Saturday of the crisis, as Robert Kennedy later reported, there was "almost unanimous agreement that we had to attack early the next morning with bombers and fighters and destroy the SAM [surface-to-air missile] sites."

Still, the president wanted to give Khrushchev time to deal with his own hard-liners. "It isn't the first step that concerns me but both sides escalating to the fourth and fifth step—and we don't want to go to the sixth because there is no one around to do so," he told his aides.

And perhaps most important, throughout the crisis, he left the door open for negotiations with Khrushchev, calling upon the Soviet leader "to join in an historic effort to end the perilous arms race and to transform the history of man." The result was that Kennedy scored a great personal triumph that overshadowed the humiliation of the Bay of Pigs.

But even so, the Soviets remained dangerous adversaries, and the New Frontier's domestic agenda was still bogged down in a balky Congress. Meanwhile, Kennedy needed to sustain the public's approval of his presidency. And for this he relied on the attraction of his style and the force of his personality. He had not been in the White House for very long before he had made his voice and his face, his manner and his habits, his staff and his family, seem one and indivisible with the office he held. It was a phenomenon unmatched since Franklin Roosevelt's tenure. And Kennedy accomplished figuratively overnight what it had taken Roosevelt years to achieve, with the great help of television.

Kennedy's presidency marked the onset of television into national politics. Kennedy's quick wit, virile good looks, and crisp manner were ideally suited to the camera. The first president to risk having his press conferences televised live, he converted the reporters in attendance into a cast of supporting players who complemented his starring performance. "We couldn't survive without television," he once remarked. Enhancing the authority of television was the response of the other media. His press conferences, because they were on television, became news events in themselves, receiving more coverage in the printed press than those of any of his predecessors, including Franklin Roosevelt.

And Kennedy saw to it that print reporters and columnists got their share of special attention. Indeed, Arthur Krock, the venerable Washington columnist of the *New York Times*, accused Kennedy of news management in the form of "social flattery . . . on an unprecedented scale."

Kennedy's efforts to influence the press worked two ways. For those he liked or hoped to win over, there were invitations to tête-à-tête luncheons or state dinners or to the occasional "deep background" confidence. But for those who challenged or threatened him, there was a darker side. His cancellation of the White House subscription to the *New York Herald Tribune* because of the paper's criticism of his domestic policies was the most conspicuous evidence of that. Behind the scenes, Kennedy sought to suppress information that he regarded as threatening either himself or the national security or both. He persuaded the *New York Times* to play down a story that described preparations for the Bay of Pigs assault, a maneuver he later regretted. And he also tried, but failed, to convince the *Times* to remove David Halberstam from his assignment in Vietnam, where his reporting contradicted the rosy picture Kennedy wanted to create.

Nevertheless, for most of the media, Kennedy remained a heroic figure. The air of urgency created by Kennedy and his New Frontier team as they plunged themselves and the country into one crisis after another gave journalists covering the White House a vicarious sense of importance. And Kennedy enriched the environment by conspicuously hobnobbing with luminaries of the arts and academe, linking his administration with the world of culture and ideas.

Kennedy clearly did not take this effort lightly. When aide and longtime crony Paul Fay asked him who had painted two canvases on a White House wall, Kennedy retorted: "My God, if you have to ask a question like that, do in it a whisper or wait till we get outside. We're trying to give this administration a semblance of class."

"The glow of the White House was lighting up the whole city," Arthur Schlesinger boasted of the heyday of the New Frontier. "It was a golden interlude." And the press corps basked in the glow.

Kennedy heightened this sense of drama by injecting himself prominently into public controversies. When the big steel companies announced a rise in prices despite what Kennedy had taken to be a pledge of restraint made personally to him, he struck back. In addition to publicly questioning the patriotism of their corporate leadership, he encouraged investigations into their economic power by the Justice Department and Congress. After the companies rescinded the increase, Robert Frost, the unofficial poet laureate of the New Frontier gloated: "Oh, didn't he do a good one. Didn't he show the Irish, all right."

Kennedy returned the sentiment in a tribute to Frost not long after his death, saying that he was impressed by many of Frost's qualities but "also by his toughness." As the British journalist Henry Fairlie observed: "Even the poets on the New Frontier had to be tough."

The infatuation of the press with the Kennedy persona extended to his family. His wife, Jacqueline, set new styles in women's coiffures and dress and, having redecorated the White House amid much fanfare, showed off her handiwork in a televised tour. Caroline Kennedy, three years old when her father was inaugurated, was the subject of innumerable articles and even of a cover story in *Newsweek*.

As powerful as it was during his lifetime, the legend Kennedy wove around his personality took on new vitality after his assassination and left a mark on the presidency that endured long after the abrupt ending of Kennedy's own tenure. In part, this was because of the circumstances of his death, which came to be seen as prefiguring a long period of national trauma and pessimism and thus as a watershed in the nation's twentieth-century history. Indeed, in notable contrast to our formal remembrances of Washington, Lincoln, and FDR, which take place on their birthdays, the nation pays tribute to JFK on the anniversary of his assassination.

But beyond the perceived historical significance of his death, as Thomas Brown points out in *JFK: History of an Image,* many people had reasons for perpetuating and embellishing the Kennedy legend. For Kennedy's brothers, Robert and Edward, the Kennedy myth represented a powerful boost for their own ambitions and for their offspring. For Democrats in general, the exalted memory of Kennedy has been a valuable asset in attracting young people, Catholics, and blacks—who came to view him more favorably after his death, when his civil rights proposals were enacted, than during his life, when he had been criticized for not promoting these ideas with sufficient vigor. Finally, but not least in importance, a multitude of journalists and political historians found the dramatic story of Kennedy's life irresistible.

The combined energies of these various individuals and groups generated a picture somewhat larger than life but very much resembling the image that Kennedy had cultivated of himself. Among the qualities emphasized were Kennedy's reasonableness, his pragmatism, his capacity for growth, his good taste, his youth and his vigor.

This image has persisted in the face of contradictory disclosures. For one thing, despite the perception of ruggedness he sought to create, he suffered for most of his life from chronic ill health as a result of a variety of afflictions. Some were injuries from sports, some from his wartime experience, and some just the result of a weak constitution. At Choate, he was absent due to illness more than any boy in his class. At Harvard, he cracked a leg bone and ruptured a spinal disk. PT-109's fatal collision with a Japanese destroyer aggravated an old college back injury; he also got malaria in the service and dropped down to 125 pounds. After he returned to civilian life, he was afflicted with Addison's disease, making him vulnerable to other infections. And during his Senate career, he twice underwent back surgery with his life on the line.

"At least half the days he spent on this earth were days of constant pain," his brother Robert wrote. "We used to laugh about the risk a mosquito took in biting Jack Kennedy—with some of his blood the mosquito was almost sure to die." Then came gradually over the years the revelations of Kennedy's sexual misconduct, knowledge of which he had managed during his presidency to keep hidden from all but a few members of his inner circle.

In the wake of the revelations of Kennedy's freewheeling sexual activities, some of his intimates sought to explain his behavior by linking it to his ailments. Kennedy used sex as a distraction from the considerable physical pain he suffered much of the time, he claimed. Biographer Herbert Parmet suggests this might have been the case with his most notorious paramour, Judith Campbell Exner, with whom, by her own account, Kennedy conducted a steamy affair before he learned of her close relationship with Mafia chieftain Sam Giancana. Her visits to Kennedy, according to Exner, were concentrated in the summer of 1961, when Kennedy was in great physical discomfort as a result of having injured his back in the spring and contracting a severe viral infection.

Others have contended that Kennedy's at times consuming interest in sex may have been intensified by the cortisone shots he received for Addison's disease. More generally, others have conjectured that Kennedy, having been told by a British doctor that he would probably die before he reached the age of forty, was determined to make the most of the years remaining to him. Sorensen reports that Kennedy had adopted this rationalization during his first year in the Senate. "Having borne more pain and gloom than he liked to remember, he enjoyed in his bachelor days carefree parties and companions on both sides of the Atlantic Ocean. There was a natural temptation to spend the limited number of days in which he could count on enjoying full health in pursuit of pleasure as well as duty."

Kennedy's court historian, Arthur Schlesinger Jr., has contended that the accounts of Kennedy's illicit behavior have been greatly exaggerated. "If half the claims were true," Schlesinger wrote in a retrospective on the New Frontier, "he would have had time for little else." Anyway, Schlesinger testifies that based on his own experience in the White House, "if anything untoward happened at all, it did not interfere with Kennedy's conduct of the presidency."

Despite the self-serving nature of Schlesinger's comment, the truth is no one has offered persuasive evidence to the contrary, though the journalist Seymour Hersh tried very hard to do so in his muckraking book, *The Dark Side of Camelot.*

Because Kennedy was "obsessed with sex, and willing to take enormous risks to gratify that obsession," he was vulnerable to blackmail, Hersh contended. And he cited an unpublished memoir by Hyman Raskin, a Chicago lawyer and political operative who claims Kennedy was forced to pick Senator Lyndon B. Johnson as his running mate in 1960 when Johnson and his fellow Texan, House Speaker Sam Rayburn, threatened to divulge some unidentified episode from Kennedy's past. "Those bastards were trying to frame me," Raskin claimed Kennedy told him, referring to Johnson and Rayburn. "They threatened me with problems, and I don't need more problems. I'm going to have enough problems with Nixon."

But there is too much evidence of Kennedy's solid political motivation for offering the number-two slot to Johnson, whom he hoped would help the Democratic ticket carry Southern states, and of Johnson's and Rayburn's reluctance to accept, to make Raskin's account in any way credible.

So far as Kennedy's own presidency was concerned, the sexual adventures of the 35th president unlike those of the 42nd, Bill Clinton, were like a tree falling in the forest. Since the public had no knowledge of his behavior, his reputation and moral authority were undamaged.

But in another part of the forest, occupied by Kennedy's legacy, the exposures of his behavior have made quite a noise that will likely reverberate as long as the presidency lasts. As even Schlesinger admits, the revelations created "disappointment edging into bitterness, resentment bordering on rage," among some of those who had accepted Camelot at face value and had pursued the same high-minded causes the Kennedy legend had helped to foster. The macho standards disclosed to have governed Kennedy's life and his presidency contravened the qualities of moralism and idealism that he purported to represent.

Others shrugged off the revelations as trivial gossip. "All very interesting—even engrossing. But so what?" contended *Washington Post* columnist Richard Cohen. The reports of Kennedy's behavior, as Cohen saw it, merely demonstrated "that a person can really be conventionally immoral in his personal life and at the same time be just a swell person in his public life. In other words, it may just be irrelevant to history what precisely Kennedy did after he concluded work. It's the work that matters."

Of course, this is sheer sophistry. What Kennedy did off duty, if a president is ever off duty, is scarcely "irrelevant to history." Indeed, it is vitally important in understanding what he did during whatever period Cohen thinks of as his regular working hours. The private and public Kennedy are not really contradictory personalities but rather different layers of the same individual. And on close inspection, the two dimensions are consistent, not contravening.

Privately and publicly, Kennedy lived and governed at the edge. His self-control was not illusory but linked to his self-indulgence. The challenge that ruled his days was in testing how far he could let himself go without losing control of himself and the country he led. Just as he ran risks by his womanizing, so he gambled with his stewardship of the country. As president, he urged his fellow citizens on to the moon; as a lover, he captured the heart of Marilyn Monroe, who was evidently entranced by Kennedy's dualism. "Marilyn Monroe is a soldier," the actress once said. "Her commander in chief is the greatest and most powerful man in the world. The first duty of a soldier is to obey her commander in chief. He says, 'Do this,' you do it."

The net result of the Kennedy revelations has been strange indeed. The news media have been relentless in publicizing the misconduct of the Kennedy family, whose members have provided plenty of raw material, from the tragic, such Edward Kennedy's auto accident at Chappaquiddick, to the trivial, such as Michael Kennedy's alleged affair with the family baby-sitter. Yet the disclosures have had relatively little impact on Kennedy's own image. He remains, according to the polls, one of the most popular of presidents. It may be, as Thomas Brown suggests, that "in a period of widespread cynicism and distrust, many Americans needed a symbol—no matter how tarnished—to cling to for reassurance." Whatever the reasons, the Kennedy myth has had a powerful and enduring impact on character and the presidency, as his successor soon discovered.

As president, Lyndon Johnson was continually tormented by the Kennedy legacy and the endless comparisons with his more stylish and elegant predecessor, contrasts that invariably worked to his disadvantage. These memories of Kennedy, greatly enhanced by his admirers, Johnson came to believe cast discredit on himself and greatly injured his own presidency.

The anxieties and resentment Johnson felt toward Kennedy, which were much greater after Kennedy's death than during his lifetime, added to Johnson's deep-rooted insecurities, shaped by his upbringing and early career. The consequence was that character shaped Johnson's presidency fully as much as it had Kennedy's, but with a glaring difference. Unlike Kennedy, Johnson was unable to control and establish his image and use it to his advantage. Instead, character was a weapon used against him with devastating effect. The spotlight that John Kennedy had drawn to the presidency was now focused on Lyndon Johnson, who was totally unprepared to deal with it and who became the first president to be destroyed by the character issue.

What made the Kennedy legacy particularly painful for Johnson was that he was forced by political necessity to exploit his successor's memory, most notably during his succession to office. Then, he captured the imagination of a grieving nation when he recalled Kennedy's assertion in his Inaugural Address: "Let us begin," and added poignantly, "Let us continue."

By pledging himself to carry out the other man's public testament, Johnson elevated both himself and Kennedy to a moral level neither could otherwise have reached. His purpose, Johnson later explained in a phrase that might have been drawn from Shakespearean tragedy, was to "take a dead man's program, and turn it into a martyr's cause."

All this was particularly difficult for Johnson, who was an exceedingly proud man. His shirts were all monogrammed with the LBJ initials, like the cattle on his ranch, and when a young aide suggested it would be unwise for him to campaign in the Texas hustings wearing a monogrammed shirt and French cuffs, Johnson retorted: "Son, they take me like I am or they find themselves another boy."

For a man with an ego roughly as large as his native state, subordinating his identity to that of the younger man who had preceded him in office, after besting him for the nomination, was an act of great discipline. Just as hard was the necessity for retaining the services of Kennedy loyalists. On the day of Kennedy's funeral, he felt obliged to plead with two of Kennedy's key lieutenants, Lawrence O'Brien, his chief liaison with Congress, and Kenneth O'Donnell, his appointments secretary, to stay on at the White House.

"Needless to tell you, I'm most anxious for you to continue just like you have been, because I need you a lot more than he did," Johnson said. Then Johnson added plaintively, "I don't expect you to love me as much as you did him, but I expect you will, after we've been around a while."

Meanwhile, though, Johnson raged in private against those who had been close to Kennedy—too close he often felt for Johnson's own good. When Harry McPherson, one of Johnson's own trusted aides, sent him a memorandum suggesting that Johnson should make more use of former Kennedy people, the president responded by suggesting that McPherson transfer to another job outside the White House.

Resentful of the treatment he received in William Manchester's chronicle of the Kennedy assassination, *Death of the President*, Johnson bitterly contrasted the reputed skill of the Kennedys in manipulating the press with what he professed to be the ineptitude of himself and his allies.

"We are not equipped by experience, by tradition, by personality or financially to cope with this," Johnson complained to one of his aides. "I just do not believe that we know how to handle public relations and how to handle advertising agencies, how to handle manuscripts, how to handle book writers, so I think they're going to write history as they want it written."

For himself and his staff, there was little to do, Johnson added, except "to try to refrain from getting into an argument or a fight or a knockdown, and go on and do our job every day, as best we can."

Yet try as he might, he could not resist striving to win over the press. "He was enormously preoccupied with the press," Douglass Cater, one of his speechwriters, observed. He lavished time and attention and flattery on reporters and was almost invariably dissatisfied with the results.

To make matters worse, Johnson had to contend against not only the memories of John Kennedy but the living embodiment of his legacy in the person of Robert Kennedy, who had remained in Johnson's cabinet as attorney general, a position he clearly hoped to use as a stepping-stone for his own presidential ambitions.

At this point in his life, Robert Kennedy had never held or even sought elective office. On many public issues, his views were unknown to the public and, in fact, still largely unformed. Yet the simple fact of his close identification with the myths woven about his brother made him a major act on the political stage with whom Lyndon Johnson had to contend. To squelch the idea then actively being promoted by Kennedy's partisans that the attorney general should be Johnson's running mate in 1964, when he would seek the presidency in his own right, Johnson publicly announced that he would not consider any official of cabinet rank for his running mate, thus effectively eliminating Kennedy.

Johnson's tension with the Kennedy legacy compounded the conflicts that had shaped his character since childhood. Johnson's mother was a woman of some cultural pretension, in contrast to his father. As a child, Johnson was caught between his mother's encouragement of intellectual and artistic interests and his father's rejection of such notions as unseemly for a young man. "My mother soon discovered that my daddy was not a man to discuss higher things. To her mind his life was vulgar and ignorant," Johnson later said. "She felt very much alone. Then I came along and suddenly everything was all right again. I could do all the things she never did." But Rebekah Johnson aggravated young Lyndon's tensions by seeming to make her love for her son dependent on his measuring up to the goals she set for him.

Thus, when he quit taking the violin and dancing lessons she had arranged, she retaliated, Johnson remembered, by in effect "pretending I was dead . . . and . . . being especially nice to my father and sisters."

Johnson's father, Sam Ealy Johnson, was a schizoid personality. On the one hand, he took the side of the downtrodden in the legislature to which he had been elected on the Populist ticket. Yet, on the other hand, he himself was a middle-class striver who saw himself and his family as country gentry. If he did not rise in the capitalist world, it was for bad luck and maladroitness rather than for any lack of trying. He poured nearly all his earnings into purchasing property and investing in what he took to be promising enterprises, but nearly all of these ventures turned into financial disasters.

His son, Lyndon, seemed born to fulfill the unsatisfied dreams of his father for material success. "With Lyndon there was an incentive that was born in him to advance and keep advancing," a childhood neighbor of the family recalled." "Sam had that. But he didn't have it anywhere near like Lyndon did."

From infancy, he was quick, bright and restless. His mother, spurred her firstborn's spirit and drive, teaching him the alphabet from blocks when he was two and Mother Goose and Tennyson by the time he was three. At ten, he liked to analyze current affairs for the crowd at the barbershop, where he had established a shoeshine stand, to his father's mortification. He started school at four, and at fifteen, he graduated from high school, where his classmates prophesied that he would rise to the governorship of their state.

But then the young man hit a bump on his road to success. An ill-advised investment by his father led to financial ruin. Sam Johnson owed money to banks and storekeepers that he could not pay and would remain in debt for the rest of his life. His family, though not on the brink of starvation, had to struggle to get by. What made all this even more painful was that the elder Johnson had cut an expansive and self-confident figure in Johnson City, driving big cars, even hiring a chauffeur and a housemaid, boasting of big business deals that he was on the verge of carrying off. From a respected and envied citizen, Sam Johnson became a despised and ridiculed figure. And of course all of this fell heavily on his family, including his son, Lyndon.

All this seemed only to make Johnson strive even harder. "Restless, energetic purposeful, it is ambition that makes of the creature a real man," he wrote as a student editor at Southwest Texas State Teachers College at San Marcos. "It is direction behind force that makes power . . . if one wishes to make something of his life he must have steadfast purpose, subordinate all other hopes to its accomplishment and adhere to it through all trials and reverses." At San Marcos and elsewhere, Johnson practiced what he preached. He dominated campus politics at college, gaining enough confidence so that he could tell a fellow student: "Politics is a science, and if you work hard enough at it, you can be president. I'm going to be president."

But Johnson's striving had another objective besides achieving the success that he always sought—and this was also a goal that reflected his upbringing. Buffeted as a child by the conflicts between his parents and between his mother and himself, Johnson sought to avoid such tensions by assuring himself of control of his environment and the people around him.

Sometimes he bullied, as he did with Senator Hubert Humphrey, taking advantage of Humphrey's desperate yearning to be Johnson's vice presidential running mate in 1964. "Some damn Republican nominated you against me today," Johnson chided Humphrey in the spring of 1964, after a GOP Senator had speculated that Humphrey might run for president against Johnson that year.

"By God, Mr. President, I'll tell you . . . I am not a candidate," Humphrey exclaimed, "so you can sleep better tonight."

But of course Johnson could not dominate every political situation. As he went on in life, Johnson relied more on a strategy of seeking consensus to achieve his goals without open conflict, while papering over or ignoring real differences between various political groups.

For Johnson, consensus was the Holy Grail of politics. "To me," Johnson explained in his memoirs, "consensus meant, first, deciding what needed to be done regardless of the political implications and, second, convincing a majority of the Congress and the American people of the necessity for doing those things."

Johnson had learned to practice consensus politics in his home state of Texas. Like other Southern states, Texas had a tradition of Democratic Party supremacy dating back to the Civil War. With the social and economic changes that followed World War II, Republicans began to stir in the state. But Johnson and other party leaders managed to forestall the emergence of Texas Republicanism for years by catering to the business interests, which normally would have supported the GOP, and by overlooking the economic grievances of less advantaged constituencies in the Democratic ranks.

Although the Republicans in the U.S. Senate were a more formidable force than they had been in Texas, Johnson found when he won election to that body that his consensus approach could still operate among the lawmakers. By taking care of the personal concerns of individual senators and by devising convenient compromises, he could generally avoid open clashes with the opposition party and also with his fellow Democrats. His skill at dealing and maneuvering helped him become majority leader and brought him unprecedented power in that position.

The tragic circumstances that elevated Johnson to the presidency were ideally suited to the building of consensus. The mourning nation rallied behind the successor to its fallen leader, and partisanship was subdued. Johnson was quick to take advantage of the situation. A few days after the assassination, he called the Republican leader in the Senate, Everett Dirksen of Illinois, and asked him to persuade his fellow Republicans "that it was essential to forget partisan politics, so that we could weather the national crisis in which we were involved and unite our people."

Dirksen, an old Johnson crony from the president's Senate days, was not hard to convince. "Well, Mr. President," he replied, "you know I will."

Johnson had many other similar conversations; as he later boasted: "I brought people together who under ordinary circumstances would have fled at the sight of each other." With them all, he stressed his basic consensus theme: "People must put aside their selfish aims in the larger cause of the nation's interest." Yet the resolution of these so-called selfish aims was actually supposed to be the task of political process, whose normal workings had been muzzled by consensus. In these circumstances, it seemed left to Lyndon Johnson alone to define the nation's interest.

Having turned his succession into a triumph for consensus, Johnson managed to achieve the same result with the 1964 election campaign, thanks in no small measure to the nomination of Barry Goldwater as the Republican standard-bearer. By selecting a candidate so far removed from what was then considered to be the mainstream of their own party, the GOP left Johnson free to spend his days on the stump defending motherhood and the flag. "I just want to tell you this," he assured a crowd in Providence, Rhode Island, "we're for a lot of things and we're against mighty few."

Brandishing a poll that showed him winning favorable ratings from liberals, middle-of-the-roaders, and conservatives, he boasted to White House visitors: "They all think I'm on their side."

In the interest of preserving that belief, Johnson sought to avoid as much as possible the controversial subject of Vietnam. Johnson had nurtured grave doubts about Vietnam from the early days of his presidency, as he revealed in a telephone conversation with his one-time Senate mentor, Richard Russell of Georgia, in the spring after Kennedy's assassination.

"It's one of those places where you can't win," Russell remarked. "Anything you do is wrong."

"I don't believe we can do anything," Johnson agreed.

"If we had a man running the government over there [South Vietnam], that told us to get out, we could sure get out," Russell said.

"That's right," Johnson said, "but you can't do that [pull out]. I just haven't got the nerve to do that."

Reluctant to push forth into the Indochinese quagmire, yet, as he had acknowledged to Russell, lacking the nerve to withdraw, Johnson defused the issue during his campaign against Goldwater by getting the Congress to pass the Gulf of Tonkin Resolution, granting him free rein in Southeast Asia.

On election day, not only did Lyndon Johnson himself win the presidency in his own right by more than 15 million votes but the Democrats gained the biggest advantage they had enjoyed in Congress since the heyday of Johnson's early hero, Franklin Roosevelt. Mindful of his far-reaching Great Society legislative objectives, Johnson rushed to take advantage of what he regarded as a golden opportunity, but also a fleeting one.

"I have watched the Congress from either the inside or the outside, man and boy, for more than forty years," Johnson told the administration's lobbyists assembled in the White House only a few weeks after this great victory. "And I've never seen a Congress that didn't eventually take the measure of the President it was dealing with. I was just elected president by the biggest popular margin in the history of the country, 15 million votes," he reminded his listeners.

But he calculated that he had already lost about 2 million as the voters recovered from their panic over Goldwater. And he warned, if he got into a battle with Congress or escalated the War in Vietnam (as he would indeed decide to do only a few months later), "I may be down to 8 million [votes] by summer."

Eight million must have sounded like a large number at the time. But as it turned out, this was an underestimation of the toll Vietnam took on Lyndon Johnson's presidency. Johnson's obsession with the race of his popularity against the clock cast a shadow over the glow from his great victory. It meant that as he roared ahead full throttle toward the Great Society programs he thrust upon Congress, he had little time to consider priorities, little time to build public understanding and support for the vast new programs he demanded.

Johnson's response to the challenge of Vietnam developed over a period of nearly a year, beginning with the August 1964 attack on U.S. warships in the Tonkin Gulf and culminating with his July 1965 announcement that he was sending 50,000 more troops to South Vietnam. During that period, even as he dealt with Indochina, at home he won a great election victory, established the agenda for the Great Society, and saw its first legislative seeds come to fruition.

By the time he was sworn in for his elected term, he had already achieved impressive legislative results, notably the enactment of the Kennedy civil rights program and the initial measures in his own war on poverty. But these turned out to be only appetizers in the far-reaching menu of demands he now imposed upon the Congress.

Consensus required something for nearly every national interest of consequence. Medicare for the elderly and federal aid to education for young middle-class families were the major components of the Great Society blueprint; they headed a laundry list of other programs in areas ranging from the arts to Appalachia, from water pollution to weather forecasting.

An added and momentous starter was voting rights. After gaining enactment of the 1964 law striking down segregation in public accommodations, new civil rights legislation was the last thing on Johnson's mind. But the voting rights issue took on a life of its own, as a result of Negro demonstrations in the South, and Johnson did not merely support the legislation. He made the Negro's cause, and its stirring battle cry, his own. "We shall overcome," he declared in a memorable address to Congress, and voting rights became another Johnson accomplishment.

To gain approval of these and other measures Johnson relied, as he had in the past, on consensus. But altered circumstances created unforeseen obstacles to success. With the memory of the assassination fading and Goldwater eliminated as an opponent and as a threat, Johnson struggled to find new ways to preserve harmony behind him. He sought to adapt the techniques he had used in the Senate, where his success was derived from his reliance on personal relationships and on his elevation of results to an importance making the means employed to achieve them irrelevant. "He doesn't believe that the end justifies any means," Harry McPherson argued. But he acknowledged: "He believes it justifies quite a few means."

As president, though, Johnson was forced to deploy his resources over a much broader arena covering the nation and the world. As the stakes increased and the battlefield expanded, so did the difficulties of maintaining the control that was the lifeblood of Johnson's consensus. "This was a man who . . . had found total mastery of the communications system in a confined environment of Congress was essential to the kind of job he was capable of doing," Douglas Cater said. "When it got on the presidential level it was no longer possible."

The celebrated "Johnson treatment"—the nose-to-nose, hand-to-lapel administering of persuasion and bully-ragging that had won him countless triumphs in the Senate cloakrooms—could not be brought to bear on Ho Chi Minh, or even on Martin Luther King.

His attempt to establish and maintain consensus in the White House was also handicapped by the need to achieve results, the cement that held consensus together. To enact the mind-boggling domestic agenda he proposed, Johnson could no longer count on winning support with something as minor as a post on a key committee. He had to deliver rewards to one after another of the many diverse groups he needed to bring into his ever-widening tent. Success with one group meant that he had to find at least a comparable reward for another group. This of course soon proved to be impossible; unlike Johnson's ambitions, the total of federal revenues was finite. In other words, as he nailed each new coonskin to the wall, as LBJ himself liked to put it, Johnson was competing with himself, and this was a game he was bound to lose.

Johnson put his personal stamp on the presidency as much as, or arguably more than, had his two immediate predecessors, Eisenhower and Kennedy. But he used his personality differently and got different results. Eisenhower and Kennedy had great personal advantages. Johnson could not match Ike's fatherly dignity or Kennedy's youthful vigor and flair, qualities that gained them a popular following. Lacking such traits, Johnson sought to focus his powerful personality internally. With rare exceptions, such as his appeal for voting rights in a crisis atmosphere, he tried to engineer support through private persuasion rather than public pressures.

Johnson was more comfortable dealing with the leaders of groups than appealing directly for the support of the members of these groups. The leaders, Johnson believed, could handle their followers for him. He liked to tell the story of the prominent Baptist who called the White House to complain to the president that the Aid to Education Bill, then before the Congress, unfairly benefited Catholics. The aide who took the call mentioned that the president at the moment was relaxing in the White House pool with none other than Billy Graham. After a pause, the caller asked: "Is that our Billy?"

Yes, it was, he was told. Did he want the president to come to the phone?

"Oh no," the mollified Baptist replied. "Just give the President my very warm regards."

In this case, and in a number of others, Johnson's cultivation of interest-group leaders paid off. But there were limits to the loyalties these leaders could command on a personal basis. And later on, as many of the programs ran into trouble, these leaders could not deliver the support of their own rank-and-file adherents, which weakened the political backing for the Great Society at a time when Johnson's own popularity was in decline because of Vietnam.

In 1965, with the war going badly for the United States, Robert McNamara returned from the latest in a series of inspection trips to Indochina and offered the president a choice between withdrawal, which McNamara contended would be "humiliating," maintaining the status quo, which the defense secretary contended would only be putting off the decision that the president had to make, or escalation, which was McNamara's own preference.

The choice Johnson made was to escalate. But the decision was so blurred by his concern with consensus that its ultimate effect was not much different than if he had maintained the status quo—except for the increasing toll that would be taken in the coming months of lives, treasure, and the president's own credibility. Most of his advisers wanted Johnson to sound a more certain trumpet—to put the economy on a war footing, activate the reserves, and ask Congress for a tax cut to finance the war effort. They wanted this not just for the practical results but for political reasons, in the best sense of the word, in hopes of rallying the country and unifying it behind the effort in Vietnam.

But Johnson did no such thing. Instead of delivering a prime-time television address to rouse the country, he said what he had to say about Vietnam at an afternoon press conference, with of course a much smaller audience. Instead of the 200,000 men he was committed to send to General William Westmoreland in Vietnam, he mentioned only an immediate increase of 50,000.

Would the country have to choose between guns and butter? he was asked. He could not foresee the future, the president said. But he added: "At the moment we enjoy the good fortune of having an unparalleled period of prosperity with us, and this Government is going to do all it can to see it continue."

Johnson's nondecision on Vietnam was the culmination of consensus. It was a policy shaped to avoid controversy that would have threatened Johnson personally, not only because of his troubled emotional make up but also because it would put in jeopardy the Great Society programs that were the cherished jewel of his presidency.

"I knew from the start," Johnson would say later, "that if I left the woman I really loved—the Great Society—in order to get involved with that bitch of a war on the other side of the world, then I would lose everything at home. All my programs."

Lyndon Johnson's sin was not that he made the wrong decision. Rather, it was that because of his inner conflicts he did not make any honest decision at all. As a result, the Great Society crumbled, and Vietnam turned into the first war the United States had ever lost. More than that, he divided and damaged his country and his party, causing wounds that endured long after his presidency had concluded. And he set the stage for Richard Nixon and Watergate.

7

THE PUNCHING BAG

I ORDERED THAT THEY USE ANY MEANS NECESSARY including illegal means to accomplish this goal," Richard Nixon confessed to his cronies in 1973 as the horrors of Watergate began to unfold. But then Nixon added: "The President of the United States can *never* admit that."

In the fall of 1997, more than twenty years after he was driven out of the White House, disclosures based on a new batch of Watergate tapes made clear that the great Watergate cover-up that brought down the Nixon presidency was inspired by more than the desperate need to obstruct the wheels of justice. Powerful motivation also came from Nixon's convoluted character, particularly his unwillingness to face the conflict between his own conspiratorial conduct and the high-minded code that he had publicly preached on his stormy journey to the Oval Office.

Nixon had spent most of a political lifetime depicting himself as a paragon of middle-class values. Thus it was that even though he perceived the potentially fatal danger from trying to suppress exposure of the Watergate outrages—"Far worse than the facts here is the cover-up," he told his close aide John Ehrlichman—Nixon continued to resist disclosure as a threat to his cherished reputation. Instead of making a clean breast of things, as many Republicans urged him to do, Nixon sought to placate his foes by putting the blame on one underling or another. He justified his conduct by recalling how the highly esteemed President Dwight Eisenhower, under whom Nixon served as vice president, had fired his chief of staff, Sherman

Adams, after Adams had been tainted by accepting a vicuña coat from a favor seeker.

"He [Adams] did a lot that made it pretty easy to do so," Nixon acknowledged. "But . . . Eisenhower felt, properly so, that the presidency had to be protected. And I feel the same way. I mean . . . you cannot figure the President is covering up this Goddamn thing."

Whether in his unyielding strategy of diversion and denial Nixon actually deceived himself is not clear, even from the tapes. But he certainly was willing to delude almost everyone else—including such renowned allies as the evangelist reverend Billy Graham. When Graham called to cheer him up while the Senate Investigating Committee, led by Sam Ervin of North Carolina, was putting the heat on Nixon's White House, Nixon airily sought to pin the sole blame for the ever-widening scandal on his reelection campaign organization.

"The main thing . . . I can assure you nobody in the White House is in on this," he said, "but the campaign, they sometimes do silly things."

Nixon's unwillingness to confront the truth about himself was closely linked to his feelings about the office he held. Master of realpolitik that he was, Nixon realized that his own public perception was enhanced by the exalted view many Americans held of the presidency. But beyond that calculation, Nixon, like many of his predecessors, came to see himself and his fate as intertwined with the presidency.

As Nixon himself later acknowledged, it was the cover-up more than the overt acts of Watergate that drove him from the White House. If he had early on made disclosure of the White House's connection to history's most notorious bungled burglary, a forgiving public might have allowed him to salvage his presidency. But as his own remarks on the tapes made clear, whatever the legal and political barriers to such a course, Nixon's self-image and his identification with the office he held also stood in the way. "You've got to be always thinking in terms of the presidency, and the president should not appear to be hiding and not be forthcoming," Nixon told White House counsel John Dean, who would ultimately abandon his scheming to shield Nixon from the scandal and become instead the most devastating single witness against his former chief.

The sycophants among his visitors learned that the easiest way to please Nixon was to reinforce his conviction that the duties of his office transcended in importance the cloud of scandal over his presidency. "It's inhuman, Mr. President," his national security adviser, Henry Kissinger, said of the charges made against him. "You were carrying a bigger load than any president has."

Nixon could not have agreed more. "Good God, we were going to Russia and China and ending the war and negotiating," he said. "I wasn't even thinking about the Goddamn campaign, you know. That's the tragedy. I wish to Christ maybe that I had but if I'd been spending time in the campaign," he added, "maybe we couldn't have pulled off Vietnam."

But for all the what-ifs and might-have-beens that Nixon sought for solace in his darkest hours, the truth was that Watergate was no aberration but the culmination of career shaped by the twists of his character. An introspective, brooding personality, Nixon managed through enormous self-discipline to make himself into a successful politician. His natural somberness and defensiveness helped him fulfill his chosen role as a defender of middle-class interests, which was the key to his political success.

Through his upbringing, Nixon had a ready claim on middle-class values—free enterprise, individual rights, the sanctity of the family, and the like. But to advance himself and his beliefs politically, he found it easier to identify these values more by contrast with the forces that threatened them—communism, big government, and the Eastern elite.

Whittier, California, where Nixon lived from the time he was nine until the age of twenty-one, was outwardly at least a tranquil place, resembling the sort of small town in Ohio that Nixon's father, Frank, had been raised in late in the nineteenth century. And in the prosperous twenties, as Nixon was coming of age, the mood of Whittier was confident and complacent, its townspeople secure in the belief that the rewards of life went to those in the town who worked the hardest.

Nixon's own recollections are redolent of classic middle-class culture. "Three words describe my life in Whittier: family, church, and school," he later wrote. In fact, he left out another word that was equally reflective of the middle class and of his boyhood: business, specifically his father's grocery store, a "mom-and-pop" operation, in which the whole family worked day and night.

But economic and technological changes that posed a threat to the old order in politics also imperiled traditional middle-class values that had been imported from the Midwest. The Midwest style of

Protestantism was not vigorous or dramatic enough to satisfy the spiritual needs of bustling Southern Californians, even of Quakers like the Nixons. They often drove to Los Angeles to hear Aimee Semple McPherson, billed as the "evangelist of a Four Square Gospel made in California," and her arch-rival, Bob Shuler.

The Quakers had chosen to settle in Whittier because it seemed an unlikely location for railroads. Little did they imagine the onset of the automobile and other threats to the tranquillity of the Communists, such as the proliferating Hispanic society in its environs and the burgeoning in nearby Hollywood of the movie industry, with its enticements of glamour and make-believe.

The social ferment in California was part of a national upheaval in manners, morals, and values that started during the Roaring Twenties and then gained fresh impetus from the stock market crash, when lives were wrecked for causes and reasons that were almost impossible to fathom.

For Richard Nixon, who was in his teens when the Great Depression struck, the trauma of this calamity was made harder to bear by conflicts within his own family. Nixon would later heap praise on both his parents publicly. Yet Nixon's own account of his growing up makes clear that both were deeply troubled personalities who passed on their problems to their offspring.

Discouraged and frustrated by his struggles to earn a living, Frank Nixon became ill-tempered, quick to take out his resentments on his offspring. "It was his temper that impressed me most as a child," Nixon wrote later. "He was a strict and stern disciplinarian and I tried to follow my mother's example of not crossing him when he was in a bad mood." In an attempt at self-analysis, Nixon suggests that "perhaps my own personal aversion to confrontations stems"— he was referring to personal, not political, encounters—from his father's belligerence.

Hannah Nixon, serious of mien, strong in her Quaker faith, had her own way of punishing the children. "She would just sit you down and she would talk very quietly and then when you got through you had been through an emotional experience," Nixon later recalled. "In our family, we dreaded far more than my father's hand, her tongue."

Nixon's youth was also jarred by the death of two of his brothers, his younger brother, Arthur, from tubercular meningitis when Nixon was twelve and his older brother, Harold, after a long siege by tuberculosis, when Nixon was twenty. After Harold's death, Richard sank into a deep silence that even his parents could not penetrate. From then on, Hannah Nixon recalled, "it seemed that Richard was trying to be three sons in one . . . to make up to his father and me for our loss."

Richard Nixon developed into a shy, intense personality who did not make friends easily. In college, where he was notably successful in his courses and in extracurricular activities, he was generally respected, but some students resented his ruthless cocksureness. Despite his shyness and introspection, Nixon made himself into a successful school politician at Whittier College. First, he won election as class president. Then he got himself elected student body president, building his campaign around a promise to lift the college's ban on campus dances, a pledge he kept, despite the fact that Nixon himself had little use for dancing.

Nixon also went all out for college football, even though he lacked any real skill for the sport and was too small. His coach, Wallace "Chief" Newman, whom Nixon idolized, later said: "We used Nixon as a punching bag. If he'd had the physical ability, he'd have been a terror."

In sum, Richard Nixon's greatest character strength was that he could make himself do almost anything he felt needed to be done to make his way in the world. This pattern, established in his student days, carried over into his political career, during which he made himself seek confrontations and polarize sentiment because he knew by doing this he could arouse emotions and enthusiasm for himself that he could accomplish in no other way. Nixon allowed himself to be used "as a punching bag" by the football team so that he could gain the friendship that was otherwise denied him.

The punching bag was the father of the politician. For three decades in national politics, Nixon made himself into a target so he could gain power that would otherwise be denied him. "Courage— or putting it more accurately, lack of fear—is a result of discipline," Nixon wrote in *Six Crises*, after losing his first run for the presidency. "Any man who claims never to have known fear is either lying or else he is stupid. But by an act of will, he refuses to think of the reasons for fear and so concentrates entirely on winning the battle." By an act of will, Nixon throughout his career was able to shut out not just fear but also pride, shame, and other fundamental emotions so that he could win the endless battles he staged and fought.

During his long political career, Nixon dramatized his role as a defender of middle-class values most effectively by opposing and attacking people and forces that threatened these values. Probably the most rewarding of these targets from Nixon's standpoint was Alger Hiss, whom Nixon took on when he was a young congressman, an encounter that turned out to be the making of Nixon's future. Handsome, educated in the best schools, accustomed to holding the best jobs and associating with the best people, Alger Hiss was the very model of the midcentury American elitist. A Harvard Law School classmate, Lee Pressman, once said of Hiss: "If he were standing at the bar with the British Ambassador and you were told to give a package to the Ambassador's valet, you would give it to the Ambassador before you gave it to Alger."

Hiss was just the sort of figure who, because of his manner and breeding, aroused instinctive resentment from many middle-class voters. He had ties not only to prominent Democratic leaders such as Dean Acheson and Adlai Stevenson but also to such a distinguished Republicans as John Foster Dulles, who, as chairman of the Carnegie Endowment, had hired Hiss as president of that philanthropy. By challenging Hiss at great risk to his own career, Nixon set himself apart from other politicians who would have been unwilling to do this because they feared the repercussions, and he thus bolstered his claim as a defender of middle-class values.

For similar reasons, during the 1952 campaign, Nixon mercilessly attacked Hiss's old colleague, Dean Acheson, who fell into the same category. "His clipped moustache, his British tweeds and his haughty manner made him the perfect foil for my attacks on the snobbish kind of foreign service personality and mentality that had been taken in hook, line and sinker by the Communists," Nixon observed.

On less substantial ground, Nixon went after Harry Truman during his 1960 presidential campaign. Responding to a question about Truman's intemperate language raised during his third campaign debate with Kennedy in 1960, Nixon said: "When a man's president of the United States, or a former president, he has an obligation not to lose his temper in public. One thing I've noted as I've traveled around the country are the tremendous number of children who come out to see the presidential candidates." If he won the election, Nixon said, he hoped that American parents would be able to look at him, whatever they thought of his policies, and say: "Well, there is a man who maintains the kind of standards personally that I would want my child to follow."

Kennedy responded with cool disdain to Nixon's homily: "I really don't think there's anything that I could say to President Truman that's going to cause him, at age seventy-six, to change his particular speaking manner," he remarked. "Perhaps Mrs. Truman can, but I don't think I can."

When he took office in 1969, Nixon was alert to the opportunity presented him by the unruly nature of the protest against the Vietnam War that then divided the country. As he analyzed the wave of protest against the war and the overall permissiveness that accompanied it, Nixon concluded that he was ready "to take a stand on these social and cultural issues. I was anxious to defend the 'square' virtues." On some issues, his opposition to funding abortion and legalizing marijuana and his support for "unabashed patriotism," Nixon claimed that "he would be standing against the prevailing social winds, and that would cause tension." But as he knew very well, it would bolster his claim as champion of middle-class values.

Confronted with the most unpopular war in modern American history, Richard Nixon used the protest movement to dramatize and reinforce his appeal to the middle class. He pursued his strategy so intensively that ultimately he could no longer separate the means from the end. Nixon's character, which had contributed to his triumph, betrayed him, causing his personal disgrace and the downfall of his presidency.

Right after his narrow election victory over Hubert Humphrey in November 1968, Nixon promised to "bring us together," a slogan that implied he would heal the deep divisions over Vietnam. The next day I phoned Henry Kissinger, whom I had met when he had been a campaign adviser to Nelson Rockefeller. Kissinger, I knew, viewed Nixon with contempt. When I asked him if Nixon could bring the country together, Kissinger snorted: "If he did, it would be the first positive thing he's ever done."

Kissinger turned out to be dead right. With Kissinger's help as his national security adviser, as it turned out, Nixon did just the opposite of what he had promised. He sharpened the polarization within the country to heighten the perceived threat to the middle class, then used himself as a rallying point for their support.

As students returned to campuses in the first autumn of Nixon's presidency, protest leaders announced a round of demonstrations.

Nixon promptly proclaimed that "under no circumstances" would he be affected by their protest. Facing a massive demonstration on November 15, Nixon knew he must strike back—or abandon his strategy for an orderly retreat from Vietnam. He delivered a major address to the nation in which he committed himself to ending American involvement in the war and appealed to the "great silent majority" of Americans to back his strategy. By morning, the White House had received the biggest response ever to a presidential speech—more than 50,000 wires and 30,000 letters, and nearly all of them favorable—and Nixon's approval ratings soared. With middle-class support secure, Nixon was positioned to call the shots on Vietnam.

Nixon made his point on Vietnam, but then he ran it into the ground. In a sense, Nixon became a victim of his own success. Because his will and his middle-class values had made his strategy of polarization pay off, he seemed unwilling or unable to make peace with his enemies for fear he would lose his middle-class supporters.

For Nixon's presidency, Vietnam turned into an institutional disaster. The will and determination that had been the prime strength of his character for most of his life ultimately became self-destructive. As biographer Joan Hoff-Wilson writes, Nixon's conduct of the ending of the war "established secrecy, wiretapping and capricious personal diplomacy as standard operation procedures in the conduct of foreign policy that ultimately carried over into domestic affairs." Nixon offered his own self-revealing analysis:

> Once I realized that the Vietnam War could not be ended quickly or easily and that I was going to be up against an anti-war movement that was able to dominate the media with its attitudes and values, I was sometimes drawn into the very frame of mind I so despised in the leaders of that movement. They increasingly came to justify almost anything in the name of forcing an immediate end to a war they considered unjustified and immoral. I was similarly driven to preserve the government's ability to conduct foreign policy and to conduct it in the way that I felt would best bring peace.

"We're up against an enemy, a conspiracy," Nixon told his chief of staff, H. R. Haldeman, in July 1971, after the publication of the Pentagon papers, the hitherto-secret Pentagon chronicle of the Vietnam War. "They're using any means. We are going to use any means. Is that clear?"

Consumed by hatred, Nixon assumed that his foes shared his passion. "Look, if we went in with sackcloth and ashes and fired the whole White House staff . . . that isn't going to satisfy those God-damn cannibals. Who are they after? They're after me, the President. They hate my guts."

Nixon's success in Indochina, heralded by National Security Adviser Kissinger's famous declaration that "peace is at hand," assured him a landslide reelection in 1972. But that victory did nothing to mellow Nixon's leadership style. Indeed, he seemed more confrontational than ever as he set about responding to his self-designated next challenge—to once and for all break the power of the "liberal establishment" and promote the beliefs of his silent majority.

"We will tear up the pea patch," he told his White House staff on the day after his election—and drove that point home by demanding the resignations from all these aides as well as from every other political appointee. Returning to tactics he had used in his first term, Nixon stepped up the bombing of North Vietnam, determined to blast that country into submission and launched a broad new program of impoundments, refusing to spend money Congress had appropriated for programs and policies he did not approve. Both these actions, in addition to their direct objectives, had the further goal of stirring up Nixon's adversaries and inciting them into public displays of opposition, which, Nixon believed, would serve to help him rally his middle-class support.

Nixon was in the midst of these machinations when he was suddenly forced to confront another sort of challenge, which turned out to be the ultimate test of his presidency—the scandal of Watergate. As the outcry against him mounted, fed by new disclosures of wrongdoing, he followed the pattern of his career, lashing out against his foes, hoping to rally his supporters. On the first day of 1974, which would be the last year of his presidency, he privately pondered whether to resign in the face of the growing drive to impeach him. "The *answer*"—he wrote in a note to himself, "*fight*." Later, he wrote: "Impeachment was not going to be decided on the basis of the law or historical precedent. Impeachment would be an exercise in public persuasion."

Yet this was a struggle he already sensed he was losing, even if he could not yet admit this to himself. Not only was he accused of managing a cover-up of a political crime but he was also charged with cheating on his income tax by taking huge bogus deductions. Nixon himself tracked his decline in the polls. In 1973, "a majority of the public still believed I was a man of high integrity," he noted later. But by 1974, the charges against him "had begun to undermine the confidence in my integrity." Through all the months of the Watergate onslaught, Nixon's will remained as strong as ever. What had collapsed was his claim to middle-class values, which above all else had made him credible as a political leader. "I am not a crook," the president startled the public by declaring at one point in his ordeal. By his conduct, he appeared to have repudiated such prime bulwarks of the middle-class code as respect for law and simple truthfulness.

In one way, Nixon resembled his immediate predecessor, Lyndon Johnson. Both men calculated and connived relentlessly, seeking every possible advantage. In strategic terms, though, the two men were polar opposites. Through consensus, Johnson sought political advantage by blurring ideological differences. Nixon, relying on polarization, depended on sharpening disagreements. When carried to extremes, both strategies ultimately distort reality and become self-destructive and damaging to the health of the nation.

Nixon spent much of his public life continually reinventing himself as a series of "new Nixons," as he sought to soften the harsh edges of the public profile his abrasive tactics etched as he climbed the political ladder. Despite the fact that his tenure in the White House was irrevocably stained by the Watergate scandal that threatened him with impeachment and forced his resignation, Nixon professed confidence about the view that posterity would take of him. "History will make the final judgment," he wrote in his memoirs. "I do not fear that judgment."

Far from being content, as he had implied in his memoirs, to wait passively for history to assess his career, Nixon launched the ultimate exercise in self-transformation after his resignation. For two decades, he churned out books on international affairs, toured world capitals, and made himself discreetly available as unofficial presidential adviser, all the while trying to create one final "new Nixon," the global elder statesman. It was an effort crowned with triumph on the evening of his death, when Democratic president Clinton delivered a glowing tribute to the late Republican ex-president, scarcely hinting that anything untoward had taken place during his presidency.

But the improved public perception of Nixon as an individual was not as significant as the effect Nixon had on the public's view of politics. Although in the eyes of many people, Richard Nixon recovered his reputation, the presidency did not. It continued to suffer from the cynicism that was his chief legacy and that the tenure of his immediate successor, Gerald Ford, both reflected and reinforced.

Wherever Ford went as vice president, the post Richard Nixon gave him after Spiro Agnew resigned in disgrace in the fall of 1973, he could not avoid the shadow of Watergate. He had to answer questions about the scandal even from conservative audiences, such as members of the Economic Club of New York, whom Ford addressed one night in the spring of 1974. Ford tried to turn the attention of his listeners away from Watergate and on to the 1974 congressional elections, still some six months in the future.

"If you really want to survive in 1974, you better start talking about the issues and not let this be a referendum on what's going on in Washington," Ford said. "Before you make a moralistic decision in senatorial and House races just bear in mind what you faced as businessmen in 1965 and 1966." During those years, when Lyndon Johnson's Democrats controlled Capitol Hill, Ford reminded them, "you had a tough time as businesspeople." And he warned, they would have a tough time again if the Democrats made similar gains in 1974. "So all I'm doing is cautioning my good friends in the business community is don't take out your moralistic attitudes vis-à-vis the executive branch on elected members of the House and Senate."

As Ford spoke that night, the Nixon presidency was crumbling fast, and he himself, as he indicated in private conversations, had grave misgivings about Nixon's ability to govern. The voice that advised the economic club members to disregard their "moralistic attitudes" was the voice of the loyalist, loyal to his party, loyal to his president. Loyalty, along with integrity, were the two chief values that shaped Gerald Ford's character. Combining these qualities helped him reach the summit of his profession. But once he arrived on the threshold of the White House, Ford found himself subject to pressures that put these values into conflict, and his inability to resolve that conflict ruined his presidency.

Until that crisis in his career, Ford seemed to be a notably stable personality, at ease with himself and with others. Not since Dwight Eisenhower had there been a president who was so determined to be liked and who succeeded so well at it. It was a quality he had amply demonstrated during his steady rise in the House of Representatives to the post of GOP leader. "He didn't keep us together with his intellectual brilliance, persuasion or pressure," said another Republican House member from Ford's home state of Michigan, Guy Vander Jagt. "He kept us together with his personality."

Ford owed much of his well-balanced nature to his mother's ability to transform her life after a stormy and unsuccessful first marriage and to the devotion of her second husband. His mother, Dorothy, divorced her first husband, Leslie King, a wealthy Omaha businessman, a few months after the future president, named Leslie King Jr., was born in 1913. When the boy was nearly three, his mother married again, to Gerald Ford Sr., a handsome Grand Rapids bachelor whom she met at a church social. Her new husband subsequently adopted her son, gave him his own name, and proved to be a strong and caring father. Gerald Ford Jr. regarded him as "the only father I ever knew."

The Ford family's life in Grand Rapids in the 1920s lived up to the idealized stereotype of middle-class Midwestern America. Both of Ford's parents were active in community life and charity work, particularly Gerald Ford Sr., who helped set up a summer camp for poor youngsters and helped run the church boy scout troop in which Jerry made Eagle Scout. The elder Ford did suffer financial reverses during the depression, but his standing in the community and the business world was such that the DuPont company kept shipping him supplies on credit and he was able to persuade his own workers to accept shrunken paychecks to keep the business afloat until conditions improved.

The moralistic attitudes Ford sought to dismiss in his remarks to the Economic Club had been an integral part of his Grand Rapids upbringing. The manners and mores of his hometown reflected the rigorous faith of the Dutch Calvinists who had settled western Michigan and remained the dominant cultural force there when Ford was young. Although Ford's parents were Episcopalians and did not fully accept all these puritanical tenets, the atmosphere in their home was nevertheless strict, Ford recalls: "The environment they created was—you darn well better tell the truth and live an honest life if you don't want to pay a penalty down the road." Seeking the endorsement of the Senate Rules Committee as Nixon's nominee to be vice president, Ford emphasized the importance of honesty to his view of politics. "Truth is the glue on the bond that holds government together, and not only government, but civilization itself," Ford said, reciting a favorite aphorism.

But if the truth holds government together, as Ford contended, then loyalty, the other foundation of his character, binds politicians to each other. Political loyalty has several levels, including mutual allegiance to shared ideals and principles. On the level on which Ford operated, the loyalty that mattered most was that of one politician to another and to the party. It was a political golden rule based on mutual trust and mutual need that served not only to nurture ambition but also to protect against risk and error.

And it was Ford's loyalty to Nixon that allowed Ford to be lured into making a fateful error of judgment by Nixon's chief of staff, Al Haig, who met with him alone a few days before the president resigned. Ford should be ready to assume the presidency within the next few days, Haig told him, because Nixon was considering resigning. If he did resign, Haig explained, Nixon had several options. He could step aside temporarily under the Twenty-fifth Amendment; he could pardon himself, and then resign.

Or as Ford recalled the way Haig put it, Nixon "could agree to leave in return for an agreement that the new President—Gerald Ford—would pardon him." At this point in their conversation, it would have been logical for Ford to remind Haig of an exchange during his Senate confirmation hearings when Senator Cannon had asked whether he believed he had the power to prevent a criminal investigation or prosecution of Nixon. He had replied: "I do not think the public would stand for it."

Had Ford made that response to Haig, then the course of the next few weeks and indeed of Ford's entire presidency might well have been very different. But that kind of rejoinder would be a total contradiction of Ford's character—his aversion to confrontation, his determination to please, his stress on personal loyalty. So instead of rebuffing Haig, he asked him about the extent of presidential pardon authority and was told that a president had authority to grant a pardon even before any prosecution had begun.

Before Haig left, Ford told him: "Well, Al, I want some time to think."

When Ford reported this conversation to Robert Hartmann, his senior aide, Hartmann exploded. "You should have taken Haig by the scruff of the neck and the seat of the pants and thrown him the hell out of your office," he told Ford. Yet Hartmann could see that Ford "had not yet grasped the monstrous impropriety" of Haig raising the pardon issue with Ford—nor did he realize the impropriety of his own failure to object immediately and forcefully.

But the truth was, the damage had been done. Ford's ambiguous response to what could only be considered to be a proposition from Haig had to be taken for a degree of assent or at least a willingness to think about what Ford had characterized as unthinkable months before. By failing to turn Haig down flat out, Ford had put himself in a position where if he did *not* pardon Nixon, his refusal could be construed by Haig and Nixon as a betrayal of his word and disloyalty to a friend. Just as important, in his own mind and conscience, Ford might find it difficult to rebut such charges.

Ford's assumption of the presidency on August 9 and his statement that "our long national nightmare is over" ushered in a period of national relief that approached euphoria. Yet while the public man seemed relaxed and confident, in private Ford was still struggling with the aftermath of Watergate and the dilemma of Nixon's fate. After he was peppered with questions about the pardon at his first press conference as chief executive, Ford asked his advisers how long reporters would continue to press him on the pardon issue. They told him the reporters would keep it up until Nixon's legal fate was resolved.

That was all Ford had to hear. Two days after the press conference, Ford met with his closest advisers and told them his mind was "about 99 percent made up" to grant Nixon a pardon. He did not even pretend to seek their views.

When he announced the pardon on September 8, 1974, the end of his first month as president, Ford claimed that he was acting to spare the American people bitterness and pain. If Nixon were forced to stand trial, Ford warned, there would be a prolonged period of delay during which "ugly passions would again be aroused." The fact is that although Watergate had been a public controversy for the better part of two years, there was no evidence that the country had been torn or divided. The main public reaction had been one of increased cynicism and alienation from the political process. That mood had been alleviated by Ford's assumption of the presidency and his reassuring statement: "Our constitution works. Our great Republic is a government of laws and not of men."

As it turned out, however, the good that had been accomplished was swiftly undone by the pardon. And it was this damage to public confidence and renewal of cynicism that had to be weighed against the supposed divisiveness that would result from continued investigation of Nixon.

Ford's action inevitably led to speculation that the pardon had been part of a sinister bargain under which Nixon would concede his presidency to Ford in exchange for Ford's promise to pardon him. Ford denied that—"There was no deal, period," he told the House investigators—and no one has produced any hard evidence to the contrary. Why then did Ford do what he did? The most plausible explanation based on an understanding of Ford's character is that he acted not for the country's sake, as he said, nor for Nixon's sake, as he may have led people to believe—but for his own sake.

"The pardon was the *real* Jerry Ford," Robert Hartmann observed. Ford's decision was consistent with the character and values that had shaped his political lifetime on Capitol Hill. To a politician whose vision of government was framed by good-natured comradeship with colleagues in both parties, by quiet cloakroom compromises sealed with a handshake, by favors sought and delivered, the issues raised by Watergate about the uses and abuses of presidential power seemed ethereal and abstract. Looking back on the pardon, Ford wrote: "It was an unbelievable lifting of a burden from my shoulders." And fifteen years after the event when a high school student asked him why he had pardoned Nixon, Ford said: "I finally decided that I should spend all my time on the problems of all Americans and not 25 percent of my time on the problems of one man."

But the problem of not being able to concentrate on the country's business was his problem, not the country's. No matter what Ford's real motives were for the pardon, the results certainly torpedoed his stated objective. He had intended, he claimed, to rid the country of a distraction. Instead, he created a whole new distraction. The pardon touched off what Watergate historian Stanley Kutler called "a convulsive reaction that seared the nation." The majority of Americans, who had gradually over the months reached a guilty verdict on Nixon, now much more swiftly condemned Ford. Ford, who had been riding high in the polls, dropped to nearly Nixon's Watergate levels. On his first postpardon trip out of Washington, demonstrators in Pittsburgh chanted: "Jail Ford, Jail Ford."

Much has been written and said about the healing service Ford supposedly performed for the country. Ford called his memoirs *A Time to Heal,* and his successor, Jimmy Carter, in his Inaugural Address said, "For myself and for our nation, I want to thank my predecessor for all he has done to heal our land." But Carter's election was in itself a measure of Ford's failure of leadership, and of character, just as Carter's own presidency would demonstrate the weaknesses of his character.

In May 1975, Jimmy Carter traveled to Concord, New Hampshire, capital of the state that holds the nation's first presidential primary, on behalf of his incipient candidacy for the White House. Although more than a year remained before the first votes would be cast in the Granite State, Carter knew that he had no time to lose. His candidacy was only a blur in the crowded field of Democratic nominees. But he had attracted attention among political professionals who thought his Southern Baptist background might help him win votes, particularly among members of the country's growing evangelical movement.

When I asked Carter about this on the plane ride to New Hampshire, it was clear that he had thought about the subject. He said the evangelical movement now included about 40 million, people like himself, "who are deeply committed to establishing government as moralistic and decent." Religion had long been a major part of his own life, he said. "That doesn't mean I'm anointed," he added carefully; "it means I have an obligation to try to discern the best qualities of the American people in government and put them into effect."

I reminded Carter that at a Democratic governors' conference two years earlier, when the full dimensions of the Watergate scandal were just beginning to emerge, he had introduced a resolution for national prayer, including prayer for Richard Nixon. The resolution was tabled by the other governors, who were more interested in Nixon's impeachment than his salvation.

Carter nodded. "I thought then that Nixon was guilty," he said. But he had felt obligated to pray for him anyway. "Religion is part of my life, part of my conscience," he said. "It may or may not be politically significant."

Despite Carter's demurrer, his religion turned out to be the defining agent of his implausible candidacy and the key to his success. It set him apart from the other candidates and infused his drive for the presidency with a moral fervor that was ideally suited for the post-Watergate era, as his visit to New Hampshire demonstrated.

At a breakfast in Manchester, Carter was very much at home. "I'm running for president because I am a deeply religious person," he said. "The most important thing in my life is my belief and my commitment in God. We should never deviate from recognizing our own unworthiness, but also our absolute strength when our hand is in the hand of God."

And for candidate Carter, God was a constant presence and a potent ally. "I don't have to be President," he told a crowd gathered for the opening of his campaign headquarters in the state. "There are a lot of things I would not do to be elected. I would never tell a lie, make a misleading statement, betray a trust or avoid a controversial issue. I ask you to give me your support on a tentative basis. If I ever should betray a trust, don't support me."

With these words, repeated over and over again around the country, Carter set a standard that invited mockery and that neither he nor anyone else could maintain. But regardless of the literal meaning of the words, the high moral tone they established was part of a brilliant political strategy.

With Jimmy Carter, the impact of character in presidential politics took another step forward. John Kennedy had used his character as background, to create an aura for his candidacy and then for his presidency. But Carter was the first to use his character, as expressed by his religious faith and accompanying morality, as a direct reason for voting for him and for supporting his stewardship.

Carter's identification with religion was doubly important to him. Not only did it give his candidacy a sense of high purpose but it helped to mask the most powerful aspect of his character, his self-absorption. As candidate Carter became President Carter, and the novelty of his religion faded, it was this trait that became more evident—and that ultimately undermined him.

In some ways, Carter's self-concern was a source of great strength for his political career, generating the discipline and the drive to succeed that carried him to the presidency. Yet it was mainly a grave defect, blinding him to the concerns and needs of others and to opportunities to fully develop his potential gifts for leadership.

Driven from childhood to prove that he was an exceptional human being, Carter was haunted by the fear that he would fail to achieve the goals he set for himself. His need to demonstrate his sense of exceptionalism seems to have stemmed from being raised as an only child until his brother, Billy, was born when Jimmy was already thirteen; from his remote rural surroundings in the little town of Archery, where the Carters were one of only two white families;

and from his keen native intelligence and the high expectations this generated in those around him.

His relationship with his parents fueled his drive to stand out from the pack but also contributed to his anxieties about his abilities. His father, Earl, had many admirable traits in his son's eyes. "My father was a natural leader in our community," Carter wrote. But Earl was also was a living reminder of the limitations that came from growing up in the rural South, handicaps that Jimmy knew he would have to overcome to fulfill his ambitions. The elder Carter had only gone as far as the tenth grade in school, although this was "the most advanced education of any Carter man since our family moved to Georgia 200 years ago."

Carter recalled his father's effort to raise his sartorial standards by ordering, for the first time in his life, a tailor-made suit. "All the family ... gathered around the fireplace while daddy began to put on his suit," which turned out to be twice Earl's size, his son later recalled. "I remember that no one in the family laughed," Carter wrote, adding that he himself "felt desperately sorry" for his father.

Earl was not the sort of father who could provide reassurance to ease his son's anxieties. "He was a stern disciplinarian and punished me severely when I misbehaved," his son recalled. Using "a small, long flexible peach tree switch," Earl whipped his eldest son six times from the time he was four until he was fifteen, experiences that Jimmy never forgot.

Carter also refers to his mother, Miss Lillian, in admiring terms, unconsciously contrasting her with her husband, a comparison in which she almost always came out ahead. He pointed out that his mother was a registered nurse, thus having attained a higher level of formal education than her husband. Moreover, "although my father seldom read a book, my mother was an avid reader, and so was I." Just as the father-son relationship lacked something in warmth because of Earl's stern and aloof manner, Carter's relationship with his mother appears to have been inhibited by her preoccupation with her own life, particularly her vocation a nurse.

As Carter grew into manhood, his "sense of being set apart was accompanied by a high degree of reclusiveness and shyness," according to Peter Bourne, a longtime friend and adviser, who had clinical training as a psychiatrist. At the Naval Academy, he made few close friends and picked as a sport cross-country running, which required almost no contact with others.

His hero worship of Admiral Hyman Rickover, the nuclear submarine pioneer, conceived as a young naval officer, appears to have been an attempt to find a more satisfactory model for his exceptionalism than his father. As Carter acknowledges, this relationship meant much more to him than to the notoriously abrasive Rickover, who, though "he may not have cared or known it . . . had a profound effect" on Carter's life. "He was unbelievably hardworking and competent and he demanded total dedication from his subordinates."

But Rickover, by Carter's account, gave very little in return. Although the admiral never hesitated to criticize severely, "the absence of a comment" was his only compliment. Measured in some ways, Rickover's career was indeed "brilliant and remarkable," as Carter believed. But he served as an exemplar not only of great energy and intelligence but also of unconscionable egotism. It does not seem to have occurred to Carter that these traits gravely damaged Rickover's career, limited his effectiveness, and when adapted to his own political career could have disastrous results.

When Carter entered politics in 1962, running for the Georgia Senate, he brought with him into this new field the same consciousness of his own apartness and superiority that had been ingrained since childhood. He was no young stripling like Kennedy, Johnson, or Nixon. Rather, at age thirty-eight, he was already well established as a successful businessman and clearly marked as an outsider by his mistrust of parties and other politicians and his emphasis on management procedures and techniques that he believed had boosted his business career. His attitudes were reinforced by his experiences in getting to the legislature and serving there. His candidacy met with the bitter opposition of the old-line politicians who sought to defeat him by stuffing the ballot box. By waging a prolonged and bitter legal battle, Carter won a recount and the election, an outcome that he later described as the triumph of "decency" over "corrupt public officials."

Once in the Senate, he predictably found that chamber to be a den of iniquitous special interests. "The confusion and complications of state government," he wrote, offered "many niches in which special interests could hide," making it "difficult for the common good to prevail." These were the themes that would gain him the governorship in 1970 and the presidency six years later.

But first, he encountered a jarring bump in the road—defeat on his first run for the governorship in 1966, which was to have a profound impact on his character and his political style. "Emotionally devastated" by that setback, he sought help from his sister, Ruth, an evangelist, who suggested that Carter could alleviate his depression if he were to take full advantage of his natural religious conviction. What followed was his much discussed "born-again" experience, which, as Carter noted, "was no blinding flash of light" but instead a decision to "reassess my relationship with God."

Whatever other benefits his reaffirmed faith brought him, it certainly was an asset on the campaign trail. In the ideological vacuum of the 1976 campaign, Carter used religion, and the related idea of trust, in much the same way as other Democrats had earlier tapped into the Vietnam protest and civil rights movements. By stressing faith and trust, Carter turned attention away from his lack of Washington experience.

Early in his campaign, he told lobbyists for public interest groups: "I don't care how much you talk about issues, or how many numbers of Senate and House bills you name, if the people don't believe that when you're in the White House, you're going to do something about the problem and that they can trust what you tell them."

In the White House, Carter sought to carry on the trust and faith theme as president. But what had worked in helping to frame the promises of the campaign was much less effective in dealing with the realities of governing. Early in his presidency, addressing a group of Housing and Urban Development workers, he felt called upon to urge them: "Those of you who are living in sin, I hope you'll get married." Such utterances conveyed to many Americans an impression of sanctimoniousness, which proved to be politically harmful, particularly after he himself appeared insensitive to the ethical indiscretions of his budget director and confidant, Bert Lance.

As president, Carter lacked "the passion to convert himself from a good man into an effective one, to learn how to do the job," his speechwriter James Fallows contended. He seemed more concerned with self-justification than with learning from his mistakes. He was unwilling to make himself a better orator, for example, which was a severe drawback to his presidency. "If Carter had given FDR's 'nothing-to-fear-but fear itself' speech, the Great Depression would still be raging," another Democratic speechwriter, Milt Gwirtzman, once remarked.

Carter arrived in the Oval Office at a moment of unusual opportunity in the history of American politics. In a memo written to the president elect a few weeks before his inauguration, the pollster Patrick Caddell, probably Carter's deepest political thinker, advised him that "the time is ripe for a political realignment in America, for construction of a new political coalition." But this was more than just an opportunity, it was an imperative, for the same turbulence that gave Carter and the Democrats the opening to create a new majority assured that the president and his party would be doomed to defeat if they failed to seize the day.

The biggest obstacle Carter faced was economic, having to deal with the tension between the threat of inflation on one hand and the peril of recession on the other. Meanwhile, in the moral arena, the landscape was littered with the psychological debris from Watergate and Vietnam, this, too, a particularly vexing problem for the leader of the Democratic Party, with its tradition of government activism.

Although these problems were formidable, Carter was uniquely positioned to deal with them because of the high moral tone he had set as a candidate and because he was an outsider not tied to the left or the right or to any element of the existing power structure. Yet these assets existed only as potentials that needed to be exploited as part of what pollster Caddell called "a fundamentally new ideology" that would help forge a new majority coalition. But this was a challenge that Carter never really took on, indeed never even acknowledged the need for.

After he got elected, Carter remained as self-absorbed and self-satisfied as he had been as a candidate, content to gloat over the decline of traditional liberalism without trying to work out a new ideological formula of his own. Carter did not think in terms of ideology; he thought mostly about himself, as he made clear to me when we talked in his office just after he had marked his First Hundred Days in the White House. "I have a coalition of what might generically be called consumers," Carter replied, when I asked about his political base. "When it comes down to a choice between what's good for consumers and good for manufacturers, my natural inclination is to have what's good for the consumers."

Since the category of consumers took in nearly everyone in the country, I asked Carter what new ideology he had in mind to attract such a wide range of voters. Taken aback, the president referred me to his speeches. "There's an amazing amount of consistency in my speeches," he said, without explaining why this consistency should be amazing. "I'd say basic morality is there—not that I'm better than other people. It's hard for me to describe," he added, "because it's part of my consciousness."

The closest Carter came to defining his beliefs during our hour-long conversation was his reference to "basic morality." For Carter, moralism was a substitute for political convictions and principles. This was a president who viewed the political arena not as a battleground for interests with competing claims but as a struggle between good and evil in which he rarely doubted on which side he was positioned.

"Not that I'm better than other people," Carter had made a point of interjecting during our talk. In fact, an important part of his appeal, first as a candidate and then in his early days as president, derived from the impression, which he fostered, that he was a good deal better in the fealty to truth and rectitude than other politicians, particularly his recent predecessors in the White House. But this favorable aura did not survive the disclosures during the first summer of his presidency of the financial finagling of Bert Lance, his close friend and former banker, whom he had named budget director. "Bert, I'm proud of you," Carter publicly declared, despite the overdrafts and other irregularities that studded Lance's record as a freewheeling Chicago banker.

When Lance was forced to quit, his friends in the White House complained that he had been judged by an artificial standard. True or not, it was a standard Carter himself had established. The damage to Carter was enduring. "It made people realize we were no different than anyone else," Carter's vice president, Walter Mondale, later acknowledged.

Lance's disgrace demonstrated how greatly Carter leaned on the shaky pillar of morality, founded on the image of his character he had carefully cultivated. If he was no different than anyone else, the public would judge him like anyone else in the White House—on his ability to deal with the nation's problems. This was a hard test for Carter to pass because he had made great claims about what he would accomplish and was unwilling to rearrange his goals to adjust to political realities.

He hit bottom in the summer of 1979, when a severe gasoline shortage in the midst of skyrocketing inflation aggravated the public discontent. Carter spoke to the nation, telling Americans they were suffering "a crisis of confidence." "I realize more than ever that as President I need your help," he said, and added: "The gap between our citizens and our government has never been so wide." This had been a familiar theme of his campaign for the White House in 1976. But after three years in the White House, who could be blamed for this estrangement but Carter himself? The so-called malaise speech was the death knell of the Carter presidency. It reflected and reinforced Carter's failures as a leader, in large part because he obsessed with his own emotions and ego, to the exclusion of the real political world.

The malaise crisis that Carter invented was a prelude to the Iran hostage crisis in the fall of 1979, which he exacerbated and exaggerated. He inflated the importance of the event, to the point where freeing the hostages became the national purpose. The public's instinctive tendency to rally around the commander-in-chief in crisis gave Carter a brief boost. But the malaise speech's failure and the defects of his character had bankrupted his presidency.

In defeat, Carter, like Nixon, sought to rehabilitate his reputation. His efforts toward that goal reflected the same strengths and weaknesses that had carried him to the White House and then undermined his prospects for success in the presidency. By contrast with his immediate predecessor, Ford, who, following his departure from the White House, appeared to spend most of his time relaxing on the golf links and lecturing business and civic groups for handsome fees, Carter chose to devote himself to service. He gained a measure of the approbation denied him in his presidential days by using his carpentry skills in community self-help projects for the poor, while continuing to teach Sunday school class at his hometown church in Georgia.

Carter also emerged as a sort of freelance international troubleshooter, mediating foreign conflicts and monitoring elections from Nicaragua and Panama to Ethiopia and Sudan, winning praise and gratitude but also stirring controversy when his rigidity and self-absorption came to the fore. In 1994, on an unofficial mission to ease tensions with Communist North Korea over its efforts to develop the potential for nuclear weaponry, he made statements to its longtime ruler, Kim Il Sung, that misconstrued the official U.S. position and had to be disavowed by the White House. Similarly, in the course of negotiating a cease-fire in Bosnia later that year, he upset the Bosnian government and U.S. and U.N. diplomats by his public expressions of sympathy for the Serbs, generally viewed as the chief aggressors in the tangled conflict. But Carter shrugged off such criticism, vowing to continue to travel the world on peace missions, which he now described as "my life's work."

Whatever he accomplished in his postpresidential career, his main impact on his country was evident in Washington, where the new chief executive led the nation in a very different direction from the course it had taken during the decades that followed the Great Depression and Franklin Roosevelt's ascension to the presidency. By first pointing to the failures of government as a candidate and then demonstrating his inability to cope with them as president, Jimmy Carter had set the stage for a president who would make government the public's enemy and who, for a while at least, would be far better able to exploit his character to strengthen his presidency.

8

THE
TRUE BELIEVER

ON HIS WAY TO THE REPUBLICAN presidential nomination in
1980, Ronald Reagan paid a campaign visit to Plymouth Rock. For
almost any other candidate, this would have been just another photo
opportunity. But Reagan converted the stop at the site of the landing
of the Pilgrim fathers into something more. Returning to the bus, he
confronted the traveling press corps and offered this one-sentence
epiphany for the voyage of the Mayflower: "If they could come all
that way in that little boat," he asked, "how dare we be afraid of
anything?"

It was a moment to remember. With that rhetorical question, farci-
cal from almost anyone else, Reagan demonstrated the intensity that
was the secret of his political strength. That ingredient endowed him
with an aura of credibility that helped him sweep all before him in
his early days in the White House, a period that reshaped the political landscape like no other since FDR's First Hundred Days.

In the wake of four of the dreariest presidencies in American history—the tenures of Lyndon Johnson, Richard Nixon, Gerald Ford,
and Jimmy Carter—Ronald Reagan restored presidential character
to the eminence of the Kennedy days and created his own legend.
Reagan's success rested on two main components of his character.
One was his ability to convince people of his sincerity, the talent he
demonstrated at Plymouth Rock. It was not so much the ideas in
which Reagan believed as the fact that he actually believed in those
ideas that undergirded his appeal. The other character pillar on

which the Reagan legend was built was the warmth and magnetism of his personality. His charm was the spoonful of sugar that made his polarizing beliefs go down. "Look, Dick, I don't care what else you do," Michael Deaver, one of his principal handlers, told Richard Darman, a key adviser on economic policy. "Get that face on television. This is a face that when a baby sees it, the baby smiles."

More than any other of the post-FDR presidents, at least since Truman, Reagan presented himself as holding a firm ideological position. He was perceived that way by the public and the political community, by his friends and even his adversaries, who, in the case of Edward M. Kennedy, were frank in confessing their admiration, laced with envy for the strength of Reagan's convictions.

"Whether we agreed with him or not, Ronald Reagan was a successful candidate and an effective President above all else because he stood for a set of ideas," the Massachusetts senator told a lecture audience at Yale, soon after the end of Reagan's tenure in the White House. "He stated them in 1980—and it turned out that he meant them—and he wrote most of them not only into public law but into the national consciousness," Kennedy added, in drawing a pointed contrast between Reagan and the vacuum of ideas that surrounded the leadership of his own Democratic Party.

"It would be foolish to deny that his success was fundamentally rooted in a command of public ideas," Kennedy declared. "Ronald Reagan may have forgotten names, but never his goals. He was a great communicator, not simply because of his personality or his Teleprompter, but mostly because he had something to communicate."

But the distinctive quality of his political philosophy was that it was based largely on his own personal experience and character rather than on more formal sources. This was the key to his persuasiveness. The public might be hesitant to buy Reagan's arguments on one controversial policy or another. But often what ultimately clinched the political sale was the sense that Reagan himself truly believed what he was saying. As Kennedy observed about Reagan's ideas: "It turned out that he meant them."

As Reagan's political thinking veered from left to right over the years, reflecting the changes in his own experience, the remarkable aspect of these adjustments was not how much Reagan's thinking changed but how fervent a believer he was in whatever particular faith he happened to hold at the time.

Because Reagan's beliefs stemmed from his personal experiences, they had the virtue of simplicity. "You have the ability of putting complicated, technical ideas into words everyone can understand," Richard Nixon had written him in 1959. "There is no left or right, only an up or down," Reagan liked to say: "'Up' to the maximum of individual freedom consistent with law and order, or 'down' to the ant heap of totalitarianism."

As politically successful as Reagan's ideology was, at least during the early stages of his presidency, some of his admirers nevertheless sought to enhance its intellectual origins. "The essence of the comprehensive economic program he has pursued in the 1980s was derived from the classical economic principles he learned almost sixty years ago as a young man," Martin Anderson, Reagan's top domestic policy adviser in his first White House term, claimed. At Eureka College, from which Reagan graduated in 1932, Anderson writes, "The economics he was taught was the old classical variety, straight from the works of Adam Smith, Alfred Marshall, Irving Fisher, Eugene Boem-Barwek, David Ricardo and Jean-Baptiste Say."

It is true that Reagan did major in economics at Eureka College. But the evidence suggests that this experience made little impression on him. Reagan devotes fourteen pages to his years at Eureka in *Where's the Rest of Me?* his 1965 memoir, describing the walls "covered with friendly ivy" and recounting his adventures as a football player and as a leader of a student strike against a threatened cutback in the academic program. But he makes not a single reference to a single class he attended in economics or any other subject. Eureka's only professor of economics recalls that Reagan got through college without ever cracking a book, though he earned good grades by cramming before exams. Early in 1981, asked by the admiring journalists Rowland Evans and Robert Novak what thinkers influenced his presidency, Reagan claimed that he had "always been a voracious reader" and mentioned the economists Ludwig Von Mises, Friedrich A. Von Hayek, and Frederic Bastiat, none of whom were mentioned by Anderson. Nevertheless, Reagan said, "I don't know where I could put a finger on someone" as having had significant impact. And none of these names, nor the names cited by Anderson, appear in Reagan's public utterances.

A more candid assessment of Reagan's intellectual outlook, or lack of it, comes from Dinesh D'Souza, a vigorous and thoughtful conservative who served on the White House domestic policy staff.

"It must be conceded that whatever Reagan's strengths, he was not an intellectual," he writes. "He lacked the two characteristics of the liberally educated person: self-consciousness and open-mindedness." The latter was a flaw to which Reagan himself cheerfully confessed. "I always consider all proposals for government action with an open mind before I say no," Reagan used to wisecrack in his days as California's governor.

And Reagan had other flaws as a political leader that stemmed from his character. Because his beliefs were homemade, they often lacked intellectual consistency, which sometimes produced grave contradictions in his policies. During his tenure, Reagan concentrated on his short-term goal of cutting the government's taxing power. But he did nothing to diminish public expectations from government. The irony is that he might have been able to accomplish that if he tried. "The President has permitted his relentless optimism to blind him to a unique opportunity," wrote the Urban Institute's John Palmer. "The American people apparently found Reagan's personality so appealing they would have swallowed some unpleasant truths from him."

Still another drawback stemmed from Reagan's relentless good nature. This trait cloaked a tendency, verging on irresponsibility, to avoid problems and delegate authority, which led to the Iran-Contra case that stained the image of his presidency.

In later years, when he had outgrown the liberalism of his younger days, Reagan liked to trace his adopted conservative faith back to his formative years in a Midwestern small town, where the institutions of family and church, along with such virtues as hard work and patriotism, were held in high esteem.

Dixon, where Reagan grew up, was about 90 miles from Chicago and had a population of only about 10,000. Reagan's use of his small-town background, and other aspects of his past, was calculating. In the autobiographical *Where's the Rest of Me?* published just as he was starting his political career, he romanticized the circumstances of his earliest years.

"It was a good life," he wrote. "I never have asked for anything more, then or now." But of course that was not quite true, or Reagan never would have left there to become a radio sportscaster in Des Moines, first stop on the road that took him to Hollywood stardom and then the White House.

Later, in the security of the presidency, he would confess that he shared the view of myriad other exiles from small towns that life there tended to become a narrow and limiting experience.

"There was nothing in those towns," he remarked to a White House aide. "Lord, that's why I left there."

Whatever his real feelings were, it is clear that Dixon served as a matrix on which Reagan drew to define and justify his conservative faith, embodied in such values as work and opportunity. "We have taken jobs away from teenagers," he told Bill Boyarsky, one of his early biographers, recalling the summer jobs he had held when he was growing up. "We have taken them away in some instances by way of unions, but more by way of our own social legislation." Reagan recalled that for one teenage job he had held, remodeling old houses, "the boss paid you out of his pocket in cash. He didn't have to sit down and do a lot of paperwork for Social Security and all of those things. I'm not criticizing it for the legitimate workforce, but for the kids who have to go through school, it seems to me we could make some exceptions."

Yet there were other experiences in Dixon, notably the Great Depression, which for a time shaped Reagan's values in a different direction. The economic collapse gave Reagan a sense of kinship with the underdog, caused him to worship Franklin Roosevelt, and inspired in him the liberalism of his early adulthood.

Like many other small-town families in the 1920s, the Reagans had enough to live on but lacked the wherewithal to cope with hard times. "Our family didn't exactly come from the wrong side of the tracks," Reagan later recalled, "but we were certainly always within the sound of the train whistle."

In the 1930s, it was as if the train itself came crashing in. Reagan, still in college, worked part-time so he could send money home for groceries and found job opportunities drying up. Reagan's mother, Nell, took a $14-a-week job in a dress store. For Reagan's father, Jack, the depression meant the killing of his dream of owning his own business. Eventually, he also lost his job. A volunteer worker in Roosevelt's 1932 election campaign, Jack Reagan was rewarded by being put in charge of the Dixon office of the Works Progress Administration. "Practically all the unemployed were able-bodied and capable and they besieged him for chances at working for their keep, even calling on him at home," his son wrote. But the problem was that "those in charge of direct relief resisted releasing their charges to WPA," this despite the fact that, as Reagan points out, Roosevelt himself had called direct relief "a subtle destroyer of the human spirit" and declared that the federal government must discard relief programs. "He said that, but it didn't work out that way," Reagan wrote in 1965, by then reflecting the full-blown conservative scorn of government that would become the hallmark of his rhetoric. "Wheels were turning in Washington and the government was busy at the job it does best—growing."

This conflict between relief and work infuriated and frustrated Jack Reagan, his son wrote. "However, his rage was directed only at his local tormentors. Being a loyal Democrat, he never criticized the administration or the government." Neither did his son, until many years later. The acerbic comments about the follies of big government in *Where's the Rest of Me?* seem intended to blur the contradiction between the Reagan with the new conservative voice of 1965 and the earlier Reagan who memorized portions of Roosevelt's first Inaugural Address and, according to biographer Lou Cannon, "listened to all the fireside chats on radio and developed an accomplished imitation of Roosevelt, complete with imaginary cigarette holder."

In part, this behavior reflected his personal admiration for Roosevelt. But for Reagan, as for millions of other Americans at the time, the personal magic of Roosevelt fostered a broader faith in what were then the liberal values of the day. "I was a near-hopeless, hemophilic liberal," Reagan wrote later of the beliefs he held during the New Deal era. "I bled for 'causes'; I had voted Democratic, following my father, in every election. I had followed FDR blindly, though not without some misgivings."

These views, acquired during the depression in Dixon, were bolstered in Reagan's early Hollywood years; by his involvement in the Screen Actors Guild, like the rest of organized labor, a trusted ally of the New Deal; and by the outbreak of World War II, which surrounded Roosevelt with an aura of patriotism and made it seem almost seditious to challenge or criticize the commander in chief. Reagan's disillusionment with liberalism began in the postwar era when, he claims, idealistic hopes inspired by the grand struggle against the Axis were dashed by postwar realities.

"Like most of the soldiers who came back I expected a world suddenly reformed," he recalled. "I was wrong. I discovered that the rich had got just a little richer and a lot of the poor had done a pretty good job of grabbing a quick buck. I discovered that the world was almost the same and perhaps a little bit worse."

Apart from the overall state of the world, several personal factors contributed to Reagan's change of heart and mind. One was the burden of the soaring federal income tax, which took a huge bite out of the salary Reagan was earning from Warner Brothers. "The entire structure was created by Karl Marx," Reagan would say of the tax code. "It simply is a penalty on the individual who can improve his own lot."

Then there was the sudden emergence of communism as a threat, right in Reagan's own new hometown of Hollywood. In his liberal salad days, Reagan had spent little time worrying about the danger of communism. "I was not sharp about Communism," he later wrote. But ideological conflict in the movie capital in the postwar era drastically altered that perception. A Communist-controlled group moved to take over the Hollywood trade unions, and as leader of the Screen Actors Guild, Reagan was pitted against them in a bitter jurisdictional dispute. Meanwhile, the House Un-American Activities Committee began its probe of Communist influence on Hollywood. Reagan became persuaded that the Communists had intended to seize control of the movie industry so that it could be used as "a worldwide propaganda base." He concluded that "like the measles," communism "will always be with us."

Then, too, Reagan's career was running into trouble because of the postwar audience's yearning for new faces. "I was a star, but I had a sneaking suspicion that a lot of people across America hadn't stayed in a breathless state of palpitation for three and a half years waiting for my return," he wrote.

More generally, the motion picture industry was having trouble competing against the surging new entertainment medium of television, which could do everything Hollywood could do and more, and deliver it into the nation's living rooms. On top of that, as Reagan complained, the Truman administration's Justice Department forced the studios to relinquish their holdings in theater chains, and the movie industry's stability was "literally destroyed."

With his income dwindling, Reagan abandoned Hollywood and went to work as a spokesman for the General Electric Company, hosting a televised series of dramas and, more important for his political future, as a sort of corporate ambassador of goodwill to GE employees and to civic and business groups around the country. Ultimately, Reagan became more committed to his newfound faith than his employer had bargained for, even attacking such relatively sacrosanct New Deal institutions as the Tennessee Valley Authority, which happened to be a $50-million-a-year GE customer. By 1962, when his arrangement with General Electric ended, Reagan claimed that bookings for his speeches had to be canceled as far ahead as 1966. "It would be nice to accept this as a tribute to my oratory," Reagan wrote. "But I think the real reason had to do with a change that was taking place all over America. People wanted to talk about and hear about encroaching government control."

If that was what people were ready to hear, Reagan was ready to tell them. The style and thrust of his rhetoric was much the same as it had been in his liberal days. Only the targets of his indignation had changed, and this was a dramatic change. The liberal Reagan, in a 1948 campaign address for Truman, when he was still a Democrat in good standing, lamented the fact that corporate profits had soared four times faster than the wages of working people. The conservative Reagan, in his memorable 1964 campaign address for Goldwater, "A Time for Choosing," decried the alleged fact that since the beginning of the century, the government had increased in size 234 times while the gross national product had grown only thirty-three-fold.

Reagan's conservative creed, centered on his antagonism and, like his depression-born liberalism, shaped by the twists and turns in his own life, was well suited to the times, for government was increasingly the target for a range of grievances, foreign and domestic. The 1960s had started out hopefully with the promise of John Kennedy and the Civil Rights movement. By the time the decade was half over, the Vietnam War abroad and a series of economic and social dislocations at home had made it an era of discontent.

Reagan's ability to express this discontent in terms that remained on the safe side of demagoguery made him, after the debacle of Barry Goldwater in 1964, the leading conservative spokesman in the country. He had two major themes, both shaped by his own experience, a reverence for the spirit and standards that had prevailed in the nation's early days and his mistrust of government as a threat to the freedom of the individual. In *Where's the Rest of Me?* he wrote: "The original government of this country was set up by conservatives, as defined years later by Lincoln, who called himself a conservative with a 'preference for the old and tried over the new and untried.' . . . The liberals believe in remote and massive strong-arming from afar, usually Washington, D.C. ...The conservatives believe in the unique powers of the individual and his personal opinions." Within two years, he had won the governorship of the nation's largest state and was well on the road to the White House.

Serving to offset the harshness of his homemade beliefs was his congenial manner, the political value of which I saw demonstrated at a conservative conference back in the 1970s when Reagan was often forced to defend himself against the charge of extremism.

One reporter recalled Barry Goldwater's disastrous statement in his speech accepting the presidential nomination that "extremism in the defense of liberty is no vice" and "moderation in the pursuit of justice is no virtue" and asked Reagan where he stood on moderation versus extremism. "Well, it sort of depends on the circumstances," Reagan said softly, adding with a grin: "If you were an airplane passenger on a stormy night you wouldn't want a pilot who was only moderately safe, would you?"

Listening to that exchange, in my mind's eye I could see headlines blaring the news: "Reagan, Like Goldwater, Backs Extremism." But as I looked around, I noticed that none of my colleagues seemed to be paying much attention to Reagan's response. Instead, Reagan was immediately asked a question about another subject. Goldwater's defense of extremism, delivered during his acceptance speech at the 1964 Republican convention, shocked the country and assured the doom of his candidacy. Reagan had made much the same point and had escaped unscathed. His warm smile, his soft voice, his apt analogy had all served to take the threatening edge off his comments and muffle criticism.

This was a trait that his aides learned to exploit in the White House. After CBS correspondent Leslie Stahl had profiled Reagan's handling of social policies in a highly critical manner, his economic adviser, Richard Darman, thanked her for the "commercial" on Reagan's behalf.

"Didn't you hear the things we said about him?" a frustrated Stahl protested.

"Oh yes," Darman said. "But nobody paid any attention to what you said. Those shots of him were priceless."

Reagan owed much of his good nature to his mother, Nell, who was a far stronger figure in the household than her alcoholic husband, Jack. When Lou Cannon first asked Reagan about his family, "he talked non-stop about his mother for several minutes without even mentioning his father."

In his biography, Reagan recalled that when he was five, his mother taught him and his brother, Neil, to read, "following each word with a finger, while we watched over her shoulder." By contrast, Reagan describes coming home at age eleven to find his father "flat on his back on the front porch and no one there to lend a hand but me. He was drunk, dead to the world." Nevertheless, Reagan claims he felt no resentment of his father because of his mother's attitude. "She told Neil and myself over and over that alcoholism was a sickness—that we should love and help our father and never condemn him for something that was beyond his control."

Whatever the root causes of Reagan's good nature, he helped to preserve it for himself as president by his avoidance of matters that did not interest him, his tendency to delegate authority, and the forbearance of his staff.

Clare Boothe Luce once introduced Reagan at a dinner by reading passages from the memoirs of previous presidents that stressed what Jefferson called "the splendid misery" of the job. "Well, Clare, I must be doing something wrong," Reagan responded. "I'm kind of enjoying myself." He was a man, speechwriter Peggy Noonan wrote, who provided living proof that "the unexamined life *is* worth living."

The contrast could hardly have been greater with his sober-sided, extradiligent predecessor Jimmy Carter, as Carter himself noted after he briefed then president elect Reagan shortly before Reagan's inauguration on the major international challenges he would face once he took power. "Some of the information was quite complex, and I did not see how he could possibly retain all of it merely by listening," Carter wrote later in his memoirs. "I asked him if he wanted a pad so that he could take some notes, but he responded that he could remember what I was saying."

But that was a claim that, on its face, seemed dubious to Carter. "It had been a pleasant visit," Carter noted when Reagan left, after about an hour. "But," he added, "I was not sure how much we accomplished."

Reagan carried the burdens of the presidency far more easily than Carter, because he saw the nation's highest office as much like the parts he had played in Hollywood. "He saw the role and put it on like a costume," Peggy Noonan wrote. "He was really acting, but the part he played was Ronald Reagan."

When Al Haig resigned as secretary of state, Reagan seemed notably undisturbed. As he headed for a press briefing, he cracked jokes, making everyone laugh.

"Whoa there," his then chief of staff Jim Baker cautioned. "We better get serious here."

"Oh, don't worry, I'll play it somber," Reagan promised. And sure enough, when he met the reporters, he treated the departure with all the gravity Haig himself thought it deserved.

"Film is forever," Reagan, newly inaugurated as president, told the Academy of Motion Picture Arts and Sciences on Oscar night. "It is the motion picture that shows all of us not only how we look and sound but—more important—how we feel."

This suggestion, that motion pictures instead of simply inducing feelings on the part of audience reflect the audience's real feelings, helps explain why for Reagan, as a public man, the distinction between movie life and real life often seemed blurred.

Reagan was especially fond of the classic movie role of the Western hero, an image of himself shared by his admirers. "I like to think of him riding off into the sunset, a lone horseman silhouetted against the an open sky," a worshipful Dinesh D'Souza wrote later. It was an image that extended even to his Secret Service code name, "Rawhide," which soon became public knowledge.

Reagan's use of lines from old movies was varied and effective. At times he uttered lines whose origin was well known, thus benefiting from the association with the original version. Thus, he dared Congress to enact a tax increase so he could veto it by mimicking Clint Eastwood's challenge to a hoodlum threatening to shoot a hostage: "Go ahead. Make my day."

On other occasions, Reagan borrowed from a script without attribution, giving the appearance of spontaneity. "Where do we find such men?" he asked about the Americans who gave their lives in the invasion of Normandy in his D-Day speech that stirred the nation. This was the same line delivered by Frederick March, portraying the commander of an aircraft carrier in the 1954 Korean War film *The Bridges at Toko Ri*.

It was clear that Reagan did regard the presidency, as Lou Cannon put it in the title of his biography, as *The Role of a Lifetime*.

Through it all, Reagan's staff helped him maintain his detachment and his genial disposition. "You can't have people rushing in [on Reagan] and talking about mistakes," said Reagan's attorney general and longtime adviser, Edwin Meese III. "The people around you can get you down," Meese said, adding that Reagan's aides had "a responsibility not to create self-doubt."

Reagan was glad to delegate nearly everything to his staff, including how they took charge of themselves. When Treasury Secretary Donald Regan and Chief of Staff James Baker decided to switch jobs at the beginning of Reagan's second term, they went ahead with the plan on their own and told Reagan later. The president "made no inquiries," Regan said. Instead, he simply offered his assent after a thirty-minute chat.

Even Martin Anderson, Reagan's domestic policy adviser and an ardent loyalist, wrote later that the president's management style was "highly unusual" in that "he made no demands and gave almost no instructions."

> Essentially he just responded to whatever was brought to his attention and said yes or no, or I'll think about it. At times he would just change the subject, maybe tell a funny story, and you would not find out what he thought about it, one way or another. We just accepted Reagan as he was and adjusted ourselves to his manner. So everyone overlooked and compensated for the fact that he made decisions like an ancient King or a Turkish pasha, selecting only those morsels of public policy that were especially tasty.

As Anderson wrote: "In the closing years of his presidency, the high-rolling, high-risk methods that served him so well earlier now betrayed him. . . . It was a flawed style with high risk and potential for disaster. Its Achilles' heel was exposed by the Iran-Contra affair."

The virtues and liabilities of Reagan's character and values had become clear during his campaign for the presidency. Given Jimmy Carter's failures in the White House, there was no way Carter could *win* the election. The only real question was whether Reagan could lose it. And for a time, it seemed that the Republican candidate might find a way to do just that.

In the late summer weeks immediately following the Democratic convention, Reagan became involved in pointless controversies about such peripheral matters as "creationism," the merits of the Vietnam War, and the Ku Klux Klan, which diverted public attention from Carter's problems to Reagan's own mental processes, never a profitable development for any candidate. The significance of these episodes for the future was that Reagan, for all the strength of his convictions, had difficulty in sorting them into a cohesive structure during a campaign, where his views were subjected to continuous and intense examination.

Faced with the possibility that their candidate would destroy himself before he could defeat Carter, Reagan's strategists decreed that he should avoid ideology and stress instead his own personality, which was far more appealing than Carter's.

The good-natured, optimistic Reagan who now appeared on the campaign stage quickly overshadowed not only the fretful persona of the incumbent but also the image of the right-wing extremist bogeyman whom Carter had been trying to run against. The successful climax of this strategy came in the televised debate during the closing days of the campaign. Carter had prepared himself to demonstrate Reagan's weakness on a broad range of issues, and the president spent his share of the ninety minutes of airtime cutting Reagan's positions to ribbons. But all of his efforts were blown away when Reagan responded to one of Carter's attacks with a carefully rehearsed good-natured riposte: "There you go again."

The other key component of the revised Reagan campaign strategy with far-reaching implications for his presidency was his decision to promise relief and ignore the pain. In the definitive statement of his economic program, made in a September 9 speech, Reagan promised to cut taxes, boost defense spending, and balance the budget by 1983. This would be made possible, the candidate explained, by economic growth and by the tens of billions he would save by trimming "waste, extravagance, abuse and outright fraud." Then he made this key promise, which was to haunt his budget director David Stockman for years to come: "This strategy for growth *does not require altering or taking back necessary entitlements already granted to the American people.* The integrity of the Social Security system will be defended" (emphasis added).

It was a decision that reflected both Reagan's patchwork set of beliefs and his characteristic tendency to avoid unpleasant realities. Once in office, the pattern repeated itself. Reagan helped his own cause greatly by quickly grasping the various dimensions of his office, exploiting the strengths of his character to gain access to the full range of presidential power.

Felled by a would-be assassin's bullet in the first months of his presidency, he had the grace and wit to say to his doctors, as they were preparing him for the surgery that saved his life: "Please tell me you're Republicans." The jump in approval ratings following the shooting was an inevitable reflection of public sympathy. But by his command of the personal powers of the presidency, underlined by his conduct when his life was in peril, he was able to channel the public response into the debate over his economic policy proposals then in full swing and use it to help overcome his Democratic opponents on Capitol Hill.

In response to Reagan's proposed tax cuts, the Democrats proposed reductions of their own. Caught in a log-rolling competition, in order to get its version enacted, the administration wound up sponsoring reductions that would cost the treasury far more than originally contemplated. To avoid the unprecedented red ink this would produce in federal fiscal affairs, Budget Director Stockman proposed delaying the income tax cuts in return for an agreement with Congress to make more spending cuts, particularly in the entitlement programs.

But that was too complex for Reagan. "Delay would be a total retreat," he said. "We would be admitting that we were wrong." As Stockman ultimately came to realize, the president had little appetite for taking on the political challenge that cutting spending would involve. This was a manifestation of Reagan's homemade ideology, his faith in the rugged individualism of the past. "Reagan's body of knowledge is primarily impressionistic," Stockman observed. "He registers anecdotes rather than concepts."

The enactment of Reagan's economic program in the first six months of his presidency represented a signal success for Reagan's leadership. But the glow from that triumph would soon be clouded by the impact of the inconsistencies of his policies. By protecting middle-class benefits while cutting government help to the poor, Reagan exacerbated existing economic and societal inequities. The rich got substantially richer, the poor fell further behind. And over the long run, by increasing the disadvantages of low-income Americans, Reagan's policies compounded and created problems that middle-class Americans themselves had to confront—drugs, the homeless, the accelerating collapse of the cities. Moreover, the deficit created by Reagan's tax cuts left the federal government in a poor position to help deal with these problems.

Like his economic policies, Reagan's conduct of his longtime battle against communism, the other cornerstone of his presidency, was riddled with inconsistencies and based in large part on Reagan's attachment to the past. He liked to tell the story of the kidnapping early in this century of an American citizen named Perdicaris by the Berber bandit Raisuli, who vowed to hold Perdicaris hostage until the United States forced the sultan of Morocco to make certain concessions to Raisuli. Instead, President Theodore Roosevelt ordered the fleet to battle stations and declared: "This government wants Perdicaris alive or Raisuli dead."

"Perdicaris alive or Raisuli dead," Reagan repeated, savoring the words when he recounted this episode to me. "That's what this country should tell other countries today."

But Reagan's approach to foreign policy in the White House failed to recognize the dramatic changes in international power relationships that limited the scope of U.S. intervention abroad. And Reagan also failed to take sufficient account of the continuing reluctance of Americans to support such interventions for fear of becoming bogged down in another Vietnam-like morass.

Thus, the president, for all his vaunted power as a communicator, was unable to mobilize a majority of the public or of the Congress to back what became the centerpiece effort of his battle against the advance of communism—support for the Contra insurgency against the Sandinista regime in Nicaragua. And Congress refused to give the Contras the military backing Reagan wanted. Unwilling to accept the congressional "no" for an answer, Reagan's aides took matters into their own hands and the result was the Iran-Contra debacle. The portrait of Reagan that emerged from investigations by the Congress and a special prosecutor focused attention on one of the less appealing aspects of his character, his dependency on others to deal with vexing problems.

The special commission appointed by Reagan himself to investigate the affair, headed by Republican senator John Tower of Texas, put the matter as gently as possible. "President Reagan's personal management style places an especially heavy responsibility on his key advisers," its report said. In their joint review, the congressional select committees used blunter language to deal with the claim by John Poindexter, Reagan's national security adviser, that he had taken responsibility on his own shoulders to shield the president. "This kind of thinking is inconsistent with democratic governance," their report said. "The ultimate responsibility for the events in the Iran-Contra affair must rest with the president. If the president did not know what his National Security advisers were doing, he should have."

But support for counterinsurgency was only part of Reagan's struggle against communism. He was also determined to bring about an end to the Marxian creed in the heart of what he called the evil empire, the Soviet Union—an objective even his ardent admirers thought beyond his reach. "I only wish that I could get in a helicopter with Gorbachev," Reagan told a phalanx of his conservative acolytes at a Washington dinner party in 1985, "and fly over the United States. If I can just get through to him about the difference between our two systems, I really think we could see big changes in the Soviet Union."

Those in attendance, the likes of columnist George Will and author Michael Novak, did all they could to avoid snickering. "Our view," Novak later said, "was that it was foolish bordering on suicidal to think that the Soviet leaders would respond to personal initiatives. It was a bit of a shock, and an unpleasant one, to see that Reagan did not share our view at all."

The next year, Reagan's optimism seemed for a time justified, when during his Reykjavik summit with Gorbachev, the Soviet leader accepted Reagan's widely derided "zero option" proposal, calling for a drastic reduction in missiles on both sides but demanded that in return the United States agree not to deploy missile defenses, in other words that Reagan scrap his cherished Strategic Defense Initiative plan, a.k.a. Star Wars. Following his instinct, Reagan refused. "There was no way I could tell our people that their government would not protect them against nuclear destruction," he explained.

That seemed to ruin the chances for progress on missile reduction. But by 1987, Gorbachev, realizing that his country literally could not afford to stand by the position he had taken, which meant continuing the vast expenditures of the arms race, abandoned his demand that Reagan forget about Star Wars and the two superpowers reached an important accord on missile reduction.

That same year, Reagan stood before the Brandenburg Gate in West Berlin and declared: "In the Communist world we see failure, technological backwardness and declining standards. Even today, the Soviet Union cannot feed itself." "Freedom is the victor," Reagan proclaimed.

Those public comments provoked as much derision as had his private remarks at the dinner party. "If Reagan was such a fool," asks his former aide Dinesh D'Souza, "what does that make the wise men who ridiculed his pronouncements? What does that make us all?"

In predicting the downfall of Soviet communism, Reagan was doing what he did throughout his presidency—following his own natural inclinations, the thrust of his character. But however remarkable Reagan's insight into the future of communism was, that gift must be balanced against his obtuseness on economic policy, which was also an outgrowth of his personal beliefs. In other words, the blade of presidential character once again cut two ways.

9

THE
NONBELIEVER

WHEN VICE PRESIDENT GEORGE BUSH SURPRISED NO ONE by announcing his candidacy for his party's 1988 presidential nomination, hopes were high among his admirers. "It has been so long since he has been able to say what is on his mind," Nancy Ellis, his sister, told journalist Barry Bearak. "Even if it gets him creamed, I can't wait for the day he just stands back and says: 'I want to do this and I want to do that.'"

Nancy Ellis and others like her would wait in vain. George Bush did capture the Republican nomination and then, the presidency, too. He served in the nation's highest office for four years. Yet in all that time, he never said what he really believed or where he wanted to lead the country. To do so would have meant going against his character. The notion held by his sister and other admirers that for eight years as Ronald Reagan's vice president he had been forced to restrain himself totally misses the point about Bush's character. The most telling truth about Bush was that, as Eugene McCarthy said of Hubert Humphrey, "he had the soul of a vice president."

Bush brought to his presidential quest in 1988 a profound superficiality and hollowness that threatened his prospect from the outset and would ultimately wreck his presidency. But he had two prime assets, which made it possible for him to gain the White House despite his drawbacks. One was a team of cunning handlers. "We know we can't elect George Bush," Eddie Mahe, who was one of them, told me at the outset of the campaign. "But we can defeat Michael Dukakis."

The other Bush advantage was his willingness to do whatever was needed to implement the strategy proposed for him by his managers. His candidacy was built around character and values. But since his own character and values offered little appeal, he ran against the character and values of his opponent, Dukakis.

The result was another extension of the political use of character and values. Kennedy and Reagan had used character and values to help themselves. Bush used it to destroy his adversary.

But in doing what he did, he was true to his heritage and to his character. Boiled down to fundamentals, Bush amounted to an elitist version of Gerald Ford. Congeniality was his most conspicuous character trait and loyalty his most important value. Of his loyalty, as vice president to President Reagan, Bush would say: "I think it's good for the country and I think it's good for the office of the vice presidency itself, and, if it isn't good, well, that's just too bad because that's the way I was brought up."

Along with loyalty, restraint was bred into Bush, like good sportsmanship in games. One did not boast of victory. Instead, after pounding an overhead smash, one said, "I was lucky." And one did not grapple with the world. It was bad form. And anyhow, the world, or at least the people in it who counted the most, could usually be relied on to see that one was well taken care of. "He has spent a lifetime thinking in conventional terms, never reaching beyond them, never even wanting to," said Thomas (Lud) Ashley, a former Democratic congressman from Ohio and Bush's close friend of forty years. "His life has been without moral ambiguity," psychoanalyst Ray Walker, Bush's cousin, says. "He feels he has been granted goodness and that his success proves the goodness was warranted."

He followed this pattern of privilege from prep school to Yale and even when he finished college, married, and went into the world to make a living, choosing to leave his native New England for the strange terrain of West Texas. Bush liked to describe that choice as "breaking away" from his family. The reality was less dramatic. The young man got an attractive offer from an oil conglomerate on whose board, it just so happened, his father, Prescott Bush, served, and whose chairman, Neil Mallon, was Prescott's dear friend. In this way, Bush got the experience he needed in the oil business. And when he decided to launch his own venture, Uncle Herbie, an investment banker, scraped together $300,000 to get his favorite nephew started, and whenever during the course of his new enterprise young George needed extra help, Uncle Herbie saw that his needs were seen to.

And so it went for young Bush in the oil business, until he left that life to enter politics. And once again, the qualities and advantages that Bush possessed, notably a network of powerful and influential friends, assured that he would go a long way in his new profession. One appointment after another carried Bush almost to the very top of the world of politics—the vice presidency of the United States.

Bush had learned not to distract from the efforts of his friends by speaking out unnecessarily and calling unwanted attention to himself. He had been brought up to hold his tongue on most occasions, and he continued to practice that art as a maturing politician.

"George has never had a job in which he was required to take definitive positions," Mary Louise Smith, who succeeded Bush as chairman of the Republican National Committee and has been a longtime friend and supporter, told me after Bush became vice president. In this respect, the vice presidency was like every other public position Bush had held since he left Congress in 1970—U.S. ambassador to the United Nations, Republican National Committee chairman, envoy to China, and chief of the Central Intelligence Agency.

Bush had only won one election on his own in his life, that for a House seat in Texas, and the result of his breeding made it problematic that he could win any others. His political career was defined by a series of switches back and forth inspired by expedience. Thus in 1964, in his first try for public office, challenging for the Senate seat held by liberal Democrat Ralph Yarborough, he turned his back on the legacy of his father, Prescott, who was a staunchly moderate senator from Connecticut and tied himself closely to the ill-fated presidential candidacy of Republican standard-bearer Barry Goldwater. In keeping with this strategy, Bush denounced the 1964 Civil Rights Act as "politically inspired and destined to failure." And he opposed Medicare and the nuclear test ban treaty. His candidacy was overwhelmed by the Lyndon Johnson landslide.

Bush bounced back from that drubbing to run for the House of Representatives in 1966. This time, the field of battle was Texas's seventh congressional district, with upper-middle-class neighborhoods not very different from the Connecticut environs where Bush was raised and also with a fair percentage of black voters. His Democrat opponent was Frank Briscoe, the county district attorney, from the right wing of his party.

The situation called for a shift back to the center, particularly on civil rights. Bush began with his own Episcopalian minister in Houston. "You know, John, I took some of the far right positions to get elections," he said of his 1964 campaign. "I hope I never do it again. I regret it." Having thus absolved himself, Bush promised the voters "to work with the Negro and white leadership to get at the root causes of racial violence" and also pledged "not to appeal to the white backlash." He took 34 percent of the black vote, compared with 10 percent for the Republican candidate for governor, and easily defeated Briscoe. In his 1964 Senate campaign, Bush had opposed the landmark 1964 Civil Rights Act. But mindful of his 1966 campaign promises, he voted for the 1968 Fair Housing Act. It was not all that daring a move. The law had the support of a majority of House Republicans and eight other Congressman on the twenty-three-member Texas delegation.

When he ran for the Senate again in 1970, Bush prepared to campaign against the liberal Democrat incumbent Ralph Yarborough, who had defeated him in 1964. Instead, he found himself pitted against conservative Lloyd Bentsen, who had defeated Yarborough for the Democratic nomination. Bush professed to be unworried. "If Bentsen is going to try to go to my right, he's gonna step off the edge of the earth," he boasted. But Bush, who had moved right in 1964, then left in 1966, found it hard to turn himself around again in 1970. He had the backing of many liberal Democrats, who were determined to reject Bentsen as too conservative. But there were too many other Democrats in Texas, and most of them voted for Bentsen.

Even in defeat, Bush generally maintained his civil demeanor and genial disposition. But for all his good manners and cheerfulness, to many people he seemed smug, vacuous, and contrived, qualities that were connoted by the derisive term "preppy." Some of these traits might have been overlooked or offset if Bush had harbored strong convictions about the purpose of public policy. But Bush did not harbor such ideas. He had been brought up to avoid ideas—particularly those that might provoke disagreement.

Pressed in his 1980 presidential campaign to define himself as either a conservative or a moderate, Bush replied: "I don't want to be perceived as either."

"Well, you can't be both," a reporter contended.

"How do you know I can't?" Bush retorted.

What Bush did possess was ambition, a burning, consuming drive to pursue whatever in life had not come to him as his birthright but that he had somehow to achieve on his own. This made him more than willing to do the bidding of higher-ups whenever it seemed likely to work to his own advantage.

Bush's tendency toward subservience and self-denial was exemplified by his experience as national party chairman. His wife, having heard reports that following the 1972 election President Nixon wanted Bush to take the national chairman's job, argued against it.

"Do anything but that," Barbara Bush pleaded.

Meanwhile, Bush was asked by Treasury Secretary George Shultz to be his deputy. This was a far more substantive job than the party chairmanship, and Bush was intrigued. But Bush told Shultz he first had to learn what the president, Richard Nixon, wanted him to do.

He soon found out. "The job I really want you to do, the place I really need you, is over at the National Committee, running things," Nixon told him. "This is an important time for the Republican Party, George," said Nixon, who had during the course of his presidency displayed nothing but scorn for the party machinery he wanted Bush to manage. "We have a chance to build a new coalition in the next four years, and you're the one who can do it."

Bush needed to hear no more. When he broke the news to his wife, she protested bitterly.

"Boy, you can't turn a president down," Bush explained.

That was late 1972, and within a few months, the hopes of building a new Republican coalition had been buried under the wreckage of Watergate. Bush was trapped.

His aversion to questioning authority led him to accept Nixon's claims of innocence until the last hours of Nixon's presidency.

A few weeks before Nixon's final collapse, he told me, "I know a lot of people disagree, but I believe the president is telling the truth." Indeed, so firm was Bush's faith that his colleagues wondered how he would deal with the disclosure on August 5, 1974, of the taped evidence that made it clear even to Nixon's most ardent supporters that the president was involved in the conspiracy to cover up the crimes of Watergate from the beginning.

Williams Timmons, the chief White House congressional lobbyist, asked Dean Burch, one of Nixon's chief strategists, whether Bush had heard the news. "Yes," Burch replied.

"Well, what did he do?"

"He broke into assholes and shit himself to death," Burch said.

For vice presidents, self-effacement is a prime requirement for service. But even given the standards of that office, Bush's dedication to subservience attracted attention. He began right after Reagan selected him in Detroit in July 1980.

During the campaign, Bush had taken sharp issue with Reagan on economic policy—branding the supply-side economic theory Reagan advanced as "voodoo economics." More fundamentally, he had always opposed a constitutional amendment to ban abortion, which Reagan favored, and had always supported the proposed Equal Rights Amendment to the constitution, which Reagan opposed.

But all that went out the window when the second spot on the ticket, the stepping-stone to the presidency, was offered.

"George, is there anything at all about the platform or anything else, anything that might make you uncomfortable down the road?" Reagan asked tactfully but pointedly.

He saw no problems, Bush replied. The important thing, he told Reagan, was to win the election in November.

For the duration of the campaign and for the next eight years, if Bush ever disagreed with his president, the country never knew about it, nor did Reagan. Not only did he abandon any previous positions that differed from Reagan's, such as support for the right to abortion, but at times he even made a point of disparaging his presidential candidacy in 1980, when he competed against Reagan.

"When I ran against Ronald Reagan the smartest thing that ever happened was that people elected him and not me," he told a Republican fund-raiser in Philadelphia.

He never bothered to explain how, if he had been so unqualified in 1980, he could justify seeking the presidency again in 1988. Not surprisingly, Bush's behavior invited criticism and ridicule.

Doonesbury cartoonist Garry Trudeau depicted him as having "put his manhood in blind trust." Conservative columnist George Will likened him to "a lapdog" for pandering to the right wing. Bush's wimpishness became a matter for public debate, and friends rushed to defend him.

In Michigan, where the first skirmishes of the 1988 presidential campaign were fought out, Bush supporters wore tiny replicas of the Avenger torpedo bomber Bush had shot to pieces under him when, as a World War II navy pilot, he won the Distinguished Flying Cross.

Pointing to the plane pinned to his lapel, Brooks Patterson, a leader of the Bush forces, told me: "This is my answer to those who try to write George Bush off as a preppy."

Such loyalty to Bush from party workers, a reflection of Bush's own loyalty to Ronald Reagan as vice president, a job that bolstered his connections to the party's top fund-raisers and political operatives, was enough to get him nominated. But facing the Democrats in the fall, even with favorable economic winds at their back, Bush's strategists concluded they needed more than a lapel pin to get Bush to the White House.

The result was the most negative presidential campaign in modern times—a campaign built around character and values. The Republican offensive against Democratic standard-bearer Michael Dukakis did not come out of the blue. The path for this strategy had been paved for a generation. John Kennedy had broken the ground in 1960 by creating the vision of Camelot and tying it to his own persona, generating an appeal that outlasted his foreshortened tenure in the White House. Then came two horrendously negative presidencies—the regimes of Richard Nixon and Lyndon Johnson—both of whose transgressions clearly stemmed from flaws in their character as broad and deep as the San Andreas fault. Jimmy Carter made the character issue more explicit than ever when he made his promise to never tell a lie the cornerstone of his candidacy. Whatever doubts may have been raised about the relevance of character by Carter's dismal White House performance were overshadowed by the glamour of Ronald Reagan's personality as he seemed to bring renewed vitality to the presidency. Then Reagan himself stumbled, but his folly in Iran-Contra once again brought out the immense potential of presidential character for harm as well as for good.

All this was having its impact on the Democratic Party, as demonstrated in the campaign for the 1988 nomination. The first dramatic development was the forced withdrawal from the campaign for the nomination of Gary Hart, the former Colorado senator and strategist for George McGovern in 1968. On the basis of his strong challenge to Walter F. Mondale for the Democratic nomination in 1984, Hart had become the early front-runner for the 1988 nomination. But he had a reputation as a womanizer, and rumors soon swirled around his candidacy, similar to those that plagued Bill Clinton in 1992.

At first, Hart tried to brand such stories, and the issues of character and values, as totally irrelevant to the presidency. When we

talked in the spring of 1987, he sought to draw a distinction between "public" and "private" values. "Each of us has our own set of
personal values," he said. "But there also are an identifiable set of
public values. The reason I belong to the party I belong to is that my
party comes closest to the set of public values that I think this nation
stands for—equality, regardless of economic background, legal and
social justice and equal opportunity."

But didn't personal values have political significance, too?

"Only because society has a right to regulate personal behavior
that affects society as a whole," Hart said. "Otherwise people
should be free to behave as they please."

But as a matter of practical politics, I asked, didn't licentious behavior offend some groups and hurt at the ballot box.

Hart said such puritanical attitudes were held only by religious
minorities. "This nation from Jefferson on has always said no minority could impose its religious values on the community," he argued. Hart pointed out that he himself had once been a member of a
religious minority with strong beliefs, the Church of the Nazarene.
"The Church didn't believe we should go to movies. So we didn't go
to movies. But we didn't picket to try to close down the theater," he
said. "It's one thing to tell your adherents to observe your values. It's
another thing to impose those values on the community."

But Hart would soon discover that whatever might have been true
about values in Jefferson's day was no longer valid in late twentieth-
century America. Hart's problems could be traced back to 1984,
when his sudden vault into prominence in his campaign against
Mondale sent reporters scurrying to pry into his background. They
soon discovered among other things that he had shortened his
name—which used to be Hartpence; that in his campaign biography,
he had made himself a year younger than he actually was. And that
he had a reputation for extramarital involvement.

All this gave rise to what came to be called the "character issue,"
which Hart's advisers took steps to defuse at the start of his next run
for presidency. But one part of their strategy, having the candidate
submit to lengthy interviews about his background, backfired.

Hart resented the probing and prying into his personal life, not
only because he had things to hide but because he was a supremely
arrogant person. Indeed, his arrogance had as much to do with his
downfall as his libido.

"I'm going to answer about three more of these, and then I'm not going to answer any more," he told one interviewer, probing into some episode in his past. "I was thirteen at the time. It's nonsense. Who cares what Ronald Reagan was thinking when he was thirteen? Or Joe Biden?"

On another, and as it turned out, more significant occasion, during an interview with E. J. Dionne of the *New York Times,* when the question of womanizing came out, his exasperation got the better of him. "Follow me around. I don't care," he said. "I'm serious. If any-body wants to put a tail on me, go ahead. They'd be very bored."

Unfortunately for Hart, the *Miami Herald* took him at his word. Acting on a tip, it sent reporters to stake out his Washington home, where they discovered that while his wife of twenty-eight years was away, he was billeted with a twenty-nine-year-old model named Donna Rice. The inevitable outcry escalated when it soon became known that Hart and Rice had cruised to Bimini together on a yacht all too appropriately named "Monkey Business."

Hart's denials of misconduct—he claimed he was interested in Rice only as a potential campaign aide—were drowned out by in-consistencies in his own story and a barrage of questions from an unrelenting press corps. His darkest moment came when he was asked during a press conference whether he had ever committed adultery.

Hart ducked the question but then had to confront a *Washington Post* reporter who demanded on orders from his editors that he comment on information, bolstered by photographic evidence, that he had maintained a longtime affair with a Washington woman.

That was too much for Hart. He pulled out of the race, eight days after the *Herald* had disclosed his liaison with Donna Rice, but not without giving the press corps and the rest of the political world a piece of his mind. "I refuse to submit my family and friends and in-nocent people and myself to further rumors and gossip," Hart said. "I believe I would have been a successful candidate and I know I could have been a good President . . . but apparently now we'll never know."

Hart called for changes in the nation's political system—which he charged had destroyed his candidacy by slighting more significant is-sues and exaggerating the importance of his personal behavior and character. "For most people in this country," he said, "that's not what concerns them."

A good many politicians echoed his words. Reverend Jesse Jackson, who had always resisted answering questions about his own freewheeling personal life, was highly critical of the press coverage of Hart. "I think he was sabotaged," he said. "He really was set up," Jackson said. "It raises some profound questions about journalistic ethics and limits." And Charles T. Manatt, cochairman of Hart's campaign, told a reporter: "It's more the media than the public that's interested in such details of personal behavior and when a newspaper does a stakeout to get the details, that's beyond the pale, it's gone too far."

But a good many scholars took the other side. "Character is singularly important, more important in the presidency than in any other office," said Michael Robinson, a specialist on the press and the presidency at Georgetown University. He claimed Hart was being unrealistic in his condemnation of the system. "I worked hard to get Lyndon Johnson elected as the peace candidate, and then he almost shipped me off to Vietnam," Robinson said. "That was a function of Johnson's character."

And Duke University's James David Barber, the reigning academic expert on presidential character, claimed, "Hart's fantasizing about how campaigns develop. In the real world, the press is going to be looking at him. To say, 'I'm going to lead my personal life the way I want to and you guys just report on my position papers'—that's just not the way it works."

What everyone did agree on was that for better or worse, the character issue was going to be a prominent part of the 1988 presidential campaign. "It seems to me that the press and the public are going to feel after Hart's case that we have to hold all the candidates to the same standard of scrutiny," predicted David Keene, senior political consultant to Republican presidential contender Senator Bob Dole of Kansas. "It's going to create a different scenario for campaigns," warned Democratic national committeeman John Roehrich of Iowa, where his party's delegate selection process would begin next February. "The American people are going to expect their candidates to be as pure as Caesar's wife. And that's going to be the norm."

It was not long before the next victim emerged—Senator Joe Biden of Delaware, as a result of a critical misstep in John Roehrich's Iowa. Just as adultery had driven Hart of the race, in Biden's case, it was plagiarism. But underlying both episodes were deeper misgivings about both men, which revelations of their conduct seemed to confirm. With regard to Hart, this was the perception of a general unsteadiness of judgment and arrogant disregard for the possible consequences of his private actions—qualities given credence by the disclosure of his ill-fated weekend rendezvous with Donna Rice. With Biden, his vulnerability grew out of suspicions that his approach to campaigning and to the substantive responsibilities of office was tinged with superficiality—that he offered more sizzle than steak. In what is certainly the fundamental irony of his presidential candidacy, those misgivings were grounded directly in what everyone agreed was his greatest political strength—his oratorical skill.

Biden was able to rouse Democratic audiences to enthusiasm in a way none of his rivals, except civil rights leader Jesse Jackson, could match. His good looks, his lithe figure, his Irish charm all combined to provide him with what one admiring commentator called "earthy magnetism"—the promise of an electricity that the Democratic Party had not been able to offer the nation since the Kennedy brothers. But it was just this dazzle that invited the suspicion that not much lurked beneath the flashing surface.

Biden's problem was comparable, as New York governor Mario M. Cuomo once warned him in a private conversation, to that of a beautiful woman no one will credit with intelligence. "If you want to be the dumb blonde of the party," Cuomo needled Biden, "the guy who can give you a speech but can't count, I'll be glad to go around the country billing you that way."

Others warned Biden more directly. "You talk too much and you say things without thinking about them," Norman Ornstein, an American Enterprise Institute fellow and a friend and admirer, told the senator as he was gearing up for his candidacy.

"I know I've got to be more disciplined," Biden replied.

But, as Ornstein pointed out: "It's easier to say that than do that. Besides, he probably didn't believe it in his heart." His undoing came about when it was discovered that he had borrowed—without attributing it—a dramatic passage of personal reminiscence from a videotaped speech by British Labor Party leader Neil Kinnock to use in a televised campaign debate in Des Moines and in an appeal for support from the National Education Association.

Asking rhetorically why his Welsh miner ancestors had not succeeded as he himself had, Kinnock said: "Did they lack talent? . . . Was it because they were weak? . . . Of course not, it was because there was no platform on which they could stand."

In closing his remarks at a campaign debate in Iowa, Biden mimicked Kinnock's questions, applying them to his own forebears, and concluded with the same peroration that Kinnock had, almost word for word. Biden's delivery, without any reference to the source of the rhetoric, created the impression that his remarks had sprung out of his own head, and heart. And the power and passion of the original version only made Biden's use of it seem all the more reprehensible.

The uproar triggered by the Kinnock episode led to the uncovering of other unseemly events in Biden's past. It was disclosed that as a student he had plagiarized parts of a law school paper. And that he lost his temper with a New Hampshire citizen who asked him about his law school grades. It was then that Biden claimed to have finished far higher in his law school class than he did. In little more than two weeks, Biden quit the race, blaming the "exaggerated shadow" of mistakes that he complained had begun "to obscure the essence of my candidacy." He said that he was frustrated by "the environment of presidential politics that makes it so difficult for the American people to measure the whole of Joe Biden and not just the misstatements that I have made."

Yet in each case, the disclosures about Hart and Biden took on salience and significance because in each case they seemed to illuminate and confirm some larger truth about their candidacies—that each man was in his own way irresponsible and unworthy of the public trust. It was for this reason that the character issue came to dominate the 1988 campaign long before a single vote was cast.

And the circle of mishaps was not yet completed. Soon after Biden's withdrawal, Michael Dukakis's aides acknowledged—after first denying it—that it was they who had passed out copies of the Kinnock tape to reporters, thus alerting them to Biden's misstep. This led to the resignations of Dukakis's two top advisers, John Sasso and Paul Tully, departures that would cause serious damage to Dukakis's campaign over the long run. But significantly, Dukakis, unlike his two rivals for the nomination, was spared. This was because, unlike in the cases of Hart and Biden, the sins committed by Dukakis's aides were not seen as revealing some profound weakness in Dukakis himself. In fact, as his candidacy ground on its mechanical way to victory, the Massachusetts governor appeared to have no noticeable human frailty beyond excessive dullness, neither an unusual nor necessarily serious drawback for a politician. It remained for Bush's board of strategy, in what was certainly its most creative act, to find—or rather, create—a weakness in Dukakis and to use it to smother his candidacy.

But those events were still sleeping somewhere in the future in the spring and fall of 1987. During that period, while the character issue was tearing the Democrats apart, at least one Republican was mindful of the positive impact of character and values—and trying to exploit it. This was Bob Dole, the veteran Kansas senator who was Bush's chief rival for the nomination. He signaled his approach in the fall of 1987 by selecting his home town of Russell as the site for the official announcement of his candidacy.

When some of his advisers questioned the need to stage that event in this remote little community tucked away in northern Kansas, Dole's senior political consultant, Don Devine, had a ready answer, "Face it," Devine said, "Russell, Kansas, is what we are running for President."

Amid the warmth and enthusiasm generated by Russell's 5,000 citizens on kickoff day in November, it was easy to see the benefits that Dole hoped his Russell roots would bring to his candidacy. Russell—where the young Dole jerked sodas in the drugstore and earned letters on the high-school track, basketball, and football teams—is a paradigm of the sort of small town still idealized by many Americans, urban and rural alike. It was this little town where Dole's family struggled through the bitter times of the 1930s, the place to which wounded combat veteran Dole came home after World War II, his right arm and his youthful dreams shattered, and whose citizens helped him to restore his life.

In short, his was the sort of story Hollywood used to make movies of in the 1940s and 1950s. And Dole's advisers believed that their candidate's down-to-earth beginnings in Russell would make for a favorable contrast with front-runner George Bush's upper-crust origins. Unlike the vice president—a senator's son, reared in New England amid the trappings of power and wealth, who had adopted a new political home in Texas—Dole's origins were middle-class middle-American, and he still proudly claimed his initial roots.

The message of his announcement speech in Russell, Dole told me as we flew there on his chartered jet, was: "Here is a person who is successful and has a chance of being the next President and hasn't forgotten where he is from. That's a quality people like to see—that you don't forget where you're from."

Moreover, Dole said, where he is from was "sort of what it's all about," a place with which most voters can readily identify.

"This is where it's at," Dole said. "You can go to cities and get the same cross-section of people." Then he added with an unmistakable allusion to Bush's affluent background: "You don't go to country clubs."

Just as important in the thinking of Dole's strategists as the boost they hoped to get from their candidate's links to Russell in his campaign against Bush was the help they figured it would provide him in dealing with another and possibly more formidable adversary: himself, or at least the unpleasant perception of himself that he had created over the years.

Much of this perception was based on Dole's performance as President Gerald R. Ford's vice presidential running-mate in the 1976 campaign, particularly his showing in his nationally televised debate with his opposite number, Walter F. Mondale, in which he famously referred to both world wars and the Korean and Vietnam conflicts as "Democrat wars."

Not even Dole's longtime friends and admirers or the leaders of his campaign could pretend that he was really some sort of badly misunderstood Mary Poppins. "I think he's tougher than nails," said Don Schnacke, a lobbyist for Kansas oil and gas producers, one of the hundreds of Dole supporters who flocked to the VFW hall in Russell for an announcement-eve barbecue. "He came up the hard way and struggled for everything he's got." But Dole's admirers hoped that when his toughness was understood in the context of his life's experience, particularly his years in Russell, the characteristics that would emerge would be a blend of tough-mindedness and compassion.

But in the end, their efforts mainly served to demonstrate the limits of efforts to manipulate the character issue. Dole finished a weak second to Bush in the contest for the Republican nomination. Bush, of course, had huge advantages in the competition that had little to do with character. He was far better known and financed and had closer contact with party leaders down to the grass roots.

However, the character strategy failed mainly because Dole could not fill the role his strategists designed for him. The compassion and concern that his aides hoped would emerge as a result of stressing his early life remained hidden to all but his closest friends. On the surface, Dole appeared to be what he had always been—a crusty, cynical politician. And he struck the death blow to his own candidacy on the night of the New Hampshire primary when asked on national television in the bitterness of his defeat by Bush whether he had anything to say to his rival who had accused Dole of favoring tax hikes, Dole snarled: "Yeah, tell him to stop lying about my record."

Bush and his advisers considered all this as they contemplated their battle against Michael Dukakis in the summer of 1988. They swiftly concluded that their only path to victory was to turn the focus of the election from George Bush to Michael Dukakis. This meant shielding Bush from attack and then hammering Dukakis.

Recasting the Bush image by converting him from wimpish elitist into a compassionate leader was the first task. Much of this was done with his acceptance speech at the convention, carefully crafted by Reagan speechwriter Peggy Noonan for maximum likability. Her challenge was twofold, first, to get Bush out of the shadow of Ronald Reagan and establish his own identity, and second, to recast the view of Bush's character as wimpish elitist into that of compassionate leader. At the start came a touch of self-deprecating humor. "I'll try to be fair to the other side," Bush joshed. "I'll try to hold my charisma in check." There followed a note of wholesome spirituality: "There is a God and He is good and His love, while free, has a self-imposed cost; we must be good to one another." Finally, and of particular importance as a counter to the by then offensive greediness that had characterized the Reagan era, Bush sounded the theme of compassion.

"The fact is, prosperity has a purpose," Noonan had Bush contend. "Prosperity with a purpose means taking your idealism and making it concrete by certain acts of goodness." The newly minted nominee acknowledged that "some would say it's soft and insufficiently tough to care about these things."

But as for himself, he declared in a phrase clearly intended to serve as the chief line of demarcation between himself and his predecessor: "I want a kinder and gentler nation." Having more or less recreated himself with his acceptance speech, Bush now faced the equally essential task of targeting his foe—Democrat Michael Dukakis. But this was no easy task. The Democratic standard-bearer presented himself as ideologically neutral, a sort of "Governor Goodwrench" who could fix whatever was wrong in the country. "This election is not about ideology," Dukakis had said in his own acceptance speech. "It's about competence."

As for his character, this was no easy target either. Dukakis was a temperate and disciplined man. The worst that could be said about him was that he was methodical to a fault and dreary, the sort of man, a friend remarked, who spent his time rearranging his socks in his drawer. Of course, there was a rumor that Dukakis had once received psychiatric treatment, which, though groundless, gained wide exposure when Ronald Reagan, asked about the story, maliciously replied: "I'm not going to pick on an invalid."

The damage that episode did—Dukakis dropped eight points in the polls—underlined the potency of the character issue. But the fact that Reagan immediately apologized—"I don't think I should have said what I said," he remarked—also demonstrated that direct personal attacks could backfire.

Out of his dilemma emerged the ingenious Bush strategy for attacking Dukakis. In a way, the thinking of Bush's advisers paralleled Gary Hart's views. Hart had drawn a distinction between public values and private values, suggesting that private values were strictly personal, while public values were a fit subject for political debate.

The Bush campaign, reasoning that way, saw public values as an opening to make their case against Dukakis. They launched a massive attack on Dukakis public values as a way of indirectly attacking his character. By focusing on several controversial aspects of Dukakis's gubernatorial record—such as his veto of the law requiring teachers to lead their classes in the pledge of allegiance, his opposition to capital punishment, and the weekend furlough he had granted to convicted killer Willie Horton—Bush sought to define his opponent as outside of what Bush called "the mainstream" of American beliefs and values—in other words, that he was not fit to be president.

It was clear from the nature of the charges lodged against Dukakis that the attack had little to do with substance or public policy. As the veteran political journalists Jack Germond and Jules Witcover asked in *Whose Broad Stripes and Bright Stars,* their chronicle of the campaign, about the capital punishment issue, "Was a candidate's position for or against capital punishment the acid test for the presidency? More important, did issues like the flag pledge, prison furloughs and the death penalty warrant crowding out such ostensibly transcendent issues of national importance as the stability of the economy, homelessness, global trade imbalance and relations with the Soviet Union?"

The answer is that these seemingly trivial values issues mattered to the Bush high command, because they packed an emotional punch that the substantive issues lacked. The Bush advisers knew this because they had carefully sampled focus groups of potential voters to get their reaction to Dukakis's actions as governor. Earlier that year, hidden behind a two-way mirror, Bush campaign manager Lee Atwater and other top aides had watched as one of their researchers dispassionately told a group of thirty New Jersey Democrats all about the Willie Horton furlough, the flag salute veto, and capital punishment. By the time the presentation was over, only fifteen of the thirty still backed Dukakis. "I realized right there that we had the wherewithal to win . . . and that the sky was the limit on Dukakis' negatives," Atwater would say later.

Bush led the attack, driving the values dagger home whenever he could, specifically and in general, making the point that Dukakis's values were a reflection of Dukakis the man. "In the final analysis, the person goes into that voting booth they're going to say: Who has the values I believe in?" Bush said in his closing statement to the first presidential debate of the campaign. "Most of what this campaign is about is a question of values," he added. And with some 60 million Americans watching, he spent much of the next ninety minutes painting a highly colored portrait of the differences between his values and those of Dukakis. On the death penalty for cop killers, rapists, and drug kingpins, for instance, the Republican standard-bearer asserted: "We just have an honest difference of opinion; I support it and he doesn't." Meanwhile, as he stumped around the country, whenever he could, Bush brought up the Willie Horton furlough. "Clint Eastwood's answer to violent crime is: 'Go ahead, make my day,'" he told campaign rallies. "My opponent's answer is slightly different. His motto is: 'Go ahead, have a nice weekend.'"

Even as his poll standings dropped under the weight of Bush's barrage at his values, Dukakis denounced the attacks as "shameless," "disgraceful," and "irrelevant." But the powerful impact of the vice president's tactics reflected more than a triumph of negative political hucksterism. The so-called values issue posed all-too-real problems for the Democratic candidate and his party. Some of the difficulty for Dukakis was that his reserved personality and his pompous manner on the stump inhibited him from spelling out his values in ways that stirred voters' feelings. He seemed incapable of engaging issues emotionally. And his own attempts at symbolic communication generally fell flat or backfired. The most memorable example was Dukakis's decision to take a ride in an M-1 tank to demonstrate that despite what Bush said, he was a patriot at heart. Unfortunately, with only his head and shoulders visible and wearing a tie, an ill-fitting helmet, and a foolish grin, Dukakis appeared like a caricature of himself, in danger of being swallowed up by this mechanized monster. "I was trying to define Michael Dukakis in terms of foreign policy and he defined himself," said Roger Ailes, Bush's top media adviser, who promptly turned the news clips of Dukakis's ill-fated ride into a devastating Bush campaign commercial that lambasted Dukakis both as a hopeless dove and a hypocrite.

The limitations of Dukakis's character were compounded because the nominee and the Democratic Party as a whole were caught in a quandary over values, a dilemma that would have profound consequences for the Democratic strategy and rhetoric in the future, as Democrats sought to learn from the failings of the Dukakis effort. Dating back to the turbulent 1960s and early 1970s, the party—particularly its liberal wing—became identified with political protest, mostly centered on race relations and the Vietnam War, and with social permissiveness in areas such as crime, drugs, and sexual behavior. Those attitudes disturbed many middle-class citizens, who typically form the swing-vote segment of the electorate, and contributed to a record of four Democratic defeats in the five presidential elections preceding the Dukakis campaign and to Dukakis's weaknesses in 1988. "We're strapped with a recent history which makes people suspect that we really don't respect the flag," Democratic strategist Michael Ford, a veteran of numerous presidential contests and a consultant to the Dukakis campaign, told me.

The Democrats badly needed to establish a new set of value guideposts to match the era of change they were promising to usher in with a Dukakis presidency. But their efforts in that direction were marked not only by Dukakis's shortcomings but by the ambiguity and uncertainty that gripped other party leaders. Unable to agree on what to say, they compromised on saying as little as possible, an attitude underlined by their decision to shrink their 1988 party platform to about one-tenth the size of past platforms.

By comparison, Bush and his Republicans—as defenders of the status quo—had a much easier task, pumping hard for traditional values such as law and order, patriotism and family, which polls showed were just as revered as ever. "I don't think it's a question of whether people like you or not to make you an effective leader. I think it's whether you share the broad dreams of the American people," Bush declared, as he and his surrogates stepped up their efforts in the closing days of the campaign to cast Dukakis as "outside the mainstream." Backing up Bush in this endeavor was Ronald Reagan, whose gift for using his character to dramatize the images and symbols linked to values had greatly contributed to the advantage the GOP enjoyed in this debate. "When the left took over the Democratic Party," Reagan declared on the campaign stump, "we made the Republican Party into the party of working people, the family, the neighborhood, the defense of freedom and, yes, the American flag and the Pledge of Allegiance to one nation under God."

For Dukakis, the attacks presented a no-win situation. He found it hard to ignore them. And his campaign commissioned pollster Stanley Greenberg, who would later become a key figure in Bill Clinton's drive for the presidency, to conduct focus group research on the impact of the Republican attack. In August, when Dukakis still held a dwindling lead in the polls, Greenberg sent his campaign managers a memo warning that the Republican onslaught was taking a toll of voter support, particularly the controversy over the weekend furlough granted Willie Horton. "The furlough issue had become a very serious blockage to people wanting to find out more about Dukakis," Greenberg warned. "They had a lurid vision of Dukakis because of this issue, and they needed to be able to rationalize it before they were willing to find out more about him. I pressed them to do this."

But Dukakis was slow to act. "He was determined not to wage the campaign on their issues," one Dukakis staff worker told the *Washington Post*. "He wanted to campaign on his issues."

And the responses Dukakis did make were weak and bloodless, reflecting his character and succeeding mainly in giving more prominence to the charges the GOP made against him. For example, when Bush raised the pledge of allegiance issue, Dukakis resorted to a legalistic defense that he was obliged to veto the law requiring the pledge, bound by an advisory opinion that the statute was unconstitutional.

Republicans were delighted that he had taken the bait. "That was our Exocet missile," UCLA's John Petrocik exulted, recalling the devastation wrought by the Royal Navy against Argentine ships in the Falklands War. "We just sank that ship—pow!" Dukakis could have made a more dramatic and compelling case for the right to dissent by citing a historic Supreme Court decision that had struck down just such a law as the one he vetoed. "Freedom to differ is not limited to things that do not matter much," former justice Robert Jackson wrote in that 1943 opinion. "That would be a mere shadow of freedom. The test of its substance is the right to differ as to things that touch the heart of the existing order."

In the end, the Bush attack on Dukakis's values succeeded not because of the specific issues they raised, which had little to do with the problems facing the next president, but because of what they said about Dukakis as a human being. They painted a picture of a narrow, unfeeling bureaucrat, remote from the genuine concerns of the average citizen. It was not just the charges but Dukakis's feeble response to the charges that gave them credibility and damned him to political oblivion.

Occasionally, Dukakis showed some signs of coming out of his torpor. In the closing weeks of the campaign, speaking at Bates College, with his mother by his side, he called for renewal of "our commitment to basic American values." Alluding to the scandals that had tarnished the Reagan administration, he said: "We need a government that not only enforces the law, but that obeys the law." And, responding to Bush's "outrageous" contention that he lacked concern for the victims of crime, Dukakis cited two particular victims—his father, who was robbed and tied up in his office, and his forty-three-year-old brother, who was killed by a hit-and-run driver.

"I don't need any lectures from Mr. Bush on crime fighting or on the sensitivity of compassion we must extend to the victims of crime," Dukakis said. But such moments were few and far between and were overshadowed by Dukakis's lifeless performance in the campaign's climactic debate, when he was asked whether if his own wife were raped and murdered, he would suspend his opposition to capital punishment and demand the execution of her killer. Dukakis had been prepped before the debate to answer any such questions with the rhetoric he had used at Bates, a speech that had gotten little attention. Instead, for reasons best known to himself, he simply responded with a flat, bloodless restatement of his reasons for opposing capital punishment.

At the end, Dukakis walked off the stage and to John Sasso, who had been reinstated as his chief political adviser, delivered the definitive verdict on the debate and his presidential candidacy. "I blew it," he said.

To repair the damage of his negative campaign to the image of caring and compassion created by his acceptance speech, right after election day, Bush embarked on an intensive character rehabilitation campaign that he pursued as vigorously as his assault on Michael Dukakis. During preinaugural week, the president made a point of vowing at a prayer breakfast in honor of Martin Luther King's birthday that "bigotry and indifference to disadvantage will find no safe home on our shores, in our public life, in our neighborhoods or in our homes." To fulfill King's dream, Bush declared, "will, I promise, be my mission as president of the United States."

Then, in his Inaugural Address, Bush once again visited the lofty heights where noble sentiments dwell. "What do we want the men and women who work with us to say when we are no longer there?" he asked. "That we were more driven to succeed than anyone around us? Or that we stopped to ask if a sick child had gotten better, and stayed a moment to trade a word of friendship?"

Also evident in this speech, along with this rebuke of materialism, was Bush's sense of noblesse oblige, which he had expressed in his acceptance address to the Republican convention. "America is never wholly herself unless she is engaged in high moral principle," the president told his fellow citizens as he took the oath of office. "We as a people have such a purpose today. It is to make kinder the face of the nation and gentler the face of the world.

Bush had notable success in presenting himself, in the words of one analyst, "as warm, sincere, relaxed and secure . . . a person most people like." After he had been in the White House a year, the Gallup Poll found that more than 80 percent of those surveyed approved of him as a person. That was ten points higher even than the summit Reagan reached in the afterglow of his recovery from the attempt on his life.

To be sure, by the summer of his second year in the White House, the worsening of the savings and loan crisis, the early evidence of the recession that would eventually ravage his presidency, and, most emphatically, his decision to break his "read-my-lips" pledge not to raise taxes had begun to raise doubts about his handling of the presidency. But these misgivings were drowned out by the triumph of Desert Storm. The battlefield victory won by U.S. forces sent his poll standings soaring anew and endowed him with new personal resources of public trust and prestige for dealing with the deficit and the Democratic opposition in Congress.

Given such an opportunity following the Cuban Missile Crisis, John Kennedy pushed through the test ban treaty with the Soviets and later launched his civil rights program. Harry Truman, in the wake of his 1948 election victory, unveiled the Fair Deal, just as Lyndon Johnson exploited the momentum he gained from his 1964 landslide triumph to launch the Great Society. Housing Secretary Jack Kemp, one of conservatism's post-Reagan heroes, argued that the time was right for Bush to broaden the Republicans' appeal by waging "an audacious, aggressive kind of dramatic war on poverty," by pushing such ideas as privatization of public housing and enterprise zones. "Bush has a chance of going beyond where Ronald Reagan went," especially with minority voters, Kemp told me.

But Bush had no interest in doing any such thing. Breaking the tax promise had been hard enough to bear. True to his character, he avoided pushing any proposals that would threaten more controversy. The president resented those who criticized him for not being more vigorous. "I am sick and tired of people saying we don't have a domestic agenda, because they've got their eyes closed or because they don't want to hear," Bush told Republican Senate leaders a few weeks after victory on the Gulf had turned public attention back to domestic affairs. "We've got a good one, and with your support we can make it come to pass."

Yet his own words gave him away. His brief defensive reference to domestic proposals followed upon an lengthy exhortation to back the White House's "veto strategy." "It is very important because when we're in a minority, the only way we're going to get something done is to beat down the bad idea before they give us a shot at a good idea." But the truth was, Bush never made clear what if anything he did want to get done, nor did he offer any examples of a good idea. His moment of triumph faded away, and by the final year of his presidency, the harsh realities of an economic slowdown underlined the inadequacies of his character to meet the challenge of the Oval Office. The chief legacy of his presidency may have been one he would not wish—his ugly campaign for the office and the lessons it taught the Democrats.

10

PRESIDENT
PROTEUS

THE 1992 NEW HAMPSHIRE Democratic primary was the campaign that was supposed to be all about issues. Victory in that economically ravaged state, one of the hardest hit in the nationwide recession, was expected to go to the candidate with the most convincing agenda of economic nostrums. But as the balloting in the first-in-the-nation primary drew near, the attention of voters had shifted from the candidates' answers to the local economic distress to vexing questions of character. These went to the heart of the American political process but offered no easy answer.

No one was unhappier about this transformed state of affairs than William Jefferson Clinton, the governor of Arkansas and erstwhile front-runner in the campaign. "Far too much of the last couple of weeks of this election has been about me," Clinton complained, as he watched his once commanding lead in the polls fade. A Southerner who had honed his intellect at the best schools the North had to offer, a Rhodes scholar who exuded down-home charm, a man of boundless energy and sweeping imagination, Clinton had easily risen to the top of a mediocre field of rivals. But ever since he had burst on the national scene a decade earlier, those who had gotten to know him had come to wonder whether his admittedly formidable talents were a match for his ambition and appetites. And that question had come into sharp focus in the New Hampshire campaign, forced to the surface by allegations that this rising new star in the Democratic firmament was both a draft evader and a womanizer.

But former Massachusetts senator Paul Tsongas, the principal beneficiary of Clinton's decline, had reason to be delighted with the emergence of the character issue. In an editorial endorsing his candidacy, the *Boston Herald* praised Tsongas's "decency and strength of character" and declared, in an apparent allusion to the unfortunate Clinton: "At a time when voters are weary of candidates with feet of clay, Paul Tsongas is a man whose integrity is unquestioned."

All this emphasis on character was not without precedent in presidential campaigning. Another Southern governor, Jimmy Carter, the last Democrat to win the presidency, had made great capital of his background as a born-again Christian and his promise to never tell a lie. And among those who competed against Clinton, Senator Bob Kerrey, time and again, described the ordeal of having his leg amputated after Vietnam combat as a crucible that helped to shape his political beliefs, just as former Senator Tsongas cited his battle against cancer both as evidence of his determination and as an episode that helped him to define his values.

Still and all, some complained that the probing into a candidate's personal background obscured the real issues of the campaign, and not surprisingly Clinton's voice swelled that critical chorus. "The real character issue and the real patriotism issue in this election is, who has a vision for the country, a plan for the future and the ability to get it done," he argued. "The people whose character and patriotism is really an issue in this election are those who would divert the attention of the people, who destroy the reputations of their opponents and divide the country we love."

But this objection was rich in unintended irony, for it was Clinton's presidential candidacy that brought to fruition the character issue as a double-edged sword. No candidate in modern times had been the target for so much criticism and controversy because of his personal behavior. And no candidate before him had been so calculating and determined to use his personal life and values as a weapon on his own behalf.

Clinton had always found it easy to get attention, ever since his election as Arkansas governor in 1978 at age thirty-two made him the nation's youngest governor. His youth in no way made him shy about speaking out, as he demonstrated in July 1979, when Jimmy Carter, beleaguered by his self-generated "malaise" crisis and facing a challenge to his renomination from Ted Kennedy, sought a boost from the nation's Democratic governors. Clinton went along with the majority of his fellow Democratic governors, gathered for their annual meeting, in voting to endorse Carter's candidacy but could not resist offering him some unsolicited advice on leadership. Carter was in trouble because people "feel no sense of movement or involvement with the president," Clinton observed, and he then laid down an indictment of Carter's governance that included the limpness of his oratory and the barrenness of his policy.

Recalling the speech Carter had given early in his presidency in which he had likened the effort to deal with the energy crisis to the "moral equivalent of war," Clinton said Carter had sounded "almost like a seventeenth-century Puritan bringing bad news to the country. What people are looking for is someone who will say that this is the moral equivalent of war of the independence—and that everybody has some role and some mission to play."

Clinton's behavior at the governor's conclave was what the political world would ultimately come to recognize as a vintage performance. He managed to have things both ways—loyally voting to pledge support for Carter and at the same time bolstering his personal identity as a new figure on the national stage with strong ideas of his own. This skill underlined the gulf between their characters. The younger man was far more supple in the practice of their mutual profession; if his rhetoric was unremarkable, at least it went down easy. He was always looking ahead and behind. He dodged and ducked, bobbed and weaved, making himself a hard target. Sometimes his foes knocked him down, but they could never count him out. Carter, as Clinton suggested, tended to talk at people, or even worse down to them, his words shaped only by the particular conceit in his own mind. By contrast, Clinton's public utterances were defined by what he imagined to be the concerns of his audience, to which he sought to match whatever point he wanted to make, giving each listener, as he had said, "some role and some mission to play."

At any rate, Clinton's advice was not enough to save the president from defeat, which also victimized Clinton, who was Carter's Arkansas campaign chairman, as disgusted voters turned both men out of office after each had served one term. But Clinton also took on some blame himself, concluding that he had been too liberal for his state. Clinton came to power in Little Rock a product of his liberal educational background at Georgetown and Yale Law and of the liberal activism that had energized the Democratic Party. Inevitably, he championed such liberal causes as environmental reform, energy conservation, and a tax hike to pay for highway improvements. And he blamed these policies for his defeat. When he won back the statehouse two years later, after promising to make amends to the voters, he might have stuck by the principles he had advocated during his first term—only doing a better job of establishing priorities and selling his proposals to the electorate. Instead, Clinton's rejection by the voters encouraged his inherent proclivities to duck any controversy and hedge every bet.

In collaboration with his once and future political adviser, a New York–born and bred political consultant named Richard Morris, Clinton set his sights on issues such as education reform. In this field he could achieve modest results that would gain him the national attention he craved without stirring up voters in Arkansas against him.

Meanwhile, his natural tendency to caution was bolstered by the experience of his fellow Democrats on the national level, where their efforts to win back the presidency were getting nowhere fast. Riding a wave of prosperity, which fueled his own personal popularity, Ronald Reagan, the Republican victor over Carter in 1980, won a landslide reelection in 1984, crushing Walter Mondale, Carter's vice president. But it was not just Mondale that was the problem. It was the whole liberal ethos that had once dominated the party that Clinton now faulted. At the convention in San Francisco that nominated Mondale, when Democratic governor Richard Lamm remarked that he had been moved by Mario Cuomo's impassioned keynote speech that had electrified the delegates, Clinton responded, "Come on, what did it really say about the issues we're trying to raise?"

Clinton began readying himself to run for the 1988 Democratic nomination, in part by carving out a niche for himself as one of the founders of the Democratic Leadership Council (DLC), created to put some space between Democratic officeholders and the likes of Cuomo. He was in the midst of those preparations when the political world was shaken by the forced withdrawal from the Democratic presidential field of Gary Hart, following the disclosure of his weekend assignation with a Miami model.

Hart's departure left the Democratic competition wide open. That was the good news. The bad news was that it made certain that any candidate would have to face intense scrutiny of his private life. And if there was any politician for whom such inspection posed a threat, it was Clinton.

Since his undergraduate days, Clinton had earned a reputation as a lady-killer. He was "amazingly successful with women," a friend from that period told Gary Wills. "You would hear him and say to yourself, 'No one is going to believe that line,' but they all did."

Becoming governor did not seem to slow him down. Nearly everyone in politics or journalism in or out of Arkansas whose business it was to know and care about prominent politicians had heard stories of Clinton's womanizing. Reporters did not have to ask politicians about the issue—politicians asked *them*. While Clinton brooded about what to do, his longtime aide Betsey Wright confronted him with a list of women whose names had been linked to his own. After a lengthy session, she advised him, by her own later account, not to run out of consideration for his wife and their daughter, Chelsea. That was enough for Clinton. He let it be known that he would sit out 1988.

In the wake of Dukakis's defeat, Clinton remained a potent presence on the national stage. In the spring of 1989 he seemed a logical person to interview for a story I was doing for the *Los Angeles Times* about economic nationalism—the movement then gaining support among Democrats to regain the economic ground the United States had lost in the world in the past two decades to Japan and other trading nations. I knew Clinton had spoken out on this subject often and I assumed he would welcome the chance to give his views on a matter of substance, as distinguished from the superficial and tactical aspects of politics that politicians often complain journalists concentrate on. To my surprise, Clinton resisted, claiming he was either too busy or had little to say on the issue. And when he finally did agree to an interview, after I offered to come to Little Rock at any time that suited his convenience, his continued reluctance was evident.

What I came to realize from this and later experience was that as eager was he was for national attention, he was uncomfortable dealing with the press in situations that he had not created for his own purposes and therefore could not control.

We talked for nearly an hour, seated in the coffee shop of the Excelsior Hotel on a Sunday morning, until his wife, Hillary, and their daughter, Chelsea, came to fetch him away to some family occasion. And during that time, he said about everything that could be said on the subject without actually making clear his own position. Looking back on the 1988 presidential election, Clinton offered the unremarkable guess that "if there had been a Roosevelt or a Lincoln running, they would have won in a walk."

But then he thought of still another caveat. "Keep in mind that Roosevelt ran on a balanced budget and Lincoln said slavery didn't matter." In other words, no leader could be trusted. Back to the present, Clinton said, "There is a struggle going on in both parties now—an attempt to break out of traditional molds." Could a strong leader carry this out, or would it take some crisis such as a deep recession?

"I can't answer that," Clinton said. "It's waiting for at least a clearer direction. And it may take hard times to get that."

It was clear from that conversation, and became even clearer during his candidacy for the presidency that followed two years later, that Clinton has a talent for avoiding controversy and political risk either by avoiding taking a position or by taking two or three positions, each stated with equal fervor or conviction. A classic example was his reaction to the congressional vote in 1991 authorizing President Bush to use military force against Iraq. "I guess I would have voted with the majority, if it was a close vote," Clinton said, adding quickly, "but I agree with the arguments the minority made."

As Clinton reached national prominence during the 1992 campaign, it became the fashion to attribute this behavior pattern to his turbulent childhood, a notion that Clinton himself encouraged by recounting some of the traumas he had encountered early in life. He was born three months after the death of his father in an auto accident and left in the care of his grandparents by a mother determined to finish her education in a distant city. His stepfather was a drunk, often a mean one, and Clinton himself, after he reached adolescence, intervened to prevent Roger Clinton from physically abusing his mother.

On one occasion, as he recounted the story, at age fourteen, when he was a head taller than his stepfather, he walked over to the older man's chair. "Daddy, stand up," he said. "What I have to say to you, I want you to be standing up." The boy helped the older man get to his feet. "I don't know what I will do if you ever strike my mother again," he said. "I would advise you never to strike her again." Years later recounting the incident to an interviewer, Clinton said: "I couldn't wait to get big enough to know there would be peace in my home." By his own account, as well as the recollections of friends and close associates, the bringing of peace to his mother's home was a shaping event for Bill Clinton, one that set a course for his life and his life's work.

Yet a year after this transformation had taken place, Clinton himself, in a deposition given during his mother's divorce proceedings, said that the physical abuse had continued, not ended. "On one occasion in the last month," Clinton swore, "[I] again had to call my mother's attorney because of the defendant's conduct causing physical abuse to my mother, and the police had to be summoned to the house."

While this contradiction does not alter Clinton's claim that he endured a troubled childhood and adolescence, it also shows that he and his admirers had learned to shape this experience to his political advantage. As a result of the searing experiences of his childhood, or so Clinton and his supporters sought to suggest, the young man became imbued with an impulse toward reconciliation well suited for stewardship of a fractious nation. And the calculated efforts to dramatize these youthful experiences demonstrate the extent to which Clinton and his inner circle were willing, even eager, to exploit his personal life to advance the public man. It was this reliance on Clinton's personal side, on the version of his character and values presented by himself and his allies, that would become the key to his candidacy's success, even as the candidate complained bitterly about the excessive attention paid to his personality.

This personalized strategy was grounded in the voter research of Stanley Greenberg, the pollster and political scientist who had been frustrated by the failure of Michael Dukakis to respond to his warnings about the impact of Bush's stress on values in the 1998 campaign. Greenberg's research in this area had begun after the 1984 election. In overwhelming Walter Mondale that year, Reagan drained blue-collar voters, Catholics, and Southern whites away from their traditional home in the Democratic Party, creating a new coalition of his own. What was striking about this group of voters, Greenberg found, was that they had turned to Reagan even though they objected to some of his most significant economic policies, including his tax cuts, which, as the Democrats liked to say, favored the rich and were the foundation of Reaganomics.

"He has guts," the blue-collar defectors told Greenberg about Reagan. "He's honest." "He shoots from the hip, but whatever he says he will stick by." "He has very high morals." "Reagan is straight as an arrow. He reminds you of John Wayne." Despite their sharp policy quarrels with Reagan, these voters saw in him, in contrast to Democrat Mondale, "a sense of strength and unity that is more important than specifics," Greenberg concluded.

Although lacking Reagan's combination of charisma and convictions, in 1988 Bush had picked up where Reagan left off, as Greenberg had tried to explain to Dukakis, by pounding away at Dukakis's values. In the wake of Dukakis's defeat, Greenberg pointed out in an landmark article in *American Prospect*, which would have profound impact on the Clinton campaign, that Dukakis's inarticulateness in the face of Bush's assault had left Lee Atwater's "savage caricature" as the dominant image of the Democratic Party. As depicted by Bush and Atwater, it was a political party short on patriotism, weak on defense, soft on criminals and minorities, indifferent to work values and family. It was a party, Greenberg wrote, that could now depend really only on Jewish, black, and Hispanic voters. The historic models for the party's liberals, the New Deal and the Great Society, had become discredited and irrelevant.

Yet Greenberg's surveys on 1988 voting turned up the same paradoxical pattern he uncovered in his studies of the 1984 Mondale-Reagan campaign. Even though the country was supposedly caught up in a pervasive conservative mood, Greenberg's data showed that voters favored an activist agenda for government, supporting more spending for a range of supposedly out-of-favor social programs from day care to Social Security to AIDS research and wanted to help pay for it by boosting taxes on corporate polluters and the wealthy.

What was needed to take advantage of these liberal impulses, Greenberg argued, was a new model to replace the New Deal and the Great Society, a model that could be made vital and compelling by linking it to "common historical experience" and explaining it with "a convincing story" that could reach the middle-class voters who had left the party. Middle-class voters saw themselves as squeezed "between the rich and the poor, neither of whom play by the rules, but seek their rewards through shortcuts and special claims—tax breaks, windfalls, and welfare," Greenberg wrote. Even though they "play by the rules," middle-class voters believe they get few of the benefits. From this diagnosis emerged the New Democrat model for the 1990s, which Bill Clinton rode into the White House.

Greenberg's model consisted not only of a policy agenda—proposals such as health care, education, and welfare reform, most of which had been part of the Democratic canon since Jimmy Carter— but also "a convincing story," in Greenberg's phrase. And this story, constructed of clues from Greenberg's polling, relied heavily on character and values, as embodied by Clinton, for emotional reality.

The seed work for this candidacy began long before Clinton's announcement, when the Democratic Leadership Council, the self-styled centrist group that Clinton had helped found after Mondale's defeat, designed its new Democratic Agenda, proclaimed in 1990, to affirm support for "the moral and cultural values that most Americans share." "We wanted to make it clear that Democrats believed in those values," Al From, president of the DLC, explained.

Echoing Greenberg, Clinton and other DLC leaders argued that Dukakis's failure to make that point clear had brought on his doom. In an speech at a Chautauqua lecture series in the summer of 1991, Clinton called Bush's values attack on Dukakis on such issues as the pledge of allegiance and the Willie Horton furlough "devastating," adding, "he didn't understand, as I tried to tell him, that where I come from people won't vote for you for President if they think you don't like to pledge allegiance to the flag."

To help avoid repeating Dukakis's mistakes, Clinton had spelled out his New Democratic principles in an address to the DLC convention in the spring of 1991, a talk that would actually serve as the keynote for his as yet unannounced candidacy. Why have the Democrats been shut out of the White House for all these years?" Clinton asked. "I'll tell you why," he said. "Because too many of the people who used to vote for us, the very burdened middle class we're talking about, have not trusted us in national elections to defend our national interests abroad, to put their values in our social policy at home or to take their tax money and spent it with discipline."

To get back into the good graces of the electorate, Clinton said, the party needed to embrace the idea of economic opportunity rather than dependence on government. It must also be ready to insist on greater responsibility from citizens, for example, welfare mothers. "We must demand that everybody who can go to work do it," Clinton said. "For work is the best social program this country has ever devised." This collection of homilies was more of a lecture than a political speech. It was part of an effort to rehabilitate the Democrats' reputation, intended to demonstrate to the "middle class," i.e., white voters, that Democrats had broken with the soft-headed permissiveness that had marked their past.

That speech and similar Clinton utterances during this period leading up to the announcement of his candidacy had a dual purpose—not only to rally the middle class but to inoculate Clinton against the kind of values warfare Bush had waged on Dukakis. But still another type of inoculation was needed—against revelations of the womanizing that had marked his personal life and kept him from running for president four years earlier. In the past when this issue had been raised, Clinton had brushed off the questions, contending that candidates should be allowed "a privacy zone." But that defense had not really settled anything, and now that he was about to formally declare himself, his advisers convinced him that something more ought to be done—all the more so because any such hint of personal scandal would certainly undercut his appeal to the middle class and give ammunition to the GOP's values warriors.

In midsummer, he arranged to be the guest at a press breakfast in Washington, surprising his hosts by bringing with him his wife, Hillary. Clinton was clearly braced for questions about his personal life, and when the first one was asked, he jumped on it like a cleanup hitter going after a fat pitch. First of all, he dismissed the question as unworthy of discussion in a presidential campaign. "This is the sort of thing they were interested in in Rome when they were in decline, too," he said.

Then, with Hillary Rodham Clinton at his side, he laid down his position.

> What you need to know is that we have been together for almost twenty years and have been married almost sixteen, and we are committed to our marriage and its obligations, to our child and to each other. We love each other very much. Like nearly anybody that's been together twenty years, our relationship has not been perfect or free of difficulties. But we feel good about where we are. We believe in our obligations. And we intend to be together thirty or forty years from now, regardless whether I run for president or not. And I think that ought to be enough.

And yet the problem would not go away. At a reception for state party leaders in Chicago that fall, a woman from the Carolinas confided in me that not too long before at another party gathering that Clinton had also addressed, of the ten women present, she knew he had slept with at least two. "That's a ratio of one in five," she pointed out, wondering whether that proportion prevailed generally and what this would mean if Clinton were the nominee.

She was not the only one concerned about Clinton's womanizing. "A lot of us are worried that this could turn out to be a problem," Jeff Neubauer, the Wisconsin state chairman and a Clinton admirer, told me at the meeting. "If this stuff is going to come out we would rather it come out now than when he is so far in front that it would be too late to do anything about it."

Which is more or less what happened. The "stuff" Neubauer feared about Clinton's extramarital activities came to light. And so did other stuff that Neubauer had not even imagined, disclosing Clinton's tortured but ultimately successful efforts to avoid military service while the Vietnam War raged. And yet Neubauer and his Democratic colleagues concluded that it was too late to turn their backs on Clinton, who polls showed was well in front in New Hampshire's first-in-the-nation presidential primary and whose face was already on the cover of the newsmagazines.

They decided this even though when the first stories broke about Clinton's alleged relationship with a Little Rock nightclub singer named Gennifer Flowers and about his avoidance of the draft, not a vote had been cast in the Democratic delegate selection process. The acceptance by these professional politicians of Clinton as their party's candidate despite the disturbing evidence of his character flaws was a reflection not of their inherent commitment to tolerance and fair play but rather of their own character defects—their dedication to avoiding controversy and their fear of deserting a front-runner.

In the wake of the Gennifer Flowers disclosures, I called the Southern party leader, who in Chicago had expressed concern about Clinton's extramarital involvements. Was she still troubled? "I thought about it some more," she said, "and I decided that if we had used that standard in the past, John Kennedy would never have been president. I think Clinton is our best candidate."

Even with the willingness of his Democratic leadership to close its eyes to his sins, Clinton would not have survived the womanizing controversy without the forceful support of his wife and future first lady. Fully as ambitious as her husband, Hillary Rodham Clinton had promised him in advance that she would stand by him if scandal broke to defend his White House candidacy. And she proved to be as good as her word.

"From my perspective, our marriage is a strong marriage. We love each other," she said, in response to a question planted by Clinton aides in New Hampshire. "We support each other and we have had a lot of strong and important experiences together that have meant a lot to us. In any marriage, there are issues that come up between two people who are married that I think are their business," she said.

Then she made two points that were central to the Clinton campaign defense against allegations into his personal life, arguments that would persist, along with the charges, into his presidency. One was privacy. "It is very important to me that what I care about most in this world—which is my family, what we mean to each other and what we've done together—have some realm of protection from public life," she said. The other counter was that the allegations were essentially a distraction from the main purpose of the presidential campaign, which in the case of this state was to find ways to relieve the economic distress of its citizens. "Is anything about our marriage important enough to the people of New Hampshire as whether or not they will have a chance to keep their own families together?"

The Flowers charges were followed by the draft controversy, when the world learned that Clinton had schemed to get himself admitted to the ROTC program at the University of Arkansas in 1968 while he was a Rhodes Scholar, in order to avoid induction. But then, Clinton passed up the chance to join ROTC and reentered the draft pool. But he never did get drafted, and circumstances suggested he probably could have assumed that he would not be.

Clinton said he hoped voters would see his actions as those of a "conflicted and thoughtful young man" who "loved his country but hated the war." But many saw its convoluted and self-serving logic as portraying a young man so consumed by expediency and ambition that he lacked the courage either to serve his country or to openly resist the draft for a war in which he professed not to believe.

Moreover, Clinton's attempt to blame the controversy on unnamed political enemies added to the odium of the affair. "Let me tell you where I go over the edge on this thing," Bob Kerrey, a Medal of Honor winner as a navy seal who had lost a leg in Vietnam, told reporters. "It should not surprise you to discover that it was the men and women who went to Vietnam who suffered. All of a sudden in this campaign the sympathy is going to someone who didn't go." In the most damning indictment that any Democrat of prominence had yet leveled at Clinton, Kerrey warned that if Clinton were to become the nominee, "he will be the issue and he will not be able to win." In a phrase that lingered in memory after his own candidacy had evaporated, Kerrey predicted that if Clinton was the party's choice to run against Bush in the fall, "he is going to be opened up like a soft peanut."

In the wake of the draft controversy came revelations of the free-wheeling financial dealings of Bill and Hillary Clinton back in

Arkansas, particularly of their joint investment in a real estate development in an Ozark resort called Whitewater.

But the charges were complicated and hard for the public to grasp. And Clinton, now made confident by the ability to face down his accusers, fought back even more vehemently. When, during a campaign debate two days before the Illinois primary vote, Jerry Brown attacked the Clintons for their alleged conflicts of interest in Arkansas, Clinton, without answering the charges, called Brown a liar who was "not worthy of being on the same platform" with Hillary Rodham Clinton. "Let me tell you something, Jerry," said Clinton, shaking his finger in anger at Brown. "I don't care what you say about me. But you ought to be ashamed of yourself for jumping on my wife."

Once again, as in New Hampshire, Clinton turned to the theme of the attacks on his past behavior as representing a digression that was against the public's interest. "The American people can spot somebody who's on their side and they desperately want this election to be about them," he said in Chicago. "They're tired of the politics of personal destruction. They would like to have one election where the focus would be on them and their future instead of all these things that divert our attention."

Blessed with remarkably weak opposition, bolstered by the reluctance of political leaders to resist inertia, Clinton stumbled through to the nomination. But he was "damaged goods," as his pollster, Stanley Greenberg, later admitted, and to repair that damage, his advisers set out by hook and by crook to change the public's view of Clinton himself. "We had decided that biography was critical," Greenberg said.

Clinton himself played the dominant role in this makeover. Whereas once he had complained that "too much of this election has been about me," now he could hardly get enough of himself into his speeches. At every turn he stressed his humble origins and the fortitude he displayed in rising above such handicaps. "My life is a testament to the fact that the American dream works," he cried. "I got to live by the rules that work in America and I wound up here today running for President of the United States of America."

His choice of a running mate was a key part in the defusing of the character issue so that he could use character to reclaim the middle-class irredenta for the Democratic Party. The usual purpose of vice presidential candidates is to balance the ticket, to compensate for some weakness or bias, usually geographic or ideological. In Gore's case, the balancing was more subtle, though just as critical. Famed in the political world for his wooden demeanor and pedestrian thinking, Al Gore nevertheless possessed one glittering asset for Bill Clinton—he was unassailably wholesome. A Vietnam War veteran, no one had ever had reason to doubt his loyalty to his country or his fidelity to his wife, Mary Elizabeth, called "Tipper." In her own right, Gore's spouse presented a helpful contrast with the Democratic candidate for first lady, Hillary Rodham Clinton, who, during the course of the campaign, had once ridiculed at the idea that instead of pursuing her professional career she might have "stayed home and baked cookies." For her part, Tipper Gore was widely known for her battle against pornography in popular music and her devotion to her own children and seemed like just the sort of person who would take delight in whipping up a batch of goodies for them and their friends. Together, the Gores provided a solid counterweight to the misgivings stirred by the past behavior of the nominee and the outspoken feminism of his wife.

The final symbolic stroke came at the convention. This was the presentation of an hour-long film biography turned out with the slickness to be expected from its producers, Harry Thomason and Linda Bloodworth-Thomason the creator of the TV sitcoms *Designing Women* and *Evening Shade*. The Clinton film focused on every obstacle the candidate had overcome, every hardship he had confronted along the long climb from his starting place in the little town of Hope, Arkansas. "I still believe in America," Clinton declared at the conclusion. "And I still believe in a place called Hope."

For all the reshaping of his image, Clinton's own view of the character issue remained unreconstructed. The candidate who urged black welfare mothers to be more responsible accepted no responsibility for his actions himself. Instead, he blamed his troubles on his political opponents and on the low esteem in which Americans held his chosen profession. "We live in a time when the politics of personal destruction have been proved very effective," Clinton told the editors of *Time* at convention time. "We also live in a time when people think pretty poorly about anybody who is in public life. You've got probably the deepest disillusionment with the American political system in my lifetime, much deeper than it was at Watergate."

Clinton contended that more important in the election than his own character was "the character of the American people and what they want for their country and whether they're prepared to make the changes it will take to turn the country around."

As for the attacks against himself, he said: "This is the way the Republicans make a living in national politics, by destroying their opponents. That's their bread and butter." For his part, he said, "I believe the best way for me to demonstrate my character is to make sure people know the whole story of my life and my work and my family and what I'm fighting for in this election. So you know, we'll just have a little contest and see who's right about the American people."

In the end, Clinton believed, the public's concern with the desperate condition of the economy would override the Republican scandalmongering based on his personal life. "I'm out here worrying about what's happening to the rest of the country. Why, with the worst economic record in fifty years, would we be having an election talking about this?"

As it turned out, Clinton was right. "Fame is a vapor, popularity an accident, riches take flight and only character endures," Bush liked to say on the stump, quoting Horace Greeley, as he stressed the importance of character. But whatever Horace Greeley may have thought, sometime during the long economic collapse that followed the triumph of Desert Storm, Bush forfeited his claim to leadership on the one aspect of the national condition that mattered most to Americans—their ability to provide for themselves and their families. With unemployment climbing, a bumper sticker summed up how far the president had fallen since his glory days: "Saddam still has his job, what about you?"

The thrust of the Republican House strategy became apparent early in the fall, when Bush addressed the National Guard Association's Salt Lake City convention and sought to renew the controversy over Clinton's Vietnam War draft record. His voice choked with emotion, Bush, by unmistakable implication, questioned whether Clinton met the "highest standard" for sending young Americans into battle as commander in chief.

This was just part of the overall scheme to exploit the public's mistrust of Clinton, echoing the question Bush had raised in his Houston acceptance speech when he had asked Americans to consider: "Who do you trust to make change work for you?" What the Republicans hoped was to fulfill Bob Kerrey's prediction, that Clinton would be crushed under a scandal barrage "like a soft peanut."

"The biggest thing that's going to happen in the next seven weeks is that people are going to know a lot more about Clinton than they do now," Bush campaign pollster Fred Steeper told me in September after both conventions were over.

But actually, the Republicans were unable to tell voters much more about Clinton than they already knew. Some would never vote for him for these reasons. But others had made their peace with Clinton because of what they already knew about Bush. In the abstract, the argument about trust seemed potent. But coming from the man who had instructed the country to "read my lips" the last time he ran for president, it became painfully hollow.

With a comfortable lead, Clinton had a chance to lay down a clear course of action for his presidency. He did not take it.

"One of the worst things we ever did for George Bush was let him get elected without a plan for what he would do as President," Clinton used to claim early in his presidential campaign. "We let George Bush get elected on the cheap . . . on 'read my lips' and 'the other guy's a bum.'"

But as election day neared, Clinton rarely used that line anymore. It would have raised questions about his own performance on the hustings. Despite his claim in the *Time* interview that the election would test whether the public was willing to make changes necessary "to turn the country around," Clinton offered little in the way of specific change. In keeping with his characteristic aversion to making specific commitments, he waged a campaign designed to bring him an electoral majority not a mandate for governing. Many other politicians have played that same expedient game—but Clinton's situation was different. He had been the clear front-runner in the race since the midsummer Democratic convention and thus had the opportunity to be explicit with minimum political risk. Moreover, by promising that his presidency would portend dramatic change in the government, he generated high expectations for himself.

Once in the White House, Clinton was forced to confront the reality he had avoided dealing with during the campaign. With the economy in crisis, he had to choose between one set of solutions reflecting the populist promises of his campaign and another set favored by Robert Rubin,* who would become his chief economic adviser, and the investment bankers who had financed his campaign and to

---

* At this writing Rubin was secretary of the Treasury.

whom he had been close as governor. For a politician who well understood the value of money, the mother's milk of his trade, there was no doubt about which course offered the least risk. In a typically protean gesture, Clinton the populist candidate, committed to "putting people first," became Clinton the budget-cutting president, dedicated to the betterment of Wall Street.

But the short-term advantages of this switch turned out to be outweighed by the political disadvantages, as Clinton seemed to lose touch with his campaign commitment to middle-class betterment. Out the window in the interest of deficit reduction went the campaign promises to expand federal investments in education, job training, and the infrastructure, along with a tax cut for the middle class. Instead of seeing their taxes reduced, middle-class wage-earning families wound up paying higher taxes on gasoline, along with a tax hike on Social Security benefits for the better-off among them, while their wages continued to stagnate.

Another big promise to improve the lot of the middle class—health reform—became a pawn in his tangled relationship with Hillary Rodham Clinton. Having helped to salvage her husband's presidential candidacy by her loyal defense of him in the midst of scandal, the first lady now claimed as her reward the leadership of the drive for health care reform, the principal item on Clinton's presidential agenda. It was an unprecedented grant of power to a first lady, who having been neither elected by the voters nor confirmed by the Congress, was accountable to no one, not necessarily even her husband. Moreover, her decision to conduct the crucial initial deliberations by her task force in absolute secrecy antagonized friend and foe alike, forfeited a badly needed opportunity to build public support, and instead fostered suspicions about her motives and purposes.

Just as significant, in keeping with his characteristic reluctance to deal directly with issues, in devising his reform plan, Clinton settled on what he hoped would be the least controversial approach to health insurance—a version of managed competition, essentially a market-oriented reform stressing the preservation of the existing system. It was designed more to placate the foes of national health insurance than to generate enthusiasm from supporters of the idea. Under the circumstances, the tortuous death of health reform was inevitable.

Just as Clinton had failed to live up to his pledges to the middle class on policy, he also had broken faith in another area, too—and that was character. Clinton's deep-rooted tendencies toward dissembling and deviousness had shaped his conduct of his campaign, and they continued to dominate his presidency, as reflected in his handling of economic policy and health reform. And during his tenure in the White House, a series of controversies about his conduct of himself and his office highlighted other defects in his character. "Clinton had a seemingly unshakable tendency to walk away from responsibility for things that had gone wrong, and worse to put these things in self-pitying terms," wrote the veteran journalist Elizabeth Drew in *On the Edge,* her chronicle of the troubled start of Clinton's presidency.

In his first months, Clinton created an unnecessary headache for himself by dismissing out-of-hand the veteran employees of the White House Travel Office and putting his own cousin in charge.

The reaction to this episode, which came to be dubbed "Travelgate," led to a White House inquiry, the rehiring of most of the dismissed staffers, and the reassignment of the president's cousin.

The most troublesome questions about his character stemmed from the Whitewater controversy. This controversy arose from an investment the president and his wife, Hillary Rodham Clinton, had made in an Arkansas real estate venture by that name back in 1978, shortly before he became governor. Partners with the Clintons in this venture were James B. McDougal, who also owned the Madison Guaranty Savings and Loan, a thrift that eventually failed during the savings-and-loan collapse in 1989, and McDougal's wife, Susan.

Clinton sought to dismiss the matter as nothing more than a failed effort to make a modest profit in real estate. But a subsequent investigation into allegations of mismanagement of Madison Guaranty, conducted by the Resolution Trust Corp (RTC), the federal agency created to clean up the savings-and-loan mess, raised questions about whether Whitewater had been a means for Clinton to use his position as governor to advance the private financial interests of himself and his wife and whether he had sought to cover up whatever he had done since he became president.

First it was disclosed that the Justice Department had subpoenaed documents concerning the real estate deal from the Clintons, thus shielding this material from inquiries by Congress or the news media. The ensuing uproar forced Clinton to ask for the appointment of a special prosecutor to look into the case. Meanwhile, congressional inquiry turned up the fact that a treasury deputy official, who was also acting director of the RTC, had briefed White House aides on the progress of the agency's probe.

Equally disturbing was the revelation that Hillary Clinton had made a $100,000 profit on her $1,000 investment in the commodities markets and that orders for her trades were placed by the outside counsel for Tyson Foods, one of the largest corporations in the state that Clinton then governed. That hardly squared with Clinton's ritual denunciations during the presidential election campaign of "cheating and cutting corners the way Republicans and their friends do."

Nevertheless, in the face of these contradictory disclosures of his conduct, Clinton continued to present himself as the champion of middle-class people "who play by the rules," a phrase right out of his pollster's lexicon. Godliness was also part of Clinton's middle-class values mantra, as he extended the presidential bully pulpit to the clerical pulpit, where he often deplored how far national life had strayed from the influence of the Almighty. "I think God wants us to sit down and talk to one another and see what values we share and see how we can put them inside the millions and millions of Americans who are living in chaos," Clinton told fellow Yale Law School alumni.

"He may well be the greatest practitioner of civil religion and of public theology of any President we've ever had," Clemson University political scientist Charles Dunn, editor of the anthology *American Political Theology,* said of Clinton.

On occasion Clinton seemed to contradict himself with his own words. Early in his first term in a talk to junior high school students in Washington's inner city, the president made a moving plea for sexual restraint and family values, stressing that sex was not "sport" but a "solemn responsibility." But five days later, talking to autoworkers in Shreveport, Louisiana, Clinton recalled owning a pickup truck with Astroturf in the back. Amid laughter from the audience, Clinton added: "You don't want to know why, but I did." Later, he tried to explain away the prurient implication of that remark. "I carried my luggage back there," he said. "It wasn't for what everybody thought it was for when I made the comment, I can tell you that."

And so Clinton's efforts to make himself into a symbol of middle-class values went on in the face of evidence to the contrary. "What we have tried to do and what Clinton has tried to do with us is articulate values which are the underpinning of a public agenda," Al From explained. "I think he's changed the agenda dramatically in the way he's conducted his office. I'm not going to talk about his personal conduct."

But that subject was difficult to avoid. As his first year in the presidency drew to a close, recollections of the Gennifer Flowers case that had besmirched his candidacy in New Hampshire were revived by published reports that during his tenure as governor of Arkansas, Clinton had used state troopers to act as intermediaries to arrange and conceal extramarital sexual liaisons. Not true, claimed the White House. But soon thereafter, a former state employee named Paula Jones sued Clinton for sexual harassment, charging that an Arkansas state trooper had escorted her to then governor Clinton's Little Rock hotel room, where Clinton asked her for oral sex.

For the most part, Republicans avoided attacks on Clinton on the character issue, yet some saw the inconsistencies between his conduct and his rhetoric as signs of vulnerability. "He very much wants to be a leader in moral terms," said Bill Bennett, the former secretary of education and drug war czar, whose authorship of the best-selling *The Book of Virtues* had given him special status in the political community as an authority on values. "He thinks of the pantheon of great American Presidents and wants to be in their company and knows that moral leadership is part of that."

"As he is drawn to the flame of morality, he speaks of it," Bennett said. And he warned: "As he speaks of it, he will be judged." Looking ahead to the 1994 elections, Republican strategist William Kristol told me: "If Clinton can convince people he is doing the right thing in health care and other areas, I think that would outweigh a fair amount of character flaws. But to do that a president needs trust, because you can never prove your programs will work right away, and Clinton does not have anything like that trust."

Kristol turned out to be a good prophet. Clinton's betrayal of the middle class brought down the wrath of the electorate. In the 1994 midterm elections, his Democratic Party suffered a defeat of historic proportions, giving the Republicans control of both houses of Congress for the first time in forty years. But that upheaval provided the Republicans with the tools for their own destruction.

Infatuated by their own rhetoric, the newly enthroned GOP congressional leadership set about carrying out a conservative revolution that threatened the middle class so severely that Clinton's transgressions were all but forgotten. After setting out to cut Medicare, to cut education, and to cut environmental protections for good measure, they forced a shutdown of the government. True to his nature, Clinton tried to compromise, but the leaders of the Republican-controlled 104th Congress refused to accept any terms short of unconditional surrender. "We thought that Clinton would cave," one Republican strategist told me after the showdown between the Clinton White House and the Republican Congress had ended in a GOP debacle in the winter of 1995.

But Clinton *had* caved—first by agreeing to balance the budget by a certain date, then by moving that date up from ten years to seven, then on making significant cuts in social spending—and in Medicare. But the Republicans, obsessed with what they believed to be the rightness of their cause, pushed ahead and transformed what could have been a partial victory into a debacle. In the end, it was fittingly left to House Speaker Newt Gingrich, self-proclaimed leader of the conservative revolution, to write the epitaph on the abortive Republican effort.

"It takes two elections to make a revolution real," he told Republican fund-raising audiences around the country. "It may just be that we need one more election."

Unfortunately for Gingrich and the GOP, that election was defined from start to finish by the extremism of the 104th Republican Congress. "That was the best thing that ever happened to us," Harold Ickes, Clinton's top political operative, told me. And it was the worst thing that could have happened to Bob Dole, who would be the GOP standard-bearer, as became apparent even before he had actually nailed down the nomination he was heavily favored to win.

As his quest for the votes of GOP convention delegates suffered early setbacks because of his links to the disastrous Republican performance on Capitol Hill, Dole retained his humor and perspective. "You know you have a big stake in my candidacy," he told me on board his campaign charter one day.

"What would that be?" I asked.

"If I'm elected," he said beaming, "I'll be the first president named Bob."

But Dole would need more than quips to make a dent in the lead Clinton had built up as a result of the depredations of the 104th Congress. The standard Republican issues such as spending cuts and tax cuts had lost much of whatever luster they once possessed because of the record of the 104th Congress, forcing Dole to seek new themes to spark the enthusiasm of the electorate.

Throughout his career, Bob Dole had always stressed values and character, leaning heavily on the modest circumstances of his middle-

American roots. "Six of us grew up living in a basement apartment," Dole would later tell campaign audiences about his upbringing. "That was Bob Dole's early life. And I'm proud of it because we learned a lot about values—about honesty and decency and responsibility and integrity and self-reliance, and loving your God and your family and your church and your community."

In the 1988 campaign, he had carefully staged the announcement of his candidacy in his hometown of Russell, Kansas, to dramatize his affinity with the nation's heartland. And a few weeks after announcing his candidacy in the 1996 campaign, he flew to Los Angeles, heart of the entertainment industry, to condemn Hollywood for debasing the nation's culture with movies, music, and television programs that he said had produced "nightmares of depravity" drenched in violence and sex. "A line has been crossed—not just of taste, but of human dignity and decency," Dole claimed in a speech that helped him confirm his conservative credentials as he bid for right-wing support in the competition for the Republican nomination and laid a foundation to use against Clinton in the general election.

And while Dole bolstered his own values credentials, he was joining his party in a broad offensive to exploit the defects in Clinton's character. The effort was two-pronged. Dole himself took the high road, as he did in his Hollywood speech seeking to define the office of president as the setter of moral standards for the nation—a man whom Americans can hold up as an example for their children. The other phase, led by Dole's surrogates, was more direct and negative. Its objective was to convince voters that because Clinton spoke with a forked tongue, he could not be relied on to fulfill his promises to promulgate policies that Republicans claim he lifted right out of their own agenda in the first place.

A letter to potential Republican contributors from the party's national chairman, Haley Barbour, started off with a damning statement from Clinton's old rival and fellow Democrat, Nebraska senator Bob Kerrey: "Clinton's an unusually good liar, unusually good." Following that assessment from a magazine interview with Kerrey, the letter charged: "Bill Clinton is systematically sacrificing America's future for your children and grandchildren in order to preserve his position in the polls."

On the face of it, Clinton's character seemed to be an obvious and easy target. Everett Carll Ladd, director of the Roper Center for Public Opinion Research, contended that doubts about Clinton's sincerity and integrity helped explain why the president's approval rating had rarely gone much above 50 percent during his first-term tenure in the White House, despite generally improving economic conditions. "He works incredibly hard at the job; he is bright, and pretty centrist, at least in his rhetoric and he has great communications skills," Ladd said. "But at the same time his numbers are mediocre. So I have to conclude that the character issue has held him down, though it hasn't been enough to put him down."

A *Los Angeles Times* poll taken in April of election year showed that by margins of 10 to 15 points, voters interviewed thought Dole was more honest than Clinton and more likely to stand by his convictions. "I want some morality in government, so that when you look at somebody, and he tells you something you can believe it," Seth Harter, a tractor dealer and Dole backer from Englishtown, New Jersey who came out to cheer Dole on a visit to the Garden State, told me.

But for all that, attacking Clinton on character proved a difficult task. Part of the problem with the Republican indictment of Clinton's character was that Americans have heard much of it before "and most have decided that whatever Clinton did, it probably wasn't important and it was a long time ago," argued Democratic pollster Mark Mellman.

Indeed, Republicans seemed to be at risk of giving the character issue a bad name—that is, using it so much that their tactics robbed honesty and trust of much of their meaning and even provoked sympathy for Clinton. "I think the Republicans are trying very hard to malign the man and to hold the things over him that happened years ago, and I think they are giving the man a raw deal," said Ethelyn Slifko, an office manager from La Plata, Maryland, who voted for Clinton in 1992 and intended to do so again as she watched Clinton campaign in Maryland. "And he's held his head high and done a good job of it."

But the more fundamental problem that faced the Republicans—and one they could not solve—was the need to demonstrate to voters how and why Clinton's personal behavior and mores affected his performance in office and therefore should influence their decisions at the voting booth. "There is a lot of drip-drip-drip that there is something wrong with Clinton," Don Sipple, a senior adviser to the Dole campaign, told me. "But it is hard to get a handle on it. Voters have to see a consequence for them before it becomes a relevant, salient issue."

Moreover, character is a complex and multifaceted concept, covering far more than moral behavior. It included empathy as well as integrity. And when it came to empathy, as Democrats liked to point out, Bill Clinton overwhelmed Bob Dole. Still, Republicans kept pounding away at the character theme in 1996, in part because Clinton kept providing them with ammunition. It was not just the allegations themselves, it was the response of the president and his allies that helped turn incidents they contended were merely ethical molehills into political Everests.

During the 1996 campaign, for example, seeking to stifle Paula Jones's sexual harassment lawsuit, Clinton's lawyers suggested that the president might be covered by the Soldiers and Sailors Relief Act, which allows military personnel on active duty to postpone dealing with lawsuits. That maneuver produced such a storm of ridicule, including a GOP television ad calling attention not only to the Paula Jones case but to the old controversy about Clinton avoiding military service during the Vietnam War, that the controversial brief was amended to excise any reference to the legislative shield for those in uniform.

Given his reputation as a Lothario, Clinton at times was notably imprudent in his utterances. At an election year fund-raiser, Clinton chose to make a joke about the well-preserved mummy of a thirteen-year-old girl discovered in pre-Colombian Peru and now being displayed in Washington. "I don't know if you've seen that mummy," the president said. "But you know, if I were a single man, I might ask that mummy out. That's a good-looking mummy."

The remark got a laugh from the audience, but it also served to recall a much-repeated one-liner uttered a few months before by television host David Letterman at Clinton's expense. If Clinton continued to climb in the polls, Letterman had predicted, "he's going to start dating again."

Whatever sting such humorous gibes might possess, the Republican thrust on Clinton was for the most part straight-faced and sober, heavily buttressed by comparison with Dole. A sixty-second Dole commercial, one of two shown around the country on his behalf by the Republican National Committee, leaned heavily on his upbringing in small-town Middle America, where "he learned the value of hard work, honesty and responsibility," and on his heroism in World War II combat. "Like many Americans his life experience and values serve as a strong moral compass."

Dole himself spelled out the implications of his background for his candidacy and for his service in the presidency when, in an address to the Catholic Press Association, he called the election "a referendum on the basic values of the country." "Americans look to the White House for moral leadership," he declared. But he described the Clinton White House as "fundamentally adrift, without direction or moral vision."

The other Republican National Committee commercial for Dole brought the character offensive to bear directly on Clinton, using film clips to depict the president as taking six different positions on balancing the budget. "Talk is cheap," the announcer says and concludes, "Double-talk is expensive." But the main point of this ad and similar thrusts is not fiscal policy but rather Clinton's unreliability. Republicans hoped to convince voters, said pollster Steeper, that Clinton "changes his stripes from day to day." Steeper conceded that this would be a tough case to make "because people are going to think that all he's doing is being a politician."

Meanwhile, Clinton's aides at the time reminded Dole and the Republicans that the character issue can work both ways. When Dole resigned from his Senate seat in the spring of 1996 to run full-time for president, Dick Morris, the Clinton campaign's top strategist, became alarmed at the favorable publicity Dole was getting. Instead of waiting for the public interest in the resignation to fade—which soon happened—Morris insisted on producing a television ad that labeled Dole a "quitter."

"He told us he would lead. Then he told us he was quitting, giving up, leaving behind the gridlock he helped to create." The ad, according to *Time* magazine, made Clinton uncomfortable, as well it might, since it opened the door to personal attacks on Clinton, not the sort of quarrel the president wanted to start. But the ad also served as a warning to Dole about putting great stress on the character issue.

Dole, as it became known during the campaign, had his own area of vulnerability and his own reason for concern about the character issue, a dilemma that manifested itself most obviously during the two crucial televised debates with Clinton. After the first debate, when Dole ducked moderator Jim Lehrer's open-ended invitation to make clear his differences with Clinton "in the more personal areas," this response was attributed to Dole's inherent inarticulateness. For a witty man, he lacked what the late columnist Murray Kempton, a Dole admirer, once described as Clinton's "sinuous fluency." And his ineffectiveness when he tried to revive the character issue in the second debate was blamed on the same limitation. In that encounter, Dole sought to draw much the same distinction Gary Hart had tried to make between "public" ethics and "private" behavior.

"Honor, duty and country—that's what America is all about," Dole said in response to a questioner who asked whether the president should be a role model for young people. "Certainly the President of the United States has a responsibility to young people. And when it comes to public ethics, he has a public responsibility," Dole added. "When you have thirty some in your administration who've either left or are being investigated or in jail or whatever, then you've got an ethical problem. It's public ethics—I am not talking about private—we're talking about public ethics."

Dole supporters were frustrated and mystified by the answer, which blurred the issue and blunted the impact of Dole's point. But as his top advisers well knew, Dole had strong motivation for trying to draw a distinction between public and private behavior, because his own private behavior was under question.

That summer his staff had learned that at least two publications, *Time* and the *Washington Post,* had uncovered a sixty-three-year-old woman named Meredith Roberts, an editor for a Washington trade association, who had told them that she and Dole had an affair from 1968 through 1970, when he was still married to his first wife, whom he later divorced before he wed his present wife, Elizabeth Hanford Dole.

Roberts's own behavior was ambiguous. On the one hand, she claimed that she did not want to speak for publication and felt no rancor toward Dole. Yet on the other hand, she wanted those who wrote about Dole to know that "he is not the great moral figure he's portraying himself to be."

Desperate to prevent publication, Dole's handlers met with the top editors at *Time* and the *Post,* arguing that since the affair had been over for twenty-eight years, it was irrelevant to Dole's fitness for the presidency. But Dole's own rhetoric could be used to refute their arguments. After Gary Hart dropped out of the 1988 presidential race, Dole declared: "Once you declare you're a candidate, all bets are off. Everything up to that point is fair game." More recently, in 1994, Dole had asserted that the personal lives of politicians—including marital infidelity—were "fair game." Besides, hadn't the

Dole campaign been claiming that Dole's character was superior to Clinton's?

Besides joining Dole's aides in pleading with the top brass at the *Post* not to publish, Elizabeth Dole filmed two thirty-second spots, which were apparently aimed to deflect the anticipated criticism of her husband if the tale of his past amour came to light but which also seemed to contravene the claim that the story was not relevant. In one ad, Dole's wife declared, "Honesty, doing what's right, living up to his word . . . Bob Dole doesn't make promises he can't keep." She was talking about his 15 percent tax cut, but of course the point would have broader meaning to viewers. In a second spot, she praised his small-town virtues: "The truth. First, last, always the truth."

At the *Post,* an intense debate raged over the story. Bob Woodward, who had helped bring down Richard Nixon, and many other reporters argued that Dole had made trust and character an issue and thus adultery, even from the distant past, was relevant. But the *Post* editors shied away from this controversy. The *Post* and its owners, the Graham family, did not want to get into the business of investigating the dalliances of presidential candidates, *Newsweek,* which is also owned by the *Post,* reported.

Time ultimately reached the same decision. Managing Editor Walter Isaacson said he "wasn't comfortable" with the story, particularly that late in the campaign. "The bar is a little higher a couple of weeks before the election because everything is more explosive," he said.

But the *National Enquirer* had learned about the story and, after offering to pay Roberts and being turned down, decided to go ahead and publish it anyway. But before the weekly came off the press, the *New York Daily News,* the nation's largest circulation newspaper, beat the *Enquirer* to the punch, with its own account. At this point, the *Washington Post,* the paper that had triggered Watergate but waited nearly a month to publish its first account of Paula Jones's sexual harassment complaint and that had decided against publishing the story of Roberts's relationship with Dole, fell back on one of the oldest ploys in journalism. Instead of reporting the story directly, it managed to get it into print indirectly. It noted that Dole had been questioned about the *Daily News* story by a reporter as he left his hotel on his way to his campaign motorcade. As the *Post* reported it, Dole, in a sour mood anyhow because of the final collapse of his presidential hopes, glared at his interrogator, waved his arms dismissively, and snapped: "You're worse than they are." And his press secretary Nelson Warfield issued a statement that ignored the *News* but lambasted the *Enquirer*, a much easier target.

"Last week the *National Enquirer* published stories on deep sea-diving monkeys and a cross-dressing school teacher," Warfield said. "Next week, they will trash Bob Dole. Maybe there were no UFO sightings to occupy their attention. If your news organization wants to follow the *National Enquirer's* lead, you may do so without the Dole campaign's help."

It seemed not by coincidence that on that same day, Dole launched his fiercest attack on the news media. He accused the press of giving a free "transfusion" to the president every day by refusing to investigate scandals involving foreign campaign donations and by failing to press Clinton on his refusal to rule out a pardon "for somebody who did business with him" in the Whitewater scandal. "We are not going to let the media steal this election. We are going to win this election. The country belongs to the people, not the *New York Times*," Dole said.

His tirade served as more than just a venting of frustration for a losing candidate. By blasting the press for bias, even though his attacks were seemingly unrelated to the disclosure about his own personal life, he served notice on nervous editors of what they could expect if they were to follow the lead of the *Enquirer* and the *Daily News*. Whether because of Dole's tactics or not, the story got relatively minor attention. Some news organizations—the *Boston Globe, Newsday,* the *New York Post*, the *Orange County Register, Newsweek,* and CNN—gave the matter only brief mentions. Many others ignored it, including the *New York Times, Los Angeles Times, Wall Street Journal, USA Today,* NBC, CBS, and ABC. Andrew Rosenthal, Washington editor of the *New York Times,* summed up the rationale for the papers that had ignored the story or given it short shrift. "This was a story about an alleged affair that happened thirty years ago. Big deal."

But as Howard Kurtz, media analyst for the *Washington Post,* pointed out, other behavior from the past has been deemed relevant in campaign stories—like Bill Clinton's use of marijuana in 1969 and his efforts to avoid the draft. And during the 1992 campaign, President Bush had tried to make an issue of Clinton's 1969 student visit to Moscow, suggesting that it was a sign of disloyalty to his country.

And Bill Bennett, national cochairman of the Dole campaign, seemed to take issue with the editors who did not consider the story relevant. "People should not cheat on their wives, whether they're presidential candidates or not, Democrats or Republicans," he said. "It's wrong. Last time I checked, Jews and Christians had a Commandment about that." What he might have added was that Dole's behavior was certainly a contradiction of the traditional family values he had done so much to identify himself with throughout his political life, particularly in his campaign against Clinton.

It could be argued that whether or not Dole's affair was relevant to his ability to perform in the presidency is something for each individual to decide, depending on that individual's view of the presidency. But it is hard to argue that it was not relevant to Bob Dole and the way he conducted his candidacy for the presidency.

Within two weeks of the publication of the accounts of Dole's long-ago affair, his presidential candidacy had also become a thing of the past. It was fitting that the role of the character issue in the 1996 presidential campaign should conclude with this murky event, because it served to underline the ambiguity about where character fits into presidential politics.

Throughout the campaign, from the controversies about Whitewater and Travelgate and Paula Jones to the concluding episode about Dole's long-ago affair, the conduct of the candidates and the press served only to make the character issue murkier than ever.

But the political battle over character did not end with Dole's defeat and Clinton's victory in the 1996 election. Although Clinton had won out over Dole on character by default in the campaign, events in his second term would demonstrate that he still could not conquer his most formidable adversary—himself.

11

"TELLING THE TRUTH SLOWLY"

BILL CLINTON'S PREDICTION that the 1992 presidential election would be a test not just of his character but of the character of the American people turned out to be a rare understatement. Not only the 1992 campaign for the White House but also the presidency that followed became a character test for him and for his fellow citizens, and for the political system as well. For Clinton, the test was whether his inherent gifts for leadership would outweigh the darker impulses of his nature. For the country, the issue was what standards of personal behavior Americans would accept from their president. And for the system, the challenge was whether it could respond responsibly to the tensions created by the controversies over Clinton's character.

At the beginning of this process, Clinton enjoyed important advantages, which he would ultimately waste as a result of his performance in office. Regardless of partisanship, a majority of voters wanted his presidency to succeed, for their own sake. They had little choice. There would not be another election for four years. They could either hope for the best from Clinton or consign themselves to prolonged frustration and bitterness.

On top of this, many Americans, particularly those of Clinton's own generation, which came of age in the Sixties, were willing to cut him extra slack because they viewed him as the embodiment of their own often conflicted behavior. On the one hand, they could see in his lofty rhetoric and high-minded goals echoes of the remembered idealism of the decade that had been defined by two great movements—the civil rights revolution and the Vietnam War protest. On the other hand, they could readily detect in Clinton evidence of the self-seeking and self-indulgence that had also shaped their lives. "Many who shared the President's path from the Sixties to the Nineties remain as conflicted about that journey as he is," wrote Frank Rich in the *New York Times*. "To reach a final judgment about Bill Clinton's character, we may first have to face the far harder task of coming to terms with what we think about ourselves."

Clinton himself did not understand, or at least would not acknowledge, the reservoir of goodwill for him in the country. Instead, he complained frequently in private, and sometimes in public, about his critics, particularly in the press, which he contended refused to give due recognition to his achievements. His resentment erupted dramatically in the fall of 1993 in an interview with *Rolling Stone* magazine, when he was asked a question suggesting that he lacked genuine commitment to some of the liberal causes he had advocated as a candidate. "I have fought more damn battles here for more things than any president has in twenty years and not gotten one damn bit of credit from the knee-jerk liberal press, and I am sick and tired of it," he shouted. "I have fought and fought and fought and fought. I get up here every day and I work till late at night on everything from national service to family leave to the budget to the crime bill and all this stuff, and you guys take it and you say, 'Fine, go on to something else, what else can I hit him about?'"

The president's partisans blamed criticism of his character on the right wing, whose members kept Clinton under a steady barrage of abuse, from videotapes implying that he had somehow murdered his political foes to newsletters disseminating fresh mud about Whitewater and other reputed Clinton misdeeds.

One conservative publication, the *American Spectator*, which early on took off after Clinton by reporting that he had prevailed upon Arkansas state troopers to procure sex for him in the days when he was governor of the state, subsequently, with tongue only partly in cheek, exposed his prevarications on the golf course. "A look at the president's golf habits reveals that he has little regard for the rules of the game or telling the truth about his score," the magazine claimed. "A critic might say the way the president plays golf mirrors the way he plays politics: a shaded truth here, a misunderstanding there, the occasional whopper somewhere else."

But misgivings about Clinton's character began to reach well beyond the right wing in the wake of the contradiction between the Whitewater disclosures and Clinton's claim to have played by the rules that bind middle-class Americans. Republican voter surveys in scattered congressional districts showed resentment of Clinton at an intensity level unprecedented for modern presidents. "I think it is the combination of only getting 43 percent of the vote—people are less sure of his legitimate claim to the White House—along with the sense that, look, he preaches in a moralistic tone about community and greed and values, and his own life reflects none of that," said Republican pollster Glen Bolger. "I think character is a major factor."

Regardless of whether Bill and Hillary Clinton had broken any laws as a result of their now notorious land development deal, the *New York Times* reached "the inescapable conclusion that this couple, early and late, suffered from a thematic insensitivity to the normal rules of conflict of interest. At every turn of their financial life, the then Governor and First Lady of Arkansas were receiving financial favors from individuals who had something to gain from having friends in high places."

In the spring of 1994, a NBC-*Wall Street Journal* poll showed that only about a third of Americans rated Clinton as "good" on ethical values. A *Washington Post*-ABC News poll found that only about one out of two Americans thought Clinton had the "honesty and integrity" to serve effectively as president, down from three out of four the week before he took office.

Clinton had come face-to-face with some of his critics at a so-called town meeting in Charlotte, North Carolina, in April 1994, designed to take advantage of Clinton's informal charm and seeming command of a wide range of issues. But the session backfired when Rebecca Fairchild, a local housewife, got the floor. "Are you really one of us middle-class people or are you in with the villainous, money grubbing Republicans?" she demanded.

That challenge to the foundation of his political strategy threw the President off-balance. "Well, I don't think that all Republicans are villainous," he answered lamely. "Sometimes I wonder in Washington but I don't really think that."

Such signs of distress from Clinton's middle-class constituency added to doubts even among some of his staunchest admirers in the press. "It seems increasingly, and sadly apparent, that the character flaw Bill Clinton's enemies have fixed upon—promiscuity—is a defining characteristic of his public life as well," concluded Joe Klein, then of *Newsweek,* who had celebrated Clinton's gifts as a politician in the best-selling novel *Primary Colors.* Klein pointed out that Clinton's promiscuity, in the sense that it implies inclusiveness, worked to Clinton's advantage as a politician, helping him to reach out to people of all sorts. But, Klein warned: "This wanton affability leads inevitably to misunderstandings. It leads to a rhetorical promiscuity, the reckless belief that he can talk anyone into anything (or more to the point, that he can his way *out of* anything), that he can seduce and abandon, at will and without consequence."

Mistrust of Clinton contributed to the dramatic Democratic debacle in the 1994 midterm elections. But these misgivings were soon overshadowed by the equally dramatic failure of the Republican counterrevolution on Capitol Hill in the winter of 1995. The budget showdown between the GOP Congress and Clinton not only destroyed Republican momentum but also defined the presidential campaign of 1996, assuring Clinton's victory.

But even before the votes were counted in November 1996, the character issue emerged in a new guise—the disclosure of far-reaching abuses of the campaign finance laws by the Democrats on behalf of Clinton's campaign, in which Clinton himself had played a leading role. These revelations came too late in the day for Dole to benefit significantly. But the president lost votes that might have carried him above his target of 50 percent of the popular vote, and the Democrats suffered more substantial damage—the destruction of their hopes for winning back the House of Representatives.

Moreover, in the wake of the election, new revelations kept the controversy alive and increased the focus on the president. "Bill Clinton has personally raised campaign cash like no other figure in modern history," the *Washington Post* reported. All through 1996, the public learned, Clinton had hosted monthly White House "coffee klatches" for fat-cat donors who were rewarded on a sliding scale. Those giving $10,000 got into the same dining room with the president, while $100,000 bought a seat at Clinton's table, though sometimes cheek by jowl with forty other Democratic benefactors. Such generosity also earned invitations to golf with Clinton, appointments to honorary commissions, and even invitations to spend a night in the Lincoln Bedroom.

What's more, it was revealed that Clinton himself had been part of a massive violation of at least the spirit of the law, distinguishing between "soft money," which is supposed to be spent only for party-building activities and issue advocacy, upon which there is no limit, and "hard money," which goes to promote a specific candidate. During the campaign, the president had personally directed the use of millions of soft-money dollars in television issue ads, which, while they arguably met the technical requirements of the law, were clearly intended to boost the president's standing with the electorate. By some estimates, this artifice allowed Clinton to spend about $25 million more to help his candidacy than the ceilings provided by the federal election laws. So much for playing by the rules.

As if none of this had occurred, Clinton sought to commence his second term by reasserting the moral authority of the presidency. Shortly before his second inaugural in 1997, he told a group of religious leaders that his supreme ambition was to be a leader who could persuade Americans to "reconcile their differences and come to a consensus which will push the country forward." And in an interview around that same time, he took note of the scandals that had stirred partisan bitterness in the nation's capital and vowed to use his Inaugural Address to "help flush the poison from the atmosphere."

Meanwhile, the furor over Clinton's character, extending beyond the press and traditional arenas of partisan warfare, reverberated through the political system, creating new challenges to its institutions. In response to the Paula Jones sexual harassment suit, the president's lawyers appealed to the Supreme Court to reverse a lower-court ruling and grant Clinton immunity to such suits as long as he held office. It was only the third time in the history of the Court and the presidency that the former had ruled on such a fundamental conflict over constitutional authority, the others being occasioned by controversies of far greater consequence than whether the chief executive had exposed himself. In 1952, the high court held that President Truman had exceeded his powers when he seized control of the steel industry to end a nationwide strike. Likewise, in 1974, the court had ordered President Nixon to hand over taped recordings of White House conversations to the Watergate prosecutor.

Despite these precedents, Clinton's lawyers, citing a 1982 ruling in which the high court held that presidents are immune from being sued over their "official acts," argued that his office endows him with "temporary immunity" from lawsuits. But in unanimously rejecting that claim, the high court declared: "The unofficial conduct of the individual who happens to be the president is not a matter of constitutional concern."

But the nation's highest tribunal was not through with the character issue yet. In another rebuff to Clinton, the justices refused to overturn a lower-court ruling that required the White House to turn over confidential notes of conversations between First Lady Hillary Rodham Clinton and two White House lawyers. The court's decision cleared the way for Whitewater independent counsel Kenneth W. Starr to obtain the disputed notes that he had sought to help determine whether Hillary Clinton had lied or obstructed justice in the Whitewater scandal.

The most dramatic impact of the character issue on the institutions of government was personified by Starr himself, who, soon after his appointment in 1994, established himself as one of the most aggressive and controversial independent counsels in the twenty-year history of that office. Underlying the existence of Starr's position is the uniquely schizoid nature of the attorney general's job and the increasing controversy over the manifestations of presidential character.

The attorney general is the guardian of the law, a posture that sets this position apart from the other cabinet jobs. But like every other member of the president's cabinet, the attorney general is also the instrument of the political will of the president, committed to the success of the president's administration and subject to dismissal at the president's will. This inherent potential for conflict of interest was carved into the Constitution, but the government managed to live with it for the first two hundred years of its history.

But the controversies swirling around the massive limestone battlements of the Justice Department, ten blocks from the White House, have heightened in recent decades, as presidential character increasingly became the focus of political controversy and legal battles. With Watergate, a crisis in large part brought on by the convolutions of Richard Nixon's character, the tension between law and politics reached a breaking point. Nixon fired the supposedly independent prosecutor, Archibald Cox, who had been appointed by then attorney general Elliot Richardson to head the investigation of the scandal, touching off the Saturday Night Massacre, which sealed Nixon's doom as president. In response, Congress established a procedure for appointment of an independent counsel to look into high-level wrongdoing by a panel of judges rather than the attorney general, thus shielding the counsel from presidential dismissal.

Critics of this scheme argued that the ground rules give an independent counsel opportunity to conduct unfettered, prolonged, and ultimately fruitless investigations. The prime example they cite is the probe into another scandal linked to presidential character, the Iran-Contra affair conducted by Lawrence E. Walsh, which consumed seven years before it was finally aborted by presidential pardons. In his own tenure as independent prosecutor, Starr came under fire for insisting on maintaining a private legal practice, including work for unmistakably conservative causes and groups, and for his decision, subsequently rescinded, to quit his post in the midst of his investigation to become a law school president. Despite the criticism, in 1997, with Clinton in his fifth year in the White House, Starr began his fourth year as independent counsel, a dagger pointed at the heart of the Clinton presidency.

In the face of these multiple embarrassments, Clinton strove to maintain the stance that he would not be distracted from his responsibilities, whatever the accusations against him. He continued to hold fund-raisers on a massive scale for the benefit of his party, occasionally using them as forums to advocate legislation that would ban just the type of soft-money contribution he was seeking. And as always, he took every opportunity to present himself as the defender of middle-class family values.

"Most of us have an instructive urge to protect our young people from danger," the president said as he stood surrounded by youngsters at a White House reception to spur efforts to curb cigarette sales to young people. "We make sure they bundle up before going out in the cold. We should wrap that same protective arm around them when it comes to resisting smoking and the advertising and marketing of cigarettes." Compared to such objectives, Rahm Emanuel, one of the president's senior press agents, argued, the fund-raising allegations were of little consequence. "We believe the American people care more about college costs than fund-raising coffees," he said. "And what we're going to continue to do is to focus on the American people's agenda."

While he struck such lofty poses in public, in private Clinton sulked and fumed about his critics, and about any threat, real or imagined to his political well-being. He treated all events, the consequential and the trivial alike, with deadly seriousness, lacking a sense of the absurd or the capacity to see the humor in his own foibles. After he had acquired a new puppy, Clinton sought to enhance the inevitable media interest by creating suspense about the name he would choose for the dog. He called a press conference to make the official announcement, but word that he had settled on "Buddy" got out beforehand. Clinton was beside himself. "I'd like to know what sorry piece of shit from my staff leaked this," the president growled at a group of his aides unfortunate enough to have gathered for a briefing right after being scooped by CNN.

Whether he wanted to admit it or not, Clinton was hindered as president by the taint on his reputation that had accumulated during his years on the national scene. What was missing from his presidency, as a result of a wide range of indiscretions, indulgences, and excesses, was the moral authority that usually accompanies the office. Its absence was particularly conspicuous soon after his reelection, when the military establishment had to confront some vexing dilemmas about sexual mores. General Joseph Ralston of the air force had to withdraw his name as candidate for chairman of the Joint Chiefs of Staff because he had previously been involved in an extramarital affair. One reason this was a problem was that Ralston's name came to the fore right after a female air force pilot, First Lieutenant Kelly Flinn, was forced to resign because of her own adulterous relationship. And at the same time, the Pentagon brass had their hands full dealing with sexual harassment charges against the army's top enlisted man, Sergeant Major Gene McKinney. Meanwhile, the president, who had just lost his much-publicized appeal to the Supreme Court to delay the Paula Jones sexual harassment lawsuit, had nothing to say on these matters. Clinton's silence refuted the claim made by his defenders that shadows in his private life had no effect on his performance in office.

If Clinton himself had not been tarnished by the brush of scandal, as *New York Times* columnist Thomas L. Friedman pointed out, he would have been able to speak to the country on the need for distinguishing between sexual misconduct, such as rape, and consensual sex. "The Commander-in-Chief is AWOL," Friedman wrote. "We know why. He fears that because of his own personal past, if he weighs in he will be labeled a hypocrite. But it is precisely because no one at the top has provided moral leadership on this issue that it has gotten so tangled."

In the political world, this moral vacuum in the Oval Office had painful implications for those in Clinton's party who considered themselves liberals. They had given their backing to Clinton in a bargain in which they had traded away some principles for power. But now it seemed that what they had bargained away was more than they realized. What Clinton's presidency had compromised was not just some particular ideological goal but, far more important, the assumption of moral superiority, the "do-goodism" defining the liberal faith and justifying government's intervention in society and distinguishing liberal idealism from conservative realism. "By the time the President and his defenders get through with explaining away his actions, they will have explained the reason for their existence away," wrote Michael Kelly in the *Washington Post* in response to the rationalizations offered by Clinton and his supporters for his abuse of the campaign fund-raising regulations. "There will no longer be two competing philosophies, moralism versus realism. There will only be Clintonism, which is the philosophy that money talks."

For six years on the national scene, Clinton had led a charmed life, dodging from one character crisis to another. "You keep playing this game of gotcha," James Carville once complained to candidate Clinton after he had just talked his way out of another tough spot. "Yeah," Clinton replied defiantly. "But they didn't get me that time, did they?"

But suddenly, as he was about to start the second year of his second term, his past seemed to catch up with him all at once. For the president, the moment of realization must have come on that bleak Saturday morning of January 17 when he arrived at his lawyer's office, two blocks from the White House, for his deposition in the Paula Jones case.

Clinton had always known this would be an unpleasant experience and had used every weapon at his command to delay it as long as he could. The circuslike atmosphere was as bad as he could have expected. Throngs of photographers, reporters, and tourists stationed themselves on the streets outside, waiting to glimpse President Clinton and his accuser, who arrived with her own spokeswoman and her own hairdresser. "I feel so proud to be an American to know that this judicial system works, to know that a little girl from Arkansas is equal to the president of the United States," she said through a spokesman, adopting just the sort of tone Clinton himself would have used had their positions been reversed. When Jones had first gone public with her complaint against Clinton, many people had dismissed her, in part because of her blowsy appearance. Some journalists sneered at her as "trailer-park trash," with "big hair." But in recent months, she had acquired a Los Angeles hair stylist who had smoothed the frizzy mane of curls once piled high on her head. The hairdresser, said to be "very much part of the defense team," had flown in from the West Coast for the proceedings, though it was made plain that like public interest attorneys, he was doing this assignment on a pro bono basis.

Clinton had expected all of this hullabaloo at the scene of the deposition, and he had also anticipated once he was inside in his lawyer's office to be grilled about his past escapades with women. He knew that Jones's lawyers had cast a wide net seeking evidence that his encounter with Jones was part of a pattern of behavior. And he had good reason to believe that he would be asked about his relationship with one particular young woman, a former White House intern named Monica Lewinsky, since she had previously been subpoenaed by Jones's lawyers. What he did not anticipate was the number and specific nature of the questions he would be asked about Lewinsky—not only whether he had ever had sex with her but whether he had ever given her gifts or whether his conversations with her had been tape-recorded.

Under oath, Clinton denied any sex with Lewinsky but gave carefully worded answers to the other questions. He acted like a man who feared he had walked into a trap. And he was right.

It was a trap of his own creation; one jaw of the trap was the Paula Jones case, the other was Whitewater. Paula Jones's suit allowed her lawyers to ask Monica Lewinsky questions about Clinton's sex life and to also question Lewinsky's friend and onetime coworker, Linda Tripp. Tripp had then become an agent of Starr and under his direction had tape-recorded her conversations with Lewinsky, providing evidence that belied Clinton's denial of a sexual relationship with the intern. Whitewater had led to the independent counsel appointment of Starr, who then found in what he learned from Tripp evidence of what seemed to him something close to the obstruction of justice by the president of the United States.

In particular, what sent Starr and his bloodhounds into high gear was learning about the activities of Vernon Jordan, Clinton's crony and adviser, a man renowned both for his charm and his deftness as a fixer behind the scenes and under the table. From the time Monica Lewinsky became a subpoena target for Paula Jones's lawyers, Jordan had talked to her on the phone and in person nearly a dozen times in an ultimately successful effort to find her a job. Jordan's involvement was a signal of how sensitive and urgent Lewinsky's job hunt was to the president. There was no one Clinton knew whom he trusted more, or considered more trusted, or more puissant. "Vernon knows a lot of stuff about the President and his personal life, but he'll never trade on it," said Dee Dee Myers, Clinton's former press secretary. "Vernon understands how power works better than anybody I know. He talks to the President about everything, I think, but it would diminish his power if he talks about it. He protects the President, his friend."

And protecting the president was just what Jordan was doing, or so Starr's investigators concluded. His efforts as employment counselor to Lewinsky followed a pattern all too familiar to Starr's investigators, who had been probing into Clinton's affairs for three years. Time after time, throughout Clinton's tenure both in Little Rock and Washington, they had turned up evidence that whenever he was in hot water, he and his cohorts had gone out of their way to find jobs or financial help for those who had information that threatened his political well-being. These included his reputed former mistress, Gennifer Flowers, his state trooper bodyguards in Arkansas, and especially Webster Hubbell, Hillary Clinton's ex-law partner and one-time unofficial guardian of Clinton's interests at the Justice Department. As Flowers told her story, when she had asked Clinton for a job while their affair was still red-hot, he picked out a post in the state government for her, got someone to help her through the interview, and even had the job description altered to better fit Flowers's resume. A few years later, when Clinton had gained the White House and reporters were digging into allegations that state troopers had arranged trysts for him during his days as governor, the president was said to have dangled offers of federal jobs before two of the troopers to gain their silence.

But by far the most significant and relevant example of such help from Starr's point of view concerned Webster Hubbell, who early in Clinton's first term had to resign as associate attorney general because Starr had charged him with bilking his clients and law partners in Little Rock. Although this case was not directly related to Whitewater, Hubbell had worked along with Hillary Clinton on disputed land transactions that were at the center of the controversy. And Starr hoped that Hubbell, in exchange for leniency on the fraud charges he faced, would help nail down their main Whitewater investigation, which could reach to the first lady.

However, before prosecutors could put pressure on Hubbell, Clinton aides and supporters rushed to help him out during the time of his legal troubles, which would eventually lead to his conviction and imprisonment. At the forefront of this effort was Clinton's then chief of staff and another longtime Arkansas crony, Thomas F. "Mack" McLarty. After getting approval from the first lady for his efforts, McLarty worked the White House phones, reaching out to prospective Hubbell benefactors. Among those who came through was the very same Vernon Jordan who had gotten Monica Lewinsky a $40,000-a-year job offer from Revlon, where he sat on the board of directors.

For Hubbell, Jordan got a consulting deal with the same cosmetics company, which paid off in more than $60,000 in fees. Also helpful to Hubbell was Mickey Kantor, then Clinton's trade representative and before that his campaign manager, who had raised money for a trust fund organized to pay costs of educating Hubbell's children and had aided Hubbell's son in landing two jobs, the first in Kantor's own shop, the U.S. Trade Representative's Office. In addition, months after Hubbell pleaded guilty to fraud and tax-evasion charges, Kantor helped pry loose a disputed $25,000 consulting fee from the city of Los Angeles.

All told, Hubbell obtained fourteen or more consulting deals, many from Clinton allies, including a $100,000 payment from a company controlled by James T. Riady, the Indonesian billionaire and Clinton friend who was a major figure in the campaign finance scandal. When Starr learned about this, he subpoenaed White House videotapes showing Clinton conferring in the Oval Office with Riady in June 1994—about the same time Riady hired Hubbell through a Hong Kong company for unspecified services—and paid him $100,000. Starr wanted to know if Clinton had asked one good friend, Riady, to help another, Hubbell.

Meanwhile, though, mindful of all the support he had received from Clinton and his allies, Hubbell, who had been released from prison early in 1997, kept his distance from Starr. The prosecutor, stymied by what he suspected was a cover-up, sought ways to break his silence. One possibility was to bring a new case against Hubbell, possibly fraud charges growing out of his consulting deal with Los Angeles; another was some kind of tax-related charge, in connection with the consulting income he received after quitting the administration.* Still

---

*In May of 1998, Starr indicted Hobbell for income tax evasion. A federal judge dismissed the case, but Starr appealed that decision.

another option was to prove that there had been a cover-up—a case that could reach high up into the White House. It was in connection with the latter possibility that Vernon Jordan's involvement with Monica Lewinsky took on extra significance. If Starr could prove that Jordan, working in cahoots with Clinton, had sought to suppress the truth about Monica Lewinsky in connection with the Paula Jones case, that evidence could help break open Whitewater.

While Starr pressed his probe, Clinton mounted a three-pronged defense—he denied the charges, he stonewalled the investigators, and he denounced his accusers. To be sure, his first denial, made January 21, 1998, the day the story broke, was so hedged that it dismayed even his strongest supporters. Asked point blank by Jim Lehrer of PBS about charges that he had encouraged Lewinsky to lie under oath about their having an affair, Clinton said: "That is not true. I did not ask anyone to tell anything other than the truth. There *is* no improper relationship."

Lehrer persisted. "You had no sexual relationship with this young woman?" he asked.

Again, Clinton was careful to keep the answer in the present tense. "There is not a sexual relationship, that is accurate."

Clinton's hope was that this cursory denial would be enough to hold off his critics until the following week, when he would give his State of the Union speech and could use that opportunity to divert the attention of the press and the public from the scandal. But by the weekend, as they were swamped with new reports of the burgeoning scandal, Clinton's aides realized that the president needed to make more of a response or his State of the Union would be overwhelmed by the scandal.

The forum, carefully chosen so that Clinton would not be exposed to questions, was a previously scheduled announcement of new child care programs in the Roosevelt Room, a few steps from the Oval Office, on the day before the State of the Union speech. Clinton talked for a few minutes about the new proposals, then shifted subjects. "Now I have to go back to work on my State of the Union speech," he said. "And I worked on it until pretty late last night. But I want to say one thing to the American people," he added, his face hardening as he glared past the audience toward the television cameras in the room. "I want you to listen to me," he began, wagging his finger for emphasis. "I did not have sexual relations with that woman, Miss Lewinsky. I never told anybody to lie, not a single time. Never. These allegations are false. And I need to go back to work for the American people." Then he turned from the lectern and left the room.

That denial left a murk of hard-to-explain behavior hovering over the nature of his relationship with Lewinsky, including questions about the gifts he had sent her—one such token, Whitman's *Leaves of Grass*, was reported to be just what he had given Hillary Rodham Clinton after their second date—about her being admitted to the White House more than three dozen times after she had left her job, and about the intensive efforts he had instigated toward finding her a job.

Still another question left unanswered by the president's denial of a sexual relationship had to do with his definition of such a relationship. According to both *American Spectator* and the *Los Angeles Times,* it was the testimony of the Arkansas state troopers, who helped tend to the servicing of Clinton's desires as governor, that oral sex, which Lewinsky implied was the basis of their relationship—"There was no penetration," she had once said on one of the tapes obtained by *Newsweek*—did not fall under the rubric of a sexual relationship. "He told me that he had researched the subject in the Bible," one trooper told David Brock of the *Spectator*, "and oral sex isn't considered adultery."

But if the president left an information void by his refusal to provide his own account of the Lewinsky affair, his supporters, led by the first lady, set out to fill that vacuum with the third prong of their strategy—the attack on their enemies, real and imagined, principally Kenneth Starr. "The great story here is this vast right-wing conspiracy that has been conspiring against my husband since the day he announced for president," Hillary Clinton declared on the day after her husband's carefully staged denial. Starr she branded as "a politically motivated prosecutor who is allied with the right-wing opponents of my husband."

All she would say about the charges against Clinton was, "That is not going to be proven true." She avoided specifics, because she said, "I've learned we need to put all of this in context." But whatever her presentation lacked in detail it made up for in smugness. Asked about the gifts the president had bestowed on Lewinsky, she responded: "Anyone who knows my husband knows that he is an extremely generous person to people he knows, to strangers, to anybody who is around him. And I think that, you know, his behavior, his treatment of people will certainly explain all of this."

And so the battle lines were set, with the future of the Clinton presidency at stake. Some of the terrain and rhetoric recalled previous battles over Clinton's character. "The people whose character is really an issue are those who would divert the attention of the people and divide the country we love," he had declared six years earlier in the winter of 1992 when his character first came under attack on the national political stage. And ever since, Clinton has used much the same argument—that what he was accused of was irrelevant to the nation's serious concerns—to shield himself from the intermittent firestorms of criticism. But the Lewinsky case amounted to the most serious character charge of his career—and the cumulative toll taken on his credibility by all these previous controversies escalated the peril to his presidency.

In a legal sense, everyone agreed that, as Independent Counsel Starr was quick to point out, the president was entitled to the presumption of innocence. But in political terms, his record raised the question of how much longer the public would give him the benefit of the doubt. "First you had Gennifer, then you had Paula, now you have Monica," Ohio University presidential scholar Alonzo Hamby told me. "It's gotten to the point where people are asking themselves, 'How can we trust this guy?'"

As a result of his past transgressions, Clinton's rating for integrity and trust had been notably low among politicians. In a 1997 Gallup Poll, Americans, asked to compare Clinton's ethical standards to other recent presidents, rated Presidents Reagan, Bush, and Carter ahead of Clinton by margins of about two to one or better. Indeed, only Richard Nixon, forced to resign in disgrace because of Watergate, trailed Clinton in this regard.

Yet Clinton had won two presidential elections. One reason was that while the public did not necessarily believe his denials, they accepted his argument that the charges about his personal conduct had nothing to do with his presidency. "Americans for some reason believe that the distinction between a president's personal conduct on one side and things that are pertinent to his public performance is one that should be taken seriously," acknowledged the opinion analyst Everett Carll Ladd.

But there was another, perhaps more important, Clinton advantage in his battle for survival: Simply put, he was more determined to stay in office than any of the other actors on the political stage were to get him out. "He has the will to withstand the attacks," said

David Keene, chairman of the American Conservative Union and a leader of the Republican right wing, which First Lady Hillary Clinton accused of "fomenting a conspiracy" to oust her husband. "Most people are willing to say that the guy is really a sleaze," said Keene. "But they know trying to get him out would involve a truly smarmy fight. And that is something they don't want any part of."

The removal of a president before his term is up has never been easy and was never meant to be, which is why the framers of the Constitution established the difficult ground rules for impeachment. And so far, only one president has been forced out because of the threat of that process, Richard Nixon, but not before an epic eighteen-month struggle over Watergate. At the time, Keene was an aide to Republican senator Jim Buckley of New York, a staunch conservative who was one of the first prominent Republicans to call for Nixon's resignation, an action that, as Buckley must have expected, cost him the support of the leaders of his party and ultimately his seat in the Senate. Yet Buckley had risked his career because in plotting his course, he had asked himself the question: "Doesn't America deserve better?" and found that the only possible answer was yes. But Keene complained that hardly any politicians were willing to act out of conscience in the Lewinsky controversy, which of course worked to strengthen Clinton's chances.

The irresolution among Clinton's opponents was evident at the annual Conservative Political Action Conference in suburban Arlington, which convened a few days after Hillary Clinton's outburst at the right wing. Assembled there were the chief movers and shakers of American conservatism, topped off by House Speaker Newt Gingrich. They seemed to be just the sort that the first lady had in mind when she decried the conspiracy against her husband. But the only kind of conspiracy in evidence at this gathering was a conspiracy of silence.

Fear of backlash tied the tongues of the most prominent among the speakers. And their references to Clinton's predicament were cryptic and oblique. Asked about "family values," Gingrich talked about curbing drug use, improving schools, and cutting taxes. "Every family I know wants a drug-free country," he said. "Every family I know wants to make sure their children really learn. Every family I know wants more money they can spend on their own needs." But if the Speaker saw any connection between the charges against Clinton and family values, it did not occur to him to mention it. His only allusion to the charges against Clinton was a hazy mention of "the difficulties we see developing around the White House," which he cited as a reason that conservatives and their GOP allies should take a positive approach rather than simply attack their foes. "As things become more unstable," Gingrich said, without explaining how this instability would develop, "people are going to want to look for someone who is stable," he said. "People are going to want somebody who cares about America first rather than about scoring partisan points."

Former Tennessee governor Lamar Alexander spoke fleetingly of recent events in the White House amounting to "a national embarrassment." But when asked to elaborate, he would only say, "It's a national embarrassment that speaks for itself." For a few speakers at the gathering, this restraint seemed excessive. "Leaders who suggest they can separate their private lives and their public actions are wrong," cried Republican senator John Ashcroft of Missouri, who was building his incipient candidacy for his party's nomination in the year 2000 on the hopes of arousing the support of Christian conservatives who presumably would be most offended by the president's behavior. "Morality is not divisible," Ashcroft insisted, in rebuttal to the claim of Clinton's supporters that the excesses of his personal life should not count against his presidency. "We have allowed the president to undermine our political strength and pervert our ideals," Ashcroft complained. "I have been criticized for speaking out," he acknowledged. But he added: "To sin by silence makes cowards of all men." It was time to tell the president, Ashcroft argued, "that if these allegations are true you have disgraced yourself, disgraced your office, disgraced this country, and you should leave. Mr. President, you cannot plead the Fifth Amendment to the country."

But as the days wore on, it became increasingly clear that Ashcroft was in a distinct minority among Republicans. The majority of their leaders stood aside from the controversy raging around the presidency and offered various rationalizations for their behavior. As the erstwhile leader of the Christian Coalition, Ralph Reed had once appeared eager to stake his future and his party's on the cause of family values. But since he had become a consultant to Republican candidates, he sang a different tune. "The overarching strategy for the Republican Party needs to be to not appear they are trying to make political capital," Reed said. "All that does is further energize the Democratic base."

Other conservatives feared the GOP risked alienating its own base in an election year if it was not more openly critical of Clinton's alleged behavior. "There is deep frustration and disappointment that there's not more moral leadership," said Gary Bauer, a conservative activist who heads the Family Research Council. "The reluctance to speak on this by politicians is a reflection of their fear to not look judgmental in an age that has elevated tolerance above all other values." But for a good many, the silent treatment for Clinton was inspired by the desire to avoid retaliation from Clinton supporters, who, Republicans feared, might try to probe for skeletons in their closets.

Allegations of sexual misconduct have long been a staple of American politics, even derailing the careers of lawmakers from Bob Packwood to John Tower. House Speaker Newt Gingrich himself is no stranger to controversy: Charges that he was involved in extramarital affairs in the 1970s have surfaced in various publications over the years. "There are a lot of folks in this town whose own lives will not stand up under scrutiny," Bauer said.

When they gathered to parley among themselves at a Southern party conference in Biloxi, Mississippi, late in that scandal-ridden winter, some Republicans were willing to raise the issue of the president's behavior, though like adolescents, they seemed most comfortable dealing with the subject with locker-room humor. In keeping with that tone, T-shirts that mocked the president with such labored slogans as "Lose One for the Zipper. Vote Republican" sold briskly. "I want to make it clear: I'm not in charge of all government affairs," quipped Senator Fred Thompson of Tennessee, chairman of the Senate Governmental Affairs Committee, who had presided over the Senate hearings on another facet of the character issue, the Democratic fund-raising abuses. "My friends," joshed former vice president Dan Quayle, "I'm proud to announce that I have a very tough anti-crime proposal for our party. And here's the centerpiece of our anti-crime plan: Three interns—and you're out!"

To be sure, Quayle devoted much of his speech to stern comments about what he called a "disgusting situation," in which, he said, Mr. Clinton had forfeited his moral authority. "The Presidency requires total focus, total commitment, total concentration," he said. "Now, we have a President who has lost credibility with the American people, who is severely distracted doing his job. This is sad—and dangerous." But the GOP's highest elected official, House Speaker Gingrich, pointedly avoided discussing the scandal, and Governor Tom

Ridge of Pennsylvania suggested that the leaders of his party had more important things to talk about. "I think the broader, more important, issue is what do Americans think today is the difference between the two parties and right now, I'll bet they're a little confused." Moreover, while gibing at Clinton served as a surefire formula for winning laughs and applause at such partisan gatherings, it was an approach that few Republicans leaders were willing to try in mixed political company, when any criticism they might make would carry greater impact but also greater risk.

While Republicans were cautious in responding to Clinton's plight, Democrats with few exceptions were downright craven. Remarkably, not a single Democratic leader of note came forward to call for the president to abandon his silence and give an honest account of himself and his behavior to the voters he was elected to serve. Instead, Richard Gephardt, the Democratic House leader, and a supposed rival to Vice President Gore in the competition for the 2000 presidential nomination, set the tone of loyalty early on. "The president explicitly denied these allegations," Gephardt said, the day after Clinton's performance in the Roosevelt Room. "He deserves the benefit of the doubt." Scolding the media for operating on "rumors and half-truths and fourth truths," Gephardt added self-righteously: "Democracy can't run on rumor mills. I think we all need to take a deep breath and back up."

Most of all, what Gephardt and his colleagues were watching carefully were the polls. And when these dubious barometers of public opinion showed the president's approval rating soaring, despite, or it seemed almost because of the charges against him, his Democratic brethren needed no further cue to embrace him fully. "I told him for all of us that we support him and more importantly, the American people support him," said Michigan congressman John D. Dingell, dean of the Democratic House Caucus at a February retreat with Clinton and Democratic House members in Wintergreen, Virginia. And Charles Rangell, claiming that there had not been "one scintilla of evidence to contradict the president's denial," said he would like to "see more outrage" directed against Starr.

That was just what the White House was trying to whip up, as the president's staff deployed an assault force on the television talk shows dedicated to turning the focus of the scandal away from Clinton and onto Starr. "I believe that Ken Starr has become corrupt in the sense that Lord Acton meant when he said, 'Absolute power corrupts absolutely,'" Paul Begala, who served as the point man for the attack, claimed on *Meet the Press*. Shrugging off the president's refusal to detail his exact relationship with Lewinsky, Begala said: "This will all come out, but it ought to come out in a way that is fair to the rights of the president. We have a situation here where an investigator is out of control," he added, using a phrase that would become a standard weapon in the White House's rhetorical arsenal.

What was particularly striking about the defense of Clinton and the attack on Starr was that it was joined by leading Democratic feminists, many of whom had been unrelenting and unforgiving in their attack on Clarence Thomas, when that Republican Supreme Court nominee was accused of sexual harassment by Anita Hill, and on Bob Packwood of Oregon, when that Republican senator was drummed out of the Senate for sexual misconduct. "I don't know what the facts are of the charges against the president," said California congresswoman Nancy Pelosi on *Meet the Press*. But what I do know is that Kenneth Starr went well beyond the constraints of ethics in his investigation of the president."

As far the rights of women were concerned, Pelosi contended that the real suspect was not Clinton, accused of seducing his intern, but rather Starr and "how he's investigating, exploiting, Monica Lewinsky, how he used Linda Tripp to do that. So I think women are reacting to Kenneth Starr in a way that says, 'You couldn't get the president on the merits of Whitewater, and now you are exploiting these women in this situation to tie, however tenuously, the president's personal life to Whitewater.'"

On the same program, Illinois senator Carol Moseley Braun picked up on the complaints made by the White House that Starr had been leaking negative information about the president. "I'm a former federal prosecutor and I can tell you that under the rules, what's coming out of Starr's investigation is absolutely unacceptable," she declared. "The Federal rules of criminal procedure say that you shouldn't leak."

When the Clarence Thomas furor was at its height in 1991, Democratic senator Barbara Mikulski of Maryland took to the Senate floor to upbraid her Senate colleagues for giving short shrift to Anita Hill's complaint against the nominee for the court. "To anybody out there who wants to be a whistle blower, the message is: 'Don't blow that whistle because you'll be left out there by yourself,'" Mikulski complained. "To any victim of sexual harassment, whether we call it sexual humiliation or whether there is overt physical aggression, sexual terrorism, the message to the private sector is: 'Cool it, guys. Even the Senate takes a walk on this one.'" Whether or not Monica Lewinsky had a legal claim for harassment, an issue she seemed totally uninterested in exploring, on the basis of what has been alleged about the intern-president relationship, as Catharine MacKinnon, the godmother of sexual harassment law, pointed out, she certainly seems to have been a victim of sexual exploitation. Yet when it came to the humiliation inflicted upon Lewinsky, Senator Mikulski and others who had previously been impassioned in the defense of the sisterhood in effect took a walk themselves, for they had nothing to say on the issue.

And when, in the wake of the allegations about Clinton's relationship with Monica Lewinsky, another former White House aide and active Clinton campaign supporter, Kathleen Willey, came forward to say that the president had groped her while she was visiting him in the White House, no one less than Gloria Steinem, founder of the National Women's Political Caucus, rushed into print to shrug off Willey's complaint. Even if Willey's charge was true, Steinem argued in the *New York Times*, Clinton's behavior did not amount to sexual harassment. All Clinton was accused of was making "a gross, dumb and reckless pass at a supporter during a low point in her life," Steinem wrote. "She pushed him away and it never happened again. In other words, President Clinton took 'no' for an answer." And in Steinem's book, that was all that mattered.

But like the Republican consensus in favor of silence, the feminist consensus against criticizing Clinton was not unanimous. Steinem's dismissal of the president's conduct with Willey because it happened only once may have been politically convenient, but it had little to do with sexual harassment law, pointed out political scientist Gwendolyn Mink. "There is no numerical threshold for harassment," she wrote, adding: "Nor does that law say each boss gets to ask each female worker for oral sex once as long as he doesn't force her when she says no."

As for Clinton's staunchest feminist defender, Hillary Rodham Clinton, feminist writer Barbara Ehrenreich contended in *Time*: "Someone needs to tell this woman that the first time a wife stands up for an allegedly adulterous husband, everyone thinks she's a saint. The second or third time, though, she begins to look disturbingly complicit." As for the Lewinsky affair, even if she had not been harassed, "feminists have plenty of reason to be concerned about a workplace where any young woman with sufficiently tart-like demeanor could reportedly enjoy the President's precious attentions, along with the career-counseling services of his closest friends. Meanwhile, who pays attention to all the other, harder-working and no doubt more productive interns whose hair is short and necklines are high?" The feminist critic Molly Haskell called the Lewinsky revelations "part of a pattern of slippery, sleazy, quasi-illegal, and grossly irresponsible behavior that has spread a thick layer of viscosity over the land. We who have voted for him or have profited from his presidency or who've made jokes about his anatomy are all in bed with Bill Clinton. Maybe it's time to get out."

Yet as Clinton's approval ratings soared in the wake of the scandal, some liberal elements sought to bond themselves to the president and to interpret his rise in public esteem as reflecting their own ideological preference. "It would behoove Democratic candidates to examine Clinton's agenda to figure out why he is so damn popular," suggested the *Nation*, which understandably had previously found little in the Clinton presidency about which to cheer. Now the *Nation* concluded that the poll ratings were due to Clinton's response to the public's desire for government to be "a positive force in their lives," though it acknowledged that "Clinton seeks to accomplish many of the historical tasks of the welfare state without using the government as his sole instrument." Of course this claim disregarded the well-grounded complaints by conservatives that Clinton had stolen most of their agenda and rhetoric and passed it off as his own. Even in the midst of its enthusiasm, the *Nation* was forced to come to terms with reality. None of the president's proposals were sufficient to deal with the nation's problems it conceded; Clinton's budget has many "offensive elements"; his trade polices "remain wrongheaded"; and "his cowardice in the face of the bloated military bureaucracy is infuriating." Still and all, the *Nation* insisted hopefully, "having done the dirty work on welfare and budget cutting on his first term Clinton is redefining himself." And then this publication, which for most of the twentieth century has been a beacon of unyielding principle on the left, concluded in an unsurpassed display of amorality: "We can retain our moral purity and continue to complain about what a bastard he is, or we can hunker down and build on his foundation."

In the public's mind, the president's shortcomings seemed obscured by the clumsiness of his principal adversary, as magnified by the White House attack team. Less than a month after the scandal broke, the polls showed that two-thirds of Americans believed that Starr had "partisan, political" motives for his investigation of the Lewinsky matter. And a substantial majority said they thought the facts were known and that Starr should drop the investigation. Encouraged by these results, the Clinton forces stepped up their assault on the independent counsel via the television talk shows. "Mr. Starr wants to indict everybody for everything," declared James Carville. "They have to keep him in check. We have an out-of-control, sex-crazed person running this thing. He has spent $40 million of the taxpayers' money investigating peoples' sex lives."

But the president's partisans did not stop with rhetoric. His legal team hired investigators to dig into the personal backgrounds of Starr's staff. Outraged when he found out, Starr struck back and in the process seemed to configure his image to match the caricature designed by the White House. Complaining that Clinton's allies were trying to bury his office under "an avalanche of lies," in what he claimed was an attempt to obstruct his investigation, Starr subpoenaed White House aide Sidney Blumenthal, a former journalist. As a writer for the *New Yorker*, Blumenthal had been known chiefly for his worshipful appraisal of the Clinton presidency. At the White House, his chief contribution had been to promote the anti-Clinton right-wing conspiracy theory to which the first lady had given prominent expression. As near as anyone could tell, Blumenthal had been doing what Starr suspected him of doing—spreading malicious gossip. But it was a long reach from fomenting stories critical of Starr to obstructing his investigation, the justification for hauling Blumenthal before the grand jury. Clinton's supporters accused Starr of "gestapo" tactics. And even Clinton's severest critics conceded that Starr had overreached himself, raising troublesome questions about the First Amendment rights of Blumenthal and the journalists he had contacted and giving more ammunition to Clinton's team. "Starr is politically tone-deaf," said William Bennett. "It's too bad, because everybody knows the central issue here should be the president."

But that was just the problem. In part, this was the responsibility of the press, which had been accused, not without justification, of rushing too quickly into print and on the air with what ultimately turned out to be exaggerations and outright falsehoods about aspects of the Lewinsky affair. The ensuing criticism, the *New York Times* complained, sent "many reporters and editors into mea culpa overdrive." The *Times* added: "A certain amount of public self-criticism is healthy in any field, especially one as powerful, diverse and unregulated as the media. But during Hurricane Monica, self-examination has morphed into unwarranted self-flagellation." Whether or not the press's treatment of Starr was motivated in some cases by the desire to make amends for whatever injustice might have been done to Clinton, the negative coverage of the independent counsel on occasion was in its own way as excessive as some of the earlier treatment of the president. Thus, the *Washington Post,* one of a handful of papers that are influential in coloring the attitudes and judgments of other journalists, on March 2 headlined its front-page lead story: "Starr Is Urged to Curtail Inquiry," a recommendation that, emanating as it did from Rahm Emanuel, one of Clinton's most energetic propagandists, seemed about as surprising and newsworthy as if the *Post* had discovered a man who had been bitten by a dog.

With Starr on the defensive, Clinton was free to maintain his silence on the case. "We are all totally in unison on the stand-pat, don't-say-a-thing strategy," one of Clinton's top political advisers told the *Post.* At first, he said for the benefit of the public, "This investigation is going on and you know what the rules are," in fending off a reporter's question. "And I just think as long as it's going on, I should not comment on the specific questions."

But as critics quickly pointed out, this was balderdash. While the federal rules of criminal procedure require the prosecutors and the grand jurors to keep silent about grand jury proceedings, witnesses and targets of the probe are allowed to talk as much as they want. Once this pretext was exposed, the president abandoned it as an excuse. But he kept his lips sealed, and his lawyers revived the claim of executive privilege, the same dubious doctrine discredited during Watergate, when it was advanced by Richard Nixon's White House to shield his aides from the grand jury investigation.

Seeking to put the best face on the president's resistance to the inquiry, Michael McCurry, Clinton's press secretary, labeled his approach, with unintended irony, "telling the truth slowly." Yet a momentary crack opened in this stone wall in the early weeks, when McCurry himself, of all people, appeared to deviate from the company line. In an interview with Roger Simon of the *Chicago Tribune,* McCurry, who, like most of Clinton's aides except for his lawyers, was almost as much in the dark as the public, suggested that Clinton's relationship with Monica Lewinsky could end up being a "very complicated story" that would not be easy to explain to the public. "Maybe there'll be a simple, innocent explanation," McCurry said. "I don't think so, because I think we would have offered that up already."

But this suggestion that the president's denial of any sexual relationship with Lewinsky might ultimately have to be qualified stirred such a furor that McCurry immediately retreated, showering himself with abuse as he did. "I goofed," he said, describing the interview as "a lapse in my sanity," for which he had placed himself in the doghouse. "I think what I was proving was that only fools answer hypothetical questions."

Yet the questions that McCurry's boss, the president, refused to answer were neither hypothetical nor irrelevant. In the Watergate scandal, to which Clinton's White House sex scandal inevitably raised comparison, the pertinent questions were what did the president know and when did he know it. In Clinton's case, the questions were what did the president do and what difference did it make. The White House and the president's supporters in the Democratic Party and the press argued that even if Clinton had had a sexual relationship with Monica Lewinsky—and it was hard to find anyone apart from his White House staff who disputed that charge—it made no difference at all. He was a public man, or so their argument went, but the allegation had to do with private conduct; both people involved were consenting adults.

Still, Clinton's own behavior contradicted this argument. Simply put, if what Clinton did made no difference, why did he bother to lie about it? Of course his behavior made a difference, and Clinton understood that. This was the reason for the carefully crafted dissembling, the months of conniving against the independent counsel, and the protracted legal defense that marked his response to the charges against him. Regardless of how citizens responded when they were asked by pollsters whether Clinton's sexual behavior matters to them, the impact of this sort of behavior cannot be measured by a simple yes or no question. The evidence of polls and focus groups since Clinton's first national campaign in 1992 is that such things matter a great deal and tend to erode credibility and trust in the president and the political system over the long run. It is true that despite the self-inflicted wounds on his reputation, Clinton won two presidential elections and it seems, as this is being written, he may be able to survive the Lewinsky controversy. But such outcomes are a consequence of a variety of factors besides character, mainly the condition of the economy and the quality of his principal adversaries, George Bush, Bob Dole, and, in effect, Kenneth Starr. Clinton's success in elections and in surviving scandal is only part of the story of his presidency. It does not reflect the damage done to the public's attitude toward political institutions and toward the political system. Nor does it take into account the opportunities lost and the potential unfulfilled for betterment of the national condition. The president, as the *Washington Post* pointed out, "has mortgaged the policies in which he ostensibly believes and the people, many of them vulnerable, whom these policies are meant to help, to his own considerable personal vulnerability and self-indulgence. There has been a lot of talk, not least within the White House, about this president's legacy. That heavy mortgage is an important part of it."

Yet another part of Clinton's legacy is the moral confusion created by his presidency and heightened by the storms that broke over the White House in 1998. Nothing so symbolized this confusion as the motion picture *Primary Colors*, released in the midst of the White House sex scandals. Like Joe Klein's novel from which it was drawn, the movie seemed to revel in the sexual exploits of its protagonist, Jack Stanton, a.k.a. Bill Clinton. But the bite that marked the best parts of Klein's book was missing from the motion picture, which was dominated by the grandly permissive view of its director, Mike Nichols.

Nichols confided to an interviewer that *Primary Colors* "is about honor. It asks the question where does honor lie now that things are as we know them to be." Interesting question. But not one that either the movie or Nichols really attempted to answer. Indeed, Nichols did not seem think an answer was required. Indeed, to Nichols's mind, somewhat clouded by half-baked Freudian concepts, the furor surrounding the president was more indicative of the immaturity of the president's critics than of anything about Clinton himself. "In France, they have no problem," he claimed. "Private acts are private acts. They long ago figured out that men who get a lot accomplished have powerful libidos. What's the problem?"

One problem with the film was that it echoed the defense strategy of the White House spin doctors, who trumpeted the idea that any sin charged against Clinton had also been committed by some of his predecessors.

"You don't think Abraham Lincoln was a whore before he was a president?" Governor Jack Stanton (a.k.a. Bill Clinton) asks a disillusioned aide who confronts him over the revelation of his latest indiscretion. But whatever wrongs Lincoln committed, Stanton contends, "he did it all just so he'd get the opportunity to stand in front of the nation and appeal to the better angels in our nature."

Although Nichols's ballyhooed movie was a box-office bust, the outlook that he and it espoused and reflected was bound to give encouragement to other men with powerful libidos—Bob Packwood, for one. Three years after he was driven from the Senate in disgrace over accusations of sexual misconduct, Packwood let it be known that he was thinking about running for office again—not the U.S. Senate, but maybe the state legislature in 2000. Deanna Smith, chairwoman of the Oregon Republican Party, could see no reason to gainsay him. "It's so ridiculous now that Clinton has been exonerated and Packwood did nothing near what Clinton did," she said. "I don't know why Packwood can't run. He was one of the best senators we ever had."

Whether or not Packwood actually does run, the environment created by the controversies over Clinton's behavior will remain to vex our culture and our politics for a long time to come, for Americans have had a hard time dealing with the test that Clinton foresaw his character would make them endure. The contradictions among the public on Clinton and the character issue were underlined in the spring of 1998 by the polling data, which show that while most Americans believe the president lied about his sexual behavior and many feel he may have even committed perjury, few want him removed from office or punished in any way. The awareness of serious wrongdoing in the nation's highest office, on the one hand, coexists with the willingness to tolerate it, on the other hand, and this represents a contflict that is bound to blur the standards of both morality and politics.

Greatly contributing to this muddle are the president's defenders, who argue that it is unfair to single him out for criticism when a number of his predecessors were later found out also to have been involved in behavior that conflicted with traditional standards. The difference is that whatever John Kennedy and Franklin Roosevelt and the others did, they did not get caught in the act while they were in office. Clinton operated under a far different system, where prying into the president's personal life and the president's exploitation of his personal life were both far more common. He knew that and should have disciplined his behavior accordingly, all the more so since he exploited the personalization of the presidency to his political advantage.

During the 1996 campaign, prompted by advice from the feminist novelist Naomi Wolf, Clinton's then chief political strategist Dick Morris sought to present Clinton as the "Good Father," defending the family home from Republicans who were determined to destroy it. Morris recalled for the president how Arkansans saw Clinton as their son who had lost his way in 1980, when he was defeated for re-election but came back to the fold, and to the governor's office in 1982. As he succeeded, the people of his state became prouder of him, because they still viewed him as their child, Morris explained.

Running for president in 1992, Morris told the president, he had campaigned as "America's buddy," a regular guy, riding around in a campaign bus, interested in helping ordinary people solve their problems. "But now," Morris told the president, "it's time to be almost the nation's father, to speak as the father of the country, not as a peer and certainly not as its child."

The net result of this image making, Peter Rubin claimed in a *New Republic* article highly sympathetic to Clinton, was to shield Clinton against the impact of the allegations against him. "A sympathetic understanding of Clinton's personality—like that we have of the members of our families—serves to distinguish him from others against whom allegations of sexual impropriety have been made," Rubin wrote, referring to Clarence Thomas and Packwood. But it is precisely because Clinton has sold himself to us as a member of the family that his personal behavior takes on relevance. What kind of father figure is it who conducts himself with women as he has been accused of doing?

The basic fallacy underlying the defense of Clinton provided by his partisans and by himself is that his private life can be separated from his public responsibilities. But John Ashcroft had it right when he said, "Morality is not divisible." The proposition that morality is irrelevant to the performance of the choices of the electorate can be simply tested. All it requires is a candidate for the presidency who is prepared in announcing his or her candidacy to say something along the following lines: "I'll do everything possible to promote prosperity and protect national security. And I will speak out vigorously in favor of truth, honor and other traditional values. But, just so you're not surprised, I want you to know that in my personal life, I feel free to cheat and lie and enjoy whatever pleasures of the flesh are available." The first time a candidate makes such a statement, the political world will know that presidential character no longer matters.

But of course this is highly unlikely to happen because it would represent a fundamental contradiction of the American political tradition. As we have seen, from the time George Washington's character helped define the presidency, the nature of that office has been inextricably linked to the character of the men who held it, sometimes for better and other times for worse.

It was in keeping with that two-centuries'-old tradition that from the time he launched his candidacy for the presidency, William Jefferson Clinton tied himself and his character to the dreams and aspirations of middle-class Americans. Inevitably, then, his prophesy that the unrelenting controversy about his character would turn into a test of the character of his fellow Americans has proven out. "President Clinton has a good deal to answer for," the social critic Gertrude Himmelfarb wrote in the wake of the White House sex scandal, "not only for his behavior, if the accusations are substantiated, but in making the public his accomplice." Whatever Clinton's legacy turns out to be, she predicted, "the public's legacy will be further vulgarization and demoralization of society."

But as even the president's own people have conceded, the public's ultimate judgment will depend on what the full story of the Lewinsky affair turns out to be. "He can't say, 'I'm doing a good job, so cut me some slack about telling the truth,'" Michael McCurry said. "He has assured the American people that he has not had sexual relations with this woman and that he never told her not to tell the truth. But if what he has said ends up not being the straight story, the American people will be troubled. They will await further explanations, but they will want to hear what the deal is."

The wait went on far longer than might have been expected, given the president's early promise to explain himself "sooner rather than later" and to tell "more rather than less." In contravention of those assurances, Clinton waged a sustained delaying action, toward that end using every tactic conceivable and some that almost went beyond conceivability. He claimed a shield of privilege for the government attorneys advising him when the crimes that were being investigated had nothing to do with official government business. Additionally, his attorney general, Janet Reno, put forward the unprecedented claim that the president's Secret Service detail should also be protected against Starr's probe on the ground that such in-

quiries would threaten Clinton's relationship with his bodyguards
and hence jeopardize his security. "When people act within the law
they do not ordinarily push away those they trust or rely upon for
fear that their actions will be reported to a grand jury," pointed out
District Court Judge Norma Holloway Johnson, in rebuffing Reno
and requiring that the agents testify.

It was not until midsummer, when all his gambits had been exhausted, after he had become the first president in history to be subpoenaed before a grand jury investigating crimes that he himself was
suspected of committing, that Clinton agreed to submit himself to
questioning by Starr. But it was clear beforehand that such guarded
testimony was not likely to answer the many questions that still
begged an answer about the Lewinsky affair and all the related
events. Democrats, like Clinton's own former chief of staff Leon
Panetta, joined in urging the president to address the nation in a setting that might encourage him to be more forthcoming than he was
likely to be while undergoing Starr's interrogation.

Indeed, politicians in both parties appeared eager for such a denouement, which would allow Republicans and Democrats to turn
their backs on what was for all of them an uncomfortable challenge.
But given the opportunity to put the Lewinsky controversy behind
him and the country, Clinton responded in character, which is to say
he followed his career-long pattern of minimizing his own culpabil-
ity while finding others to blame for whatever difficulty confronted
him. In his much heralded televised talk to the nation on August 17,
1998 he offered only a grudging, vague, and legalistic admission of
wrong doing. "While my answers were legally accurate," he said of
his deposition in the Paula Jones case, "I did not volunteer information," adding lamely: "I know that my public comments on this
matter gave a false impression." He then infuriated many of the
politicians sympathetic to his case by launching into a bitter attack
on Starr's investigation, contending that "it is time to stop the pursuit of personal destruction." In concluding his four-minute utterance, Clinton claimed that the matter was now between him, his
wife, and their daughter. But that was patently untrue. He had involved the whole country in his deception. And by the dismal nature
of his statement, he had surrendered control of his fate to Starr, who
continued to pursue his investigation, and ultimately to the House of
Representatives which awaited the independent counsel's report.

But however this drama was to play itself out, by late summer its outcome was in a sense moot. Throughout his tenure on the national political landscape, Clinton has lived by the sword of character. Now his presidency had been severely wounded by that sword. Whether or not the House of Representatives was ultimately to act against him, Clinton's potential for leadership had suffered irreparable harm, and cynicism about the political process and those charged with its stewardship had markedly heightened.

One indicator of this cynicism was the poll results, which showed a majority of Americans willing to shrug off the president's behavior and suspected mendacity as if they had little reason to expect anything better from their politicians, or, for that matter, from themselves. Pointing to those polling numbers in which Clinton's high ratings were widely attributed to reflect in large part the prevailing economic prosperity, Bill Bennett said, "Clinton's effect on the economy has been overstated. His effect on our expectations of ourselves has been understated. He has led us downhill, but too many of us have been prepared to follow him."

It could hardly have abated the rising tide of cynicism that whatever other handicaps the scandal had imposed on his presidency, Clinton's fund-raising abilities remained undiminished. By mid-August 1998, the Clinton Legal Expense Trust, established only six months earlier to help defray his legal expenses, had raised more than $2 million, with contributions ranging up to $10,000, from such entertainment luminaries as David Geffen and Steven Spielberg. Clinton is the first chief executive in history to accept such contributions, apparently untroubled by the appearance of influence buying by generous givers. Even Richard Nixon, beleaguered by Watergate, paid his own legal expenses until he left office.

As part of the fund's aggressive solicitation, a letter by former Arkansas senator David Pryor, the head of the effort, asserted: "In today's political climate, public service can exact a disturbing price. There is perhaps no better example than the financial crisis now facing President and Mrs. Clinton." The extent to which they had contributed to this "political climate" did not seem to have occurred to either of the Clintons. Indeed, the first lady, following her earlier contention that her husband's troubles had been brought on by a "vast right-wing conspiracy," later also blamed anti-Arkansas bias. "I think a lot of this is prejudice against our state," she told the

Arkansas Democrat-Gazette. "They wouldn't be doing this if we were from some other state."

Despite such protestations and favorable poll-ratings, as time passed, evidence mounted that the political winds were beginning to turn against the president. One telltale sign that did not escape the White House was the thinly veiled public warning from House Democratic leader Richard Gephardt that unless the president agreed to give evidence to the grand jury, he ran the risk of losing support among his party's hitherto loyal cohorts on Capitol Hill. Moreover, after Clinton's August 17, 1998 statement, a number of Democrats began to distance themselves from him. One member of his party, Congressman Paul McHale of Pennsylvania, asserted that "perjury is not excused by an apology compelled by overwhelming evidence," and called upon the president to resign.

Still another omen was the tack taken by Texas governor George W. Bush, the heavy early favorite to become the presidential Republican standard-bearer in the year 2000, as he prepared for his anticipated candidacy. Something of a hellion as a young man, the eldest son of the forty-first president, a member of the same baby boomer generation as Clinton, now appeared to be planning to run as a sort of anti-Clinton figure, someone who, like Clinton, had made mistakes but, unlike Clinton, had learned from them.

"People are concerned about Clinton's behavior because it undermines the idea of personal responsibility," Bush told me as he campaigned for reelection in his state in the summer of 1998 while Starr pressed his inquiry into the president's actions in the nation's capital. "We've got to get this chapter in American history behind us and move on."

Perhaps the strongest evidence of the political salience of Clinton's behavior was Connecticut senator Joseph Lieberman's now famous speech on the Senate floor denouncing that behavior as not just "inappropriate," the term favored by Clinton in his televised non-confession, but rather downright "immoral."

To understand the full significance of Lieberman's utterance, which for all its hedges and qualifications represented the first substantial reproof of Clinton by a fellow Democrat, it is important to bear in mind the ideological background. This assault on Clinton, as the White House surely perceived it, came not from the ideological left of the Democrats, the one-time bastion of discontent and dissent. Instead it was a leader of the Democratic right who spoke out.

Lieberman, it needs to be remembered, is the sort of Democrat who favors private school vouchers and who is the current chairman of the Democratic Leadership Council, the organization created fifteen years ago to steer the Democrats back toward the supposed political center. And it is of course the organization that Clinton himself used as a springboard for his march to the 1992 presidential nomination. In short, Lieberman is not just a fellow Democrat; he is a fellow *new* Democrat. And as such he spoke for the forces in the party who were most threatened by the contradiction between Clinton's conduct and the paradigm of middle-class values that had paved the way for the Democratic reconquest of the White House after the long years in the wilderness during the Reagan-Bush epoch.

"Look, part of what troubled me about this whole episode is that one of the great things the president has done for our country, and, if I may say, speaking as a Democrat, for our party, is that in his public statements and in the programs he's advocated, he has reconnected the Democratic Party to the mainstream of American values, from which we were disconnected," Lieberman explained after his Senate speech. "This misconduct, behavior that is both immoral and untruthful, undercuts that . . . "

The larger and more enduring issue was the impact the crisis that Clinton's behavior had provoked would have on the health of the office he held. As Clinton fought a series of losing legal battles against the independent counsel's office, some saw Clinton's predicament as the latest in a series of challenges that had eroded the institutional authority of the presidency. In dissenting from the court of appeals rejection of the president's claim that attorney-client privilege should shield his conversations with Deputy White House Counsel Bruce Lindsey, Judge David S. Tatel argued that one troublesome consequence of the Watergate scandal had been to increase "the President's vulnerability." Because of "aggressive press and congressional scrutiny," along with the enactment of the independent counsel statute, Tatel claimed that "no president can navigate the treacherous waters of post-Watergate government, make controversial official legal decisions, decide whether to invoke official privileges or even know when he might need private counsel without confidential legal advice," which he claimed should be cloaked with the privilege normally accorded discourse between clients and their attorneys.

But given the history of the post-Watergate quarter century, Tatel's concern for the presidency seems overstated and misplaced. As every occupant of the office, certainly including Clinton himself, has demonstrated, even during this era of the supposedly post-imperial presidency, the chief executive wields enormous power to set the national agenda and shape public opinion. The contention that presidents will constantly have to ponder whether to ask for confidential legal advice suggests that they will be operating close to the border of criminal activity, a notion that, fortunately for all of us, is contradicted by the conduct of every post-Watergate president except Clinton. Indeed, what history tells us, particularly the study of presidential character, is that the greatest threat to the welfare of the presidency comes not from Congress, or the press, or even the offices of independent counsel, but rather from presidents themselves. Or as Truman biographer Alonzo Hamby put it in prose as succinct as might have been uttered by the Man from Missouri himself, "It seems to me the presidency is going to be hurt when presidents do things that are wrong or stupid."

It needs to be remembered that the presidency is an eminently resilient and dynamic institution. From George Washington to Bill Clinton, just as the presidency has suffered from the flaws of presidents, it has thrived on their strengths and virtues. The lesson for the public is to monitor both sides of their behavior closely. In preparing to leave office, Washington, referring to the mistakes he supposed he had made, called upon God "to avert or mitigate the evils" he might have caused. Looking beyond the feckless conduct of Bill Clinton, it makes sense for Americans to join in that prayer, counting for its fulfillment not only on Divine Providence but also on their own vigilance and judgment.

12

THE ROAD TO ANOMIE

WHEN ROBERT L. LIVINGSTON OF NEW JERSEY, the Speaker-designate of the House of Representatives, rose to address that body on Saturday morning, the furor over President Clinton's dalliance with a White House intern, which had consumed nearly all of the year, appeared to have reached its apex.

The date was the 19th of December 1998, eleven months almost to the day since independent counsel Kenneth Starr had launched his investigation of the affair. Four months had passed since President Clinton had finally admitted that he had lied to the country when, in the wake of the first public knowledge of the affair, he had denied that he had a sexual relationship with White House intern Monica Lewinsky. It had been three months since Starr had submitted to the House of Representatives a 445-page summary of his investigation containing "substantial and credible information . . . that may constitute grounds for impeachment." The principal offenses cited in Starr's report were perjury and obstruction of justice. The report, which the House made public immediately, had generated a new storm.

The explicit details of Clinton's sexual encounters divulged by the report offended and embarrassed many Americans, leading some to condemn the president for his behavior and others to denounce Starr for allegedly trying to capitalize on the lurid aspects of the case. For their part, Starr's investigators claimed they had little choice but to make public such details because the details went to the heart of the charge that the president had committed perjury by denying having sex with Lewinsky—though, as he acknowledged, the two had engaged in oral sex.

In a rebuttal to the report, Clinton's lawyers accused Starr of waging a "smear campaign" because his inquiry into the Whitewater land deal had failed to yield evidence of serious wrongdoing. While conceding that the president's affair with Lewinsky had been "wrong," David Kendall, who headed Clinton's defense team, called the president's misconduct "personal, not impeachable."

In the autumn weeks that followed the release of Starr's report, the prospects for impeaching the president alternately ebbed and flowed in reaction to unforeseen events and changing circumstances. In the battle for public opinion, Clinton got an inadvertent assist from the House Republicans when they released a videotape of his testimony before the grand jury investigating the Lewinsky affair. The videotape helped the president because of the contrast between his generally calm and self-assured demeanor on the tape and previous reports that he had lost his temper during his grand jury appearance.

The net result of the tape's release was an increase in sympathy for the president from a public that polls indicated had grown weary of the Lewinsky case. Despite the polls, Republicans in the House, with some Democratic support, voted on October 8 to conduct a full-scale impeachment inquiry into Starr's charges against Clinton. The resolution to conduct an open-ended inquiry was supported by only thirty-one Democrats; most Democrats voted for an alternative resolution that would have set December 31 as a deadline for completing the probe. Yet, neither party was prepared to sweep the scandal under the rug; all told, 429 of the 435 House members voted for some form of impeachment inquiry.

A month later, Clinton's fortunes received another boost as a result of the dismal GOP showing in the November midterm elections, when the Republicans lost five seats in the House. This setback marked the first time since 1934 that the party opposing the White House had lost ground in the House in an off-year election. The president then was Democrat Franklin Roosevelt, and he was leading the nation out of the depths of the Great Depression. After their reverse in 1998, the Republicans remained in charge of the House, but with a majority of only 223 to 211.

On election night, as he patrolled the West Wing in stocking feet, monitoring computer and television screens for results on House races in which Republicans had run commercials trying to make an issue of the scandal, Clinton could scarcely contain his relief, which soon turned to exuberance. "He had five Diet Cokes and a shrimp quesadilla to celebrate," said a friend who was there. "He was chewing on an unlit cigar, loose as a goose. It was clear to everybody the whole dynamic had changed." This would turn out to be another in a string of misjudgments made by both parties.

Given the listless campaign they had conducted, the Republican House members had no one to blame but themselves for their defeat. They found it more convenient, though, to focus their resentment at their leader, Speaker Newt Gingrich, whom many sought to depose. Facing a mutiny spearheaded by Livingston—the chairman of the powerful Appropriations Committee who had announced he would seek the leadership himself—Gingrich, the architect of the great GOP victory of 1994, had abruptly announced that he would give up his post, clearing the path to the Speakership for Livingston.

The turmoil in Republican ranks, along with the president's continued strong showing in the polls, gave Clinton's supporters confidence that the impeachment drive could be turned back. Hoping to pave the way for his vindication, the president paid $850,000 to settle the Paula Jones lawsuit, which had been the root cause of his difficulties. In April, the trial judge, Susan Webber Wright, had thrown out Jones's suit on grounds that even if what Jones said was true, she had not suffered sexual harassment because she had not been demoted or otherwise punished for rebuffing Clinton's alleged advances. Two months later, though, the U.S. Supreme Court, ruling in a Chicago case, said that a female worker does not need evidence she suffered a demotion to bring a claim of sexual harassment against a male supervisor. "Severe or pervasive" sexual harassment from a supervisor is enough, the high court said. Citing the high court's ruling, Jones's lawyers had appealed Wright's dismissal of the suit, and even the president's own attorneys considered it likely that the case would be revived—and along with it the threat that Clinton would face a trial on Jones's charges of sexual harassment. In settling the case, Clinton did not apologize or admit wrongdoing. His willingness to pay $850,000 to get rid of this problem, $150,000 more than Jones had sought initially, spoke for itself.

Remarkably, neither the losses at the ballot box nor the president's legal maneuvering seemed to diminish at all the determination of the House Republicans to press on with the case for impeachment. Then their cause received important help from Clinton himself. On November 5, two days after the midterm election, Judiciary Committee Chairman Henry Hyde submitted to the White House a list of eighty-one questions bearing on the case, asking the president to either "admit or deny" the assertions made in the questions. Clinton's answers, made three weeks later, shed little new light. Instead they displayed the congenital deviousness that had helped bring on his predicament. He would not even provide a direct answer when asked whether he as president was the nation's chief law enforcement officer. All Clinton would concede on that point was that the president was "frequently referred to" in that way.

Most Republicans viewed the president's responses as nothing less than arrogant, a reaction that helped to unite them behind the two leaders of the impeachment drive, Chairman Hyde and Majority Whip Tom DeLay, both of whom insisted that their constitutional responsibility to hold the president accountable transcended public sentiment. Whether they were driven by conscience, as their admirers claimed, or sheer malice, as their Democratic detractors charged, no one could question their determination.

DeLay, a hard-eyed Texan who had once operated an exterminating business in his hometown, had in his seven terms in the House come to be known as a shrewd, ruthless, and heavy-handed operator, a reputation testified to by his sobriquet, "The Hammer." By throwing his considerable support behind Livingston's candidacy for the top job in the House at the very start, DeLay had gained the right to move in the void between the Speakerships of Newt Gingrich and Livingston. Indeed, in private, the Democrats called him "the de facto Speaker."

To throttle the efforts of Democrats to offer censure of Clinton as a substitute for impeachment, DeLay relied upon a grasp of the technicalities of House procedures that seemed an inherent gift. Even as a child, the 51-year-old DeLay had such a head for detail that his parents woke him early on Christmas morning so he could help assemble the toys for his siblings. "I read the instructions," he recalled. "I've always been a rules person."

DeLay's devotion to rules and to traditional values—he was a born-again Christian and a formidable ally of the religious right—informed his battle against the president. "Rules are rules, right is right," DeLay liked to say. As for the political consequences of the push for impeachment, to his view, those who claimed the Republicans would suffer from this push were probably Democrats at heart.

Far from damaging the GOP, leadership in the impeachment crusade against Clinton, DeLay claimed, would serve to solidify the party.

In explaining his fervor for the impeachment cause, DeLay spoke repeatedly and passionately of Clinton's dishonesty. "I don't believe a word he says," he told a reporter. And that, his friends said, was at the heart of what really bothered him about Clinton.

To keep the Republican moderates in line and away from the Democratic censure alternative, DeLay knew exactly what to emphasize: the rule of law; the comparisons to Nixon's Watergate crimes; the old Clinton sins that still ate at uncommitted Republicans like Louisiana's W. J. "Billy" Tauzin. Tauzin never forgave the president for "lying to my face" about an energy-tax vote. DeLay also understood that Clinton himself provided the best argument against censure by his refusal, based on lawyerly caution and reflexive evasiveness, to confess to wrongdoing. Without a clear admission of guilt, Clinton "wasn't giving us any choice," said Representative Brian P. Bilbray of San Diego, a moderate who had initially favored censure.

If his energies ever lagged, DeLay only had to remind himself of Clinton's widely quoted observation that he thought both Anita Hill and Clarence Thomas were telling the truth as they remembered it when Hill accused Thomas of sexual harassment and the Supreme Court-justice-to-be denied her charges during his confirmation hearings. Such a flexible notion of verity was, in DeLay's view, nothing less than outrageous.

Still and all, the main reason Clinton should be impeached, DeLay argued, was to uphold the law and the Constitution, a tiny copy of which he had carried in his pocket for almost twenty years. "I do what I believe," DeLay said. "I believe in the Constitution, I believe in this institution, and I believe in the office of the presidency—and I'm doing what I think is the right thing to do."

On Tuesday of impeachment week, four days before Livingston rose to speak to the House, DeLay took a call from an angry Massachusetts voter who demanded that Congress call a halt to impeachment and get back to more important business. "We are doing what we're supposed to do," DeLay said. "But we will impeach this president."

In manner and style, Judiciary Committee Chairman Henry Hyde was as different from his chief collaborator as impeachment architect, Tom DeLay, as the cultural and geographic distance between Hyde's suburban Chicago constituents and the voters in the outlying precincts of Houston who sent DeLay to Congress. The blunt-spoken DeLay often abraded Republicans as well as Democrats; Hyde's courtly manners and intellectual flair had won him admirers in both parties. Yet not a great deal separated the two men ideologically. Long before the impeachment challenge arose, Hyde had made his mark on the Congress—and earned the undying hatred of feminists—by his successful advocacy of the eponymous amendment that bans federal funding for abortions.

When it came to impeachment, Hyde was as committed to the cause as DeLay or anyone else on the Hill. This commitment was no easy task for him. At 74, though his intellect seemed as keen as ever, the lingering affects of prostate surgery made the long public hearings an ordeal; and his ponderous, six-foot-five-inch figure shuffled along the Capitol corridors at a pace a tortoise could have matched easily. Threats on his life were numerous enough and serious enough to compel him to allow the Capitol Hill police to chauffeur him back and forth from his home to his duty station at the Judiciary Committee. "I haven't driven my car in about a month and a half now," he wisecracked. "I hope it will start."

As the leader of the assault on the president, Hyde had learned to ignore the abuse of wild-eyed Clinton defenders—and he was forced to own up to the all too accurate findings of investigative journalists. In September, the Internet magazine Salon disclosed an adulterous affair in the 1960s with a married woman whose husband at the time came forward to accuse Hyde of breaking up his family. Hyde's attempt to dismiss the affair as "a youthful indiscretion" only stirred more hoots and jeers from his critics. "But he's 74 years old. He was 41 then. It's all relative," a sympathetic friend sought to explain.

Hyde was subject to a different form of embarrassment when Democrats who had fought against him during the Iran-Contra scandal pointed out that the congressman seemed to have a more permissive view of mendacity in 1987. Then he sought to rationalize the denials of wrongdoing by President Reagan's aides, whose sins were later exposed, as uttered in a good cause: the struggle against communism. By contrast, in 1998 he condemned Clinton's untruths about the Lewinsky affair as nothing less than perjury, warranting impeachment.

Hyde shrugged off the criticism and the self-contradictions. After nearly a quarter of a century on Capitol Hill he had learned not to waste his energy on self-doubt or self-recriminations about past conduct he could not change. In the election a few weeks before, Hyde had easily gained re-election to his own seat. But his satisfaction with is own success was dimmed by the setback suffered by his party. "It's pretty clear," Hyde remarked to reporters over the clamor of an election night victory celebration, "that impeachment dropped off the public's radar screen."

Even so, his own course seemed clear. "I can't speak for other members, but I know what I have to do," Hyde said.

The next day, he conferred with aides, with a new air of urgency. Before the election Hyde had talked about the idea of concluding the committee's probe before year's end. Now that possibility had become a necessity. Hyde could not let impeachment drag on into the next Congress when the Democratic minority would be bigger and bolder as a result of the midterm vote. The impeachment clock was running, and Henry Hyde had less than two months to deliver the goods.

"Let's just lay it out," he told his aides.

Over the next few weeks, Hyde would nurture and protect the impeachment effort like a fragile plant, tending it with all the skill and resources his seniority and prestige gave him. For Hyde this was a personal matter, and also a matter of high principle.

It was clear to the chairman, cognizant of his own role in the political system as a legislator, that the president, the nation's chief executive, had stained the office he held and the government he headed, in both a legal and symbolic sense. Not only had Clinton broken the law, Hyde believed, but he had violated the moral underpinning of the political system.

The concepts expressed by the president's actions and his utterances—"this idea that everything is relative, that stretching the truth is acceptable because everyone does it"—had defamed the values that Hyde had pledged himself to serve.

Hyde had a reputation for fairness, and in his conduct of the inquiry he lived up to it, to a point. He granted extra time to minority and White House lawyers and allowed Democrats to bring up the idea of a presidential censure. But he made plain that he did not consider censuring Clinton a viable, constitutional option.

This was a critical decision. In the early weeks of the inquiry, several Republicans on the Judiciary Committee had considered censure a possibility. But any chance for agreement on compromise was lost because they kept their short-lived interest to themselves. Moderate

Democrats never learned that the GOP had toyed with the idea. Some members in both parties met for breakfast and sometimes late at night in the interest of maintaining civility during the hearings. Nevertheless, Democrats still couldn't sell Republicans on the idea of censure—not with Hyde adamantly opposed to the idea. And ultimately most of the breakfast club members stopped showing up. The die was cast for impeachment.

The Democrats faced their own moments of torment, from the White House to Capitol Hill. In the executive mansion, the president's home—which was also, so to speak, the scene of the crime—the Starr report hit with devastating impact when it was released in mid-September. Overwhelmed by a sense of betrayal and disgust, members of the White House staff, hitherto steadfast in their loyalty to the president, for a brief period turned their backs on their chief.

When the Sunday talk shows asked for guests to defend Clinton against the allegations put forward by Starr, no one volunteered. Instead, press secretary Michael McCurry told the president's lawyers to face the cameras. "We're not going out," McCurry said. In the Senate, a half dozen or so lawmakers were believed to be on the verge of calling for Clinton's resignation. Their thoughts echoed the demands of editorials in papers large and small around the country.

"Bill Clinton should resign. He should resign because his repeated, reckless deceits have dishonored his presidency beyond repair," said the *Philadelphia Inquirer.* "It is too late for the president to make amends for his outrageous conduct with apologies. Those apologies should have come months ago, when it first became evident that he was embroiled in a tawdry affair with a woman young enough to be his daughter," said the *Reporter* of Lebanon, Indiana. "Clinton should resign and go home to Arkansas, although that is completely out of character," said the *Detroit Free Press.* "While we have supported many of his policies, we cannot say we would be devastated, since his effective days are well past gone and his judgment and veracity will be forever suspect."

For the moment the Democratic senators, with the notable exception of Connecticut's Lieberman, kept their outrage to themselves. They caucused to hear from Erskine Bowles, Clinton's chief of staff, who told them, lamely enough, "He lied to me, too."

Joe Biden of Delaware, whose own candidacy for the presidency a decade earlier had been ended by the exposure of a far milder indiscretion involving plagerism, said his preference would be for Clinton to quit. The party would be better off in the elections if the president left, Biden theorized. In almost the same breath, though, Biden discounted his own suggestion. Clinton would never quit, he conceded.

"There isn't much holding them together," John Podesta, the deputy chief of staff who had accompanied Bowles to the Senate caucus, remarked afterward. "There could be a stampede."

Bowles himself was near a breaking point. "I just want you to know that I'm not going up and doing any more defense of the president on the Hill," he told McCurry. "Never again. I can't do what I did this week. I also want you to leak it out somewhere that I'm going to be leaving when Congress leaves."

Minority Leader Tom Daschle told several Senate Democrats that the scandal might reach a point where it would be best for everyone if Clinton resigned. "But we're not there yet," he said. "Be patient, hold your fire," he counseled.

At the White House, Clinton stuck to his guns, determined never to quit. He fought to keep recalcitrant Democrats in line, relying always on the polls, which, reflecting the thriving economy, continued to show support for him. In late September, the president got word that Congressman Jesse L. Jackson Jr. had written a proposed op-ed piece that he was showing around to top Democrats. In it, the 33-year-old Jackson, like his father never shy of the limelight, suggested that Clinton "articulate the possibility that he had lied under oath," a move Jackson believed would clear the air around the White House and short-circuit the impeachment drive.

That was no part of Clinton's strategy. Traveling on Air Force One when he learned of Jackson's literary effort, Clinton immediately put through a call to the congressman.

The president wasted no time on small talk. "Jesse, listen, have you read this morning's *New York Times*?" Clinton asked pointedly.

"No I haven't, sir."

"Well the polls are in our favor," Clinton said. "This thing is backfiring on the Republicans. We need Democrats to hang in there with us."

"I do not want you to be impeached," Jackson replied. "I've come up with a strategy to support you and keep you in office."

"I appreciate that," Clinton said. "Our strategy is to keep the poll numbers up. The Republicans are going too far. We need to stick together."

When Clinton rang off, Jackson realized that Clinton saw the polls as the solution to all his problems. He wondered if Clinton had ever even read his article, which ultimately was published but with the offending suggestion smoothed over.

The polls, however, did not deter Republicans on the Judiciary Committee from carrying out what they professed to be their duty. Brushing aside the notion of censure, which had been the principal hope of the president's allies, as unconstitutional and inconsequential, and dismissing the proposal of another presidential apology as inadequate, the committee voted along party lines to send four impeachment articles to the House floor. The president was charged with perjury, both before the federal grand jury and in his Jones case deposition; obstruction of justice; and abuse of power. It was the first such action by the Judiciary Committee since 1974, when charges were brought against Richard Nixon as a result of the Watergate scandal.

In the face of the storm swirling about him, Clinton sought for the most part to behave as if none of this was really happening. His admirers raved about his ability to "compartmentalize" his time, his thoughts, even his emotions. Clinton, they boasted, had become increasingly adept at stuffing troubling issues into what he referred to as a "box," allowing him to concentrate on his other work. And always he stressed his determination, as he put it in his now discredited denial of his relationship with Lewinsky, to continue "to work for the American people."

Yet as the scandal deepened, it became increasingly difficult to separate the charges against him for personal misconduct from the official conduct of his job. That problem had been driven home in August even aborad. Several Republican senators questioned Clinton's motives when, in response to the bombings at U.S. embassies in Kenya and Tanzania, he launched antiterrorist military strikes in Sudan and Afghanistan. That was only a week after confessing to his improper relationship with Lewinsky. But Republican leaders, including Senate Majority Leader Trent Lott of Mississippi and House Speaker Newt Gingrich, quickly silenced those insinuations by unreservedly endorsing the attack.

Still, doubts lingered on, particularly in the wake of reports that the antiterrorist offensive had been a dud, missing its principal target—renegade Saudi millionaire Osama Bin Laden—and leveling a pharmaceutical plant in Khartoum in the apparently mistaken belief that it was a center for nerve gas manufacture.

All this served to heighten Republican suspicions about Clinton's motives and to remind them of the satirical film *Wag the Dog*. Released by bizarre coincidence just as the Lewinsky affair erupted in headlines, the film depicts presidential aides trying to divert attention from a sex scandal by staging a phony war on television.

Against this troublesome background, a new foreign crisis, or more precisely a recurrence of an all too familiar crisis, loomed just as the House was preparing to debate Clinton's impeachment. At the root of the challenge abroad was Iraq's intransigent ruler Saddam Hussein, who for the second time that year had balked at allowing the weapons inspections mandated by the U.N. following Iraq's defeat in the 1991 Gulf War. The earlier confrontation in February, when the Lewinsky scandal was in its incipient stages, was resolved by a negotiated compromise. This time diplomacy seemed to offer no solution, or so the president's military advisers claimed.

In the White House Situation Room, Defense Secretary William Cohen met at 7 A.M. with the principals of Clinton's national security team. It was Wednesday, December 16. The full House was scheduled to begin debate the following day on four articles of impeachment voted by the Judiciary Committee. All present recommended that the president give the green light for an attack scheduled to begin about 5 P.M. that day, the eve of the impeachment debate. "A failure to take action now will undercut our credibility," Cohen told Clinton.

And then Cohen bluntly introduced the threat of impeachment into the president's decisionmaking process. "Our word is at stake," the defense secretary and former Republican lawmaker told the president. "If we don't carry it out, we're going to be tested in the future." Weakness would be met by more of Saddam's defiance, Cohen argued. "If you don't act here, the next argument will be that you're paralyzed," he said.

Clinton ordered the bombing to begin, under the code name "Operation Desert Fox." "I can't consider anything else," Clinton said. "I have no choice."

But to many Republicans on Capitol Hill the situation hardly looked that cut and dried. The wrangling with Saddam over the weapons inspections had been going on for most of the year. On a number of occasions Clinton had threatened to attack—but then held off when Saddam seemed to give in. After all that backing and filling, the Republicans wondered, why bring matters to a head now, just when the impeachment debate was to begin?

On Wednesday, December 16, as U.S. planes began their attacks, Republican leaders postponed the debate on impeachment, which had been set for Thursday, until Friday, December 18. Instead of arguing about Clinton's misconduct, the House voted a resolution in support of U.S. troops. "We support our troops," Speaker-designate Livingston said, adding dryly: "As to the matter of timing, we would leave that to the best judgment of the American people." Trent Lott was far blunter, refusing to back the action and challenging the president's motives. "While I have been assured by administration officials that there is no connection with the impeachment process in the House of Representatives, I cannot support this military action in the Persian Gulf at this time," Lott said. "Both the timing and the policy are subject to question."

Defense Secretary Cohen was indignant: "I am prepared to place thirty years of public service on the line to say the only factor that was important in this decision is what is in the American people's best interest. There were no other factors."

But of course it was not Cohen's credibility that was under question, but his commander in chief's. And a good number of Republicans were not convinced. "Never underestimate a desperate president," said House Rules Committee Chairman Gerald B. H. Solomon of New York. "What option is left for getting impeachment off the front page and maybe even postponed? And how else to explain the sudden appearance of a backbone that has been invisible up to now?"

The nasty quarrel over the president's motives showed how deeply the impeachment crisis had dogged his ability to lead. "It's exhibit A on how much credibility the president has lost that we're even asking, is this 'Wag the Dog?'" said Representative Marge Roukema of New Jersey.

With the impeachment debate postponed until Friday, Thursday was expected to be a day of peace and quiet on Capitol Hill. It turned out be anything but that. Unrest started building in mid-afternoon when rumors swept through the House office buildings facing on the Capitol that Bob Livingston, the Republican's new Speaker-designate, was in trouble, woman trouble to be exact. The

55-year-old Livingston had been no stranger to trouble during the course of his long political career. But usually when he was around, it meant trouble for somebody else.

Flamboyant and hot headed, he had once appeared at a meeting of the Appropriations Committee he headed brandishing a machete to dramatize his intention to slash the federal budget. The proud wearer of a black belt in tae kwon do, Livingston often tangled verbally with his House GOP colleagues—including other committee chairmen—over spending priorities. One confrontation with one of his peers nearly led to physical blows with a staff aide.

During the December 1995 government shutdown confrontation with the White House, it was Livingston who took to the House floor and delivered a rambunctious speech in which he had shouted: "We will never, never give in. We will stay here until doomsday." The speech got a rousing reception from fellow Republicans, but it also became the face of the GOP intransigence in the budget war that culminated in a partial government shutdown, which proved politically damaging to Republicans.

As a young criminal prosecutor in New Orleans, Livingston celebrated his more important courtroom victories in the watering holes of the French Quarter. But one night he stayed out so late that when he got home, he discovered his wife had left his dinner out on the front stoop. That incident was soon smoothed over. But now it had come to light that the household Livingston maintained with his wife, Bonnie, and their four children had faced far more serious troubles.

It seemed that Livingston had a roving eye, which he had indulged, and on more than one occasion. This story had come to light because Larry Flynt, publisher of *Hustler* magazine, was determined to show up the critics of Clinton's behavior as hypocrites; Flynt had offered a $1 million payment to anyone coming forward with evidence of adultery by a member of Congress or other top government official. Once he knew Flynt was on his case, Livingston had little choice. That Thursday evening, hours before the impeachment debate was to start, he issued a statement: "I have decided to inform my colleagues and constituents that during my 33-year marriage to my wife, Bonnie, I have on occasion strayed from my marriage and doing so nearly cost me my marriage and my family." Confronting his fellow Republicans with this admission he told them: "My fate is in your hands."

The GOP House members rose to offer an ovation, and several left the room to tell reporters that Livingston had handled the matter with integrity and deserved to become Speaker when the next Congress convened in early January. The Republicans willing to talk to reporters insisted that Livingston's conduct had nothing to do with the allegations against Clinton—perjury, obstruction of justice, and abuse of power—and would not affect their support for impeaching the president. "He never lied under oath," Representative James E. Rogan of California pointed out.

On the other side of the House, Massachusetts Democrat William D. Delahunt predicted Livingston's disclosure would produce "turmoil and chaos" on the House floor during the impeachment debate. At the very least it must have made publisher Flynt feel his investment had paid off. Livingston was the fourth House Republican, Henry Hyde among them, who had been forced to admit past sexual misdeeds since Congress began considering impeaching Clinton because of his efforts to conceal his affair with former White House intern Monica S. Lewinsky.

Republicans tried to make the best of a bad situation. House Majority Leader Dick Armey accused unnamed forces of trying to "twist the impeachment debate" into an investigation of private lives. Some Republican lawmakers pointed fingers at the White House and Clinton allies, suggesting that Livingston had been the victim of a smear campaign. "The people trying to support Bill Clinton have done everything they can to try to intimidate people," said a fuming Representative Dana Rohrabacher of California. "This is the worst, god-awful tactic I've ever seen in the whole planet." But Rohrabacher and the other Republicans offered no evidence to back up such allegations.

For his part, Livingston was willing for the moment to accept the support of his colleagues while he absorbed the shock waves from the event. That was good enough for Thursday night. But Livingston's instincts, honed over years in the House, were too keen to accept all the expressions of good will at face value. And so on Friday, while the House debated the articles of impeachment, Livingston spent much of the day working the phones, asking his friends to find out from their friends what the House Republicans really thought. What he learned was disquieting, although for a man of Livingston's practical bent, it could hardly have been surprising.

A number of House conservatives felt they had been betrayed by Livingston, so much so that they were planning to vote against him when the official election for Speaker was held in January. Livingston knew that the "wingers" were too few in number to defeat his candidacy. And he calculated that many probably could be persuaded to vent their resentment in some other way. He also knew, though, that the House Republicans were already gravely fissured. Another reason for disgruntlement was the last thing their future leader would need.

Politics aside, there was the matter of his wife, no small matter. Bonnie Livingston was "suffering terribly," Livingston told one of his colleagues. "Devastated" was the word another House member used.

Pondering all this, Livingston's decision suddenly became quite clear. By Friday morning, when Zach Wamp of Tennessee buttonholed him on the House floor to tell him of the restlessness in conservative ranks, Livingston had already made up his mind. Now it was time to tell the world about it.

This was Livingston's moment. And having earned this opportunity the hard way, through the personal ordeal of the past forty-eight hours, Livingston was resolved to make the most of it. Rather than blurt out his decision, he began his speech with a note of amity, expressing his "fondest hopes" that the bitterness of recent days would be set aside as members returned to their homes for the Christmas holidays. He paid his respects to "our magnificent Constitution" and to the men and women in military service pitted against that "enemy of civilization," Saddam Hussein, and to the Congress itself. "I am proud to serve in this institution," Livingston said. "And I respect every member of this body." Referring again to the bitterness of the continuing debate, he regretted that this furor had become "the opening gambit" of his intended Speakership. "I most certainly would have written a different scenario, had I had the chance."

But then, moving beyond the civilities and his own personal situation, he reminded his colleagues, "We are all pawns from the chessboard and we're playing our parts in a drama that is neither fiction nor unimportant." In the next few minutes, Livingston dealt with the merits of the case against Clinton. The president had been accused of perjury, Livingston reminded his colleagues, a charge that his Democratic defenders had both denied and discounted, claiming it did not fall within the constitutional rubric of "high crimes and misdemeanors." It was true, Livingston acknowledged, that no president had ever been impeached for perjury, but three federal judges had been impeached and convicted on that charge.

Perjury was a serious business, a felony for which more than 100 persons were presently serving time in federal prison. "It is a crime for which the president may be held accountable, no matter what the circumstances," Livingston argued. And on these grounds, Livingston said, he would vote to impeach Clinton.

Now as he neared the peroration of his remarks, Livingston addressed Clinton directly. "To the president I would say, sir, you have done great damage to this nation over this past year." Noting that Clinton's defenders argued that further impeachment proceedings would only worsen this damage, he then turned this argument against Clinton. "I say that you have the power to terminate that damage and heal the wounds that you have created. You, sir, may resign your post."

This injunction, set off, as Livingston must have known it would, a chorus of boos and catcalls from the opposition.

"No," the Democrats shouted. "You resign, you resign."

"The House will come to order," cried the presiding officer as he banged down his gavel.

Livingston waited for the hubbub to subside. Those watching him closely thought they saw a flicker of a smile cross his lips.

And then his listeners, who thought that the tumult of the past eleven months, particularly the events of the past few days, had already exhausted the potential for drama in the theater of politics, had already drained their personal store of human emotions, found out they were mistaken, as Speaker-designate Livingston unveiled a stunning new development in the scenario forged by character and politics.

When Livingston resumed after the hubbub, the smile had vanished and he was in deadly earnest, still addressing the president, whom he had just urged to resign his office. "And I can only challenge you in such fashion," Livingston continued, "if I am willing to heed my own words. To my colleagues, my friends, and most especially my wife and family, I have hurt you all deeply and I beg your forgiveness. I was prepared to lead our narrow majority as Speaker . . . but I cannot do that job or be the kind of leader that I would like to be under current circumstances. So I must set the example that I hope President Clinton will follow. I will not stand for Speaker of the House on January 6."

Nor would he remain much longer in the chamber where he had served for more than two decades. Six months into the next Congress he would quit his seat and give his constituents the chance to fill it with a new face.

For a few moments, the House, only a handful of whose members knew in advance of Livingston's decision, was too stunned to react. Then slowly, in small groups, like fighters still reeling from an uppercut, they scrambled to their feet to applaud.

It was the Democrats, fearful of the symbolic impact of Livingston's dramatic stroke, who responded first, seeking to mitigate the weight of the sacrifice by the man who now would never be Speaker. Even as they rushed to the side of the fallen leader of the opposition to urge him to renege on his vow, one of their own, Jerrold Nadler of New York, whose squat figure had earned him the sobriquet of "Congressman Fireplug," sought to recast Livingston's dramatic gesture as an argument against the Republican cause.

"I believe Bob Livingston's resignation, while offered in good faith, was wrong. It is a surrender," Nadler said before he was interrupted by applause, mostly from Democrats.

> It is a surrender to a developing sexual McCarthyism. Are we going to have a new test if someone wants to run for public office: Are you now or have you ever been an adulterer? We are losing sight of the distinction between sins, which ought to be between a person and his family and his god, and crimes, which are the concern of the state and of society as a whole?
>
> But the impeachment of the president is even worse. Because again we're losing track of the distinction between sins and crimes. We're lowering the standard of impeachment. What the president has done is not an impeachable offense under the Constitution.

Henry Hyde was not about to stomach that. Having endured his own exposure earlier in the year, he was unwilling to allow his pain to go to waste. "My friends, those of us who are sinners must feel especially wretched today, losing Bob Livingston under such sad circumstances," Hyde began. "One's self-esteem gets utterly crushed at times like this. But something is going on repeatedly that has to be stopped and that is a confusion between private acts of infidelity and public acts. As a government official," Hyde said, "you raise your right hand and you ask God to witness to the truth of what you're saying. That's a public act. Infidelity—adultery—is not a public act, it's a private act, and the government, the Congress has no business intruding into private acts. But it is our business, it is our duty to observe, to characterize public acts by public officials, and so I hope that confusion doesn't persist."

Clinton's transgressions were not simply private, and he did not deserve to be spared, Hyde said. "Equal justice under the law, that's what we're fighting for, and when the chief law enforcement officer trivializes, ignores, shreds, minimizes the sanctity of the oath, then justice is wounded, and you are wounded, and your children are wounded."

The debate droned on for several hours more. But by now the battle lines were set, and everyone who had a vote knew how he or she would cast it. The four articles of impeachment approved by the Judiciary Committee were winnowed down to two. One, charging the president with perjury by misleading the federal grand jury about his relationship with Lewinsky, passed by a vote of 228 to 206. Five Democrats crossed over to vote for the impeachment; the same number of Republicans broke with their party to oppose. A second article, accusing Clinton of obstructing justice by inducing others to help him conceal his affair, passed by a narrower margin, 221 to 212.

The last echo of the roll call had hardly died down before most of the Democratic leaders had appeared alongside the president on the White House grounds. As if determined to prove by their own conduct that the entire process brought against Clinton was nothing more than a partisan exercise, they staged what they themselves chose to call a pep rally. Democratic leader Richard Gephardt, who only a few hours before, on the floor of the House, had bemoaned Livingston's resignation and declared "Let all of us here today say no to resignation, no to impeachment, no to hatred, no to intolerance of each other, and no to vicious self-righteousness," was now in far less statesmanlike mood. "We've just witnessed a partisan vote that was a disgrace to our country and our Constitution," he told the assembled Democrats.

Then it was the president's turn. "I want the American people to know today that I am still committed to working with people of good faith and goodwill of both parties to do what's best for our country, to bring our nation together, to lift our people up, to move us all forward together." This was what he intended to do, Clinton said, "until the last hour of the last day of my term."

After the bitterness of the House debate, conventional wisdom held that things would be blander and calmer in the Senate. For once, conventional wisdom was right. The reason for this was not hard to find. It all came down to the simplest arithmetic. In the Senate, Republicans outnumbered Democrats, 55 to 45. They could get their way on procedure. But the framers of the Constitution, in their wisdom, had mandated that conviction on impeachment requires a two-thirds vote of the senators—that would mean twelve more votes than there were Republican senators. No one imagined that those twelve votes would come from the Democratic side. So the fundamental reality that governed the trial in the Senate was that there would be no conviction—the president would be acquitted.

With the outcome assured, it became easier for both sides to arrange a series of compromises that helped members of each party meet certain political obligations and avoid serious political danger. The key vote came on January 27, when the Republican majority, with the addition of one Democratic senator, voted solidly to defeat a Democratic motion to dismiss the charges. On its face, this was a victory for the GOP. But the vote spelled out doom for the hopes of the House managers who determinedly argued the case against the president. With all but one Democrat voting for dismissal, it was clear to one and all that Clinton was home free.

The subsequent proceedings took on the aspects of one of those show trials for which Moscow became famous when Stalin ruled the Kremlin. The difference was that in the Soviet Union the guilt of the defendant was taken for granted. On Capitol Hill, the opposite was true. But in both cases the outcome was thoroughly predictable in advance. The sham nature of the Senate proceeding was underlined when the Senate decided not to hear any witnesses but to limit itself to the videotaped testimony of Clinton's paramour and two of his confidantes, Sidney Blumenthal and Vernon Jordan.

Even with the element of suspense removed, the attorneys for each side did far more than go through the motions. In addition to their own personal reputations, the opposing advocates had a great deal at stake. Although the press wrote a great deal about President Clinton's "legacy," White House counsel Charles Ruff had been around Washington long enough—since Watergate in fact, when he helped to prosecute malefactors involved in a scandal generated by another president, Richard Nixon—to know that the peril to the president he served was far more urgent than that. What Ruff was fighting for was not Clinton's place in history but rather his ability to govern in the two years that remained of his term.

Accordingly, in defending his client's innocence, Ruff set the bar for guilt at a dizzying height. "We know that our primary obligation, the duty we all have, is to preserve that which the founders gave us, and we can best fulfill that duty by carefully traveling the path they laid out for us," he told the assembled Senators. "There is only one question before you, albeit a difficult one," Ruff contended. "Would it put at risk the liberty of the people to retain the president in office? Putting aside partisan animus, if you can honestly say that it would not, that those liberties are safely in his hands, then you must vote to acquit."

By defining that standard for conviction Ruff opened a yawning doorway through which anyone reluctant to unseat Clinton could march with a clear conscience. If Ruff was battling for the future of Clinton's presidency, Henry Hyde was fighting for the future of his party—to avoid having Republicanism equated with intolerance and extremism. To judge the president, Hyde had a different standard in mind—not the imminent threat of tyranny, which Ruff suggested would be the only justification for voting for conviction, but instead the threat to the credibility of the presidency as an institution and to the rule of law, which both sides acknowledged as the underpinning of the Republic.

"Nothing begets cynicism like the double standard—one rule for the popular and the powerful, another for the rest of us," Hyde declared. "There is no denying the fact that whatever we decide will have a profound effect on our culture, as well as on our politics. A failure to convict will make a statement that lying under oath, while unpleasant and to be avoided, is not all that serious. Perhaps we can explain that to those currently in prison for perjury. We have reduced lying under oath to a breach of etiquette, but only if you are the president."

A few days later came the Senate verdict. The vote to acquit on the count of perjury was 55 to 45, with ten Republicans joining the solid phalanx of Democrats for acquittal. On the charge of obstruction of justice, the vote split 50 to 50, with five Republicans deserting their party. The White House could take some satisfaction in the failure of Republicans to get a majority on either count. But no one on Clinton's side could draw too much happiness from the day's reckoning. In addition to the fifty senators who had voted for conviction on the charge of obstruction of justice, another thirty-two signed on to a censure resolution, which stated that by his conduct the president had "brought shame and dishonor" to himself and to his office and had "violated the trust of the American people." The resolution was blocked from reaching the floor by a filibuster threat. But all told, eighty-two senators had gone on record, in one form or another, denouncing the president's conduct.

After the Senate trial concluded with Clinton's acquittal, Chief Justice Rehnquist, who had presided over the proceedings, declared in a brief statement to the Senate: "I leave you a wiser, but not a sadder man." If this was really the case, if Rehnquist was not merely straining to sound a note of grace out of characteristic civility, then he was certainly one of the few persons involved with Clinton's character crisis who could make such a claim. The experience left nearly everyone else on both sides not just sad but deeply depressed. And rather than bringing any wisdom with it, the outcome of the controversy left throughout the country bewilderment and anomie in its wake.

In anticipating his acquittal, some of Clinton's defenders worried that the president might gloat, as he had in the past over apparent victories in the long struggle. Thus warned, the president, by his words and his bearing, sought to convey a feeling of humility. "I want to say again to the American people how profoundly sorry I am for what I said and did to trigger these events and the great burden they have imposed on the Congress and the American people." Asked whether he could "forgive and forget," Clinton replied in the same tone, "I believe any person who asks for forgiveness has to be prepared to give it."

Actually, neither the president nor his supporters had much to gloat about, even if they had cared to so indulge themselves. Within a fortnight of his acquittal, the tarnish on his presidency was darkened by the airing in print and on television of an unprovable but nevertheless persuasive allegation by Juanita Broaddrick, an Arkansas nursing home operator, that Clinton had forced her to submit to his sexual advances in a convention hotel room more than twenty years earlier. She had confided in friends about the incident at the time but did not report it to the police. Years later, when contacted by Paula Jones's attorneys, Broaddrick signed an affidavit denying Clinton had assaulted her. But when questioned by investigators from Kenneth Starr's office, she retracted the affidavit, and then, after Clinton's trial in the Senate had begun, she decided to make the allegation public, though it did not surface in the mainstream press until after the trial was over.

The charge shook even such foes of impeachment as *Washington Post* columnist Richard Cohen: "The Clintons play by no rules. They have vanquished outrage," Cohen wrote.

Less than two months later, federal judge Susan Webber Wright, who in 1998 had dismissed the Paula Jones sexual harassment suit, found Clinton in contempt of court for lying about his affair with Monica Lewinsky in the Jones case. For this offense judge Wright later ordered the president to pay nearly $90,000 to Paula Jones's lawyers for extra work they performed because of his false testimony. "The record demonstrates by clear and convincing evidence that the president [gave] false, misleading and evasive answers that were designed to obstruct the judicial process." The judge added that Clinton had "undermined the integrity of the judicial system" and that she felt compelled to cite him with contempt to deter others from "emulating the president of the United States by willfully violating . . . orders of this and other courts." The finding was particularly significant because of its source, a jurist who had been, if anything, sympathetic to Clinton in her handling of Jones's lawsuit. Her ruling refuted the White House claim that the Lewinsky scandal was primarily the product of an overzealous prosecutor and politically motivated House Republicans.

More important, though, than whatever righteous satisfaction Clinton's detractors gained from Wright's ruling was any lesson the president might have drawn from the ordeal he had put himself and the country through. Certainly there was nothing to suggest that the experience had provided him with the wisdom that Justice Rehnquist claimed to have gained. "I think we learned that people expect their elected officials to work for them and not to be focused on themselves or their adversaries in Washington," the president told Dan Rather on national television. "And that they will reward those whom they believe get up every day and show up for work and work for them and their future and their children and they will take account of those they believe do not."

After Clinton had thus disposed of his Republican foes, he was asked by Rather whether he was ashamed of what had happened. The president soon set him straight. "I do not regard this impeachment vote as some great badge of shame," he said. "I do not. Because, I do not believe it was warranted, and I don't think it was right." And when Rather suggested that impeachment will be in the first paragraph of Clinton's obituary, the president took exception.

"Well, first of all, I'm not at all sure that's right that it will be in the first paragraph of the obituary. And secondly, if it is, if the history writers are honest, they'll tell it for just exactly what it was. And I am honored that something that was indefensible was pursued and that I had the opportunity to defend the Constitution."

If what Clinton learned from his character crisis was to blame his enemies, some of his enemies chose to blame the public. Particularly outspoken in this regard was Paul M. Weyrich, probably the most vehement moral crusader in the conservative realm. The man who had undermined President Bush's nomination of former Texas senator John Tower to head the Pentagon because of his drinking and womanizing, Weyrich had also conceived of the name, adopted by Jerry Falwell, Moral Majority. In the wake of Clinton's acquittal, Weyrich concluded that the name amounted to an oxymoron. "I no longer believe that there is a moral majority," Weyrich wrote in a letter to hundreds of thousands of supporters of his organization, the Free Congress Foundation. "I do not believe that a majority of Americans actually shares our values." Although he was "not suggesting that we all become Amish or move to Idaho," Weyrich said that "we have to look at what we can do to separate ourselves from this hostile culture."

Just as frustrated was William J. Bennett, perhaps the most articulate and unrelenting critic of Clinton's behavior, who charged that by their reaction to the president's conduct, ordinary Americans had to be considered as "complicit in his corruption." "I will not defend the public. Absolutely not," Bennett said. "If people want to pander to the public and say they're right they can. But they're not right on this one."

Some months before the denouement of the Lewinsky scandal in the Senate chamber, Bennett worried that "the history books may describe how a diffident public, when confronted with all the evidence of wrongdoing and all the squalor, simply shrugged its shoulders. And, finally, that William Jefferson Clinton really was the representative man of our time, when the overwhelming majority of Americans no longer believed that presidential character mattered, and that no man, not even a president, was accountable to the law."

The frustration and confusion on both sides about the outcome of Clinton's scandal was further evidence of the complex and potent role of character in presidential politics. As this book has argued, character is the ultimate political weapon. President Clinton demonstrated its potency for good—good for Clinton—when he used his

character to personalize his New Democrat ideology and policy proposals. His foes showed its power for harm—harm to Clinton and to
themselves—during the course of the many scandals of his presidency, climaxing with the Lewinsky affair. The exposure of Clinton's
misconduct inflicted severe damage on his presidency, robbing him
of the credibility and moral force needed to support initiatives for
significant change in American life. Instead Clinton was limited in
his second term to pleading the cause of "saving social security"—an
institution long taken for granted and that many analysts did not regard as being in any serious danger—or engaging in ventures overseas, such as his ill-conceived intervention in Kosovo.

And even in such enterprises he was handicapped by the damage
to his prestige from scandal. When he unleashed the Air Force to
punish Saddam Hussein, his critics charged him with manipulating
the crisis to preserve his political skin. Unwilling to take the political
risk of sending ground troops to fight the Serbian armies of
Slobadan Milosovic, Clinton relied solely on bombing the Serbs into
submission. As a result, he was unable to prevent 1.5 million Koso-
vars, on whose behalf the war had supposedly been fought, from being driven from their homes. And he was ultimately forced to accept
a settlement of the undeclared war that allowed indicted war criminal Milosovic to remain in power in Belgrade, retaining sovereignty
over war-torn Kosovo.

Meanwhile, Clinton's foes suffered damage themselves from their
awkward handling of the explosive character issue. The casualties
included, besides Speaker Gingrich and Speaker-designate Livingston, what had been decent prospects for increasing the Republican majority in the House.

In the aftermath, Republicans and Democrats asked themselves
two opposite questions. Republicans wondered how Clinton had
managed to win acquittal and maintain public support given the evidence against him. Democrats had a hard time understanding, given
the mood of the country, how the president had been impeached in
the first place. The answers to these questions depend on a clear-
eyed understanding of the character issue.

Character is a powerful weapon. But it is only a weapon. Its effectiveness depends on the terrain of the political battle field and the
skill of those using the weapon. In the case of Clinton, the ground
was very much in his favor because of the thriving economy, and his
Republican adversaries possessed neither the imagination nor the

courage to make him pay the ultimate political price for his personal misdeeds.

Even if they had been more gifted in this regard, the Republicans would have had a very hard time indeed. To say that the economy was in good condition is to commit a gigantic understatement. The truth is that every single economic indicator of any note—unemployment, inflation, productivity, gross domestic product, household income, stock market averages—was in a more salubrious state than at any time in recent memory. Moreover, just as the standard measures showed the economy to be robust, the gauges of the health of the society told a similar and not unrelated story: Among teens, the school drop out rate, the pregnancy rate, the suicide rate, and the use of alcohol were in decline; among the population in general, the divorce rate was headed downward and violent crimes were at our near their lowest levels in twenty-five years. It was the sum total of such measurements that bolstered Clinton's support and allowed him to survive.

It was not that Americans were naive enough to believe Clinton was responsible for all these favorable aspects of the national condition. Rather, it was that they were worried that removing him from his post might create a new and negative dynamic that would imperil the nation's well-being and their own; for in the midst of all the plenty, most Americans were still deeply anxious about their economic futures. "They live from paycheck to paycheck and worry about losing their health insurance if they are laid off," David Broder observed. And many feared that a shakeup at the highest level of government could upset the balance of economic forces and plunge them into the bleakness of hard times.

Does this mean that this generation of Americans is more selfish and materialistic than past generations? Hardly. What it does means is that it is difficult to get any group of citizens at any period of history to act against what they perceive to be their own self-interest. And this reality greatly helped the Democrats and severely handicapped the Republicans in arguing over Clinton's punishment. The heart of the Democratic case was that Clinton's conduct, as "reprehensible," "indefensible," "shameful," and "dishonorable" as it may have been—they were willing to use any adjective, no matter how pejorative, as long as they could keep their president—had nothing to do with his performance of his public duties. For their part, the Republicans had to disprove that contention—had to show that character mattered. It was the almost sublime national condition that made it impossible for the Democrats to lose, or the Republicans to win, that argument.

The thriving economy and the benign stability of society was all the evidence the Democrats needed to demonstrate that Clinton the adulterer, Clinton the perjurer, Clinton the obstructor of justice had no connection with Clinton the president of these contented United States. As for the Republicans, just those factors contravened their argument that character mattered in determining how a president performed. How could it matter if things were so good?

The point is well illustrated by what happened during Watergate, the scandal often cited by both sides during the struggle over Clinton's impeachment. Through the first months of the damaging revelations, Richard Nixon's support remained firm, both from the public and from within his own party. And it was no coincidence that the economy was booming along with low inflation and high employment. But late in 1973, the economy ran into trouble. Inflation soared to levels not seen since the end of World War II. Production began to dip, and unemployment began to climb.

Particularly troublesome, an Arab oil embargo cut into oil and gas supplies, raising prices and forcing Americans to sit in long lines outside their gas stations as they waited to fill up. Anger against Richard Nixon mounted, as I found out during a congressional recess in January 1974, when I accompanied Angelo Roncallo, a Republican congressman, on a twenty-mile walk through his Long Island district to test the mood of his constituents.

At every service station on the road from Massapequa to Cold Spring Harbor, long lines of cars waited for gas. "How are things going?" Roncallo asked a woman impatiently waiting her turn in her Cadillac. But this constituent had no interest in small talk, as Roncallo learned when she pulled down the window of her car to give him a piece of her mind. "Angelo, I'll follow you for twenty miles and drive you home on one condition," she offered.

What's that? Roncallo inquired.

"Impeach the son of a bitch," she said.

By his own reckoning, Roncallo talked to more than 250 voters, only two of whom had a kind word for the president.

"How soon people forget the good things a man does," said Mrs. Roncallo, who kept her husband company on the hike.

"If I were Nixon," the congressman said wryly, "I wouldn't run again." He went back to Washington bearing the same message from the grass roots that was being delivered to his colleagues across the country.

That summer the Judiciary Committee moved to impeach Richard Nixon, just as the lady in the gas station line wanted. And a few weeks after that, he quit.

Fortunately for Clinton, he had no gasoline shortage or any economic adversity to plague his presidency in the midst of his personal crisis. But his supporters were not content to limit their arguments to such practical and arguably crass grounds. Seeking for loftier reasons to maintain the president in office, they helped to make the debate over his impeachment part of the culture war that had raged as a backdrop to American politics since the 1960s.

To be sure they had plenty of assistance from conservatives, or "neo-puritans," as Clinton's defenders saw them. "Are we a nation based on truth or a nation based on moral relativism?" thundered Republican congressman Bob Inglis of South Carolina on the House floor, as he urged President Clinton's impeachment. The "nub of the question" raised by the charges against Clinton, Representative Inglis claimed, is, "Does the truth matter or is everything relative? Is there any truth, or is my truth different than your truth?"

But if conservatives seemed to be inspired in their animus against the president by their view of him as embodying the erosion of values rooted in the turbulent Sixties, liberals were glad to make his defense on those grounds. "A vote against impeachment is not a vote for Bill Clinton," declared Harvard law professor Alan Dershowitz, a vociferous opponent of impeachment. "It's a vote against bigotry. It's a vote against fundamentalism. It's a vote against anti-environmentalism. It's a vote against the right-to-life movement. It's a vote against the radical right. This is truly the first battle in a great culture war. And if this president is impeached, it will be a great victory for the forces of evil—genuine evil."

At a Los Angeles rally, Hollywood turned out in force on behalf of the film colony's favorite politician. More than 1,000 anti-impeachment demonstrators—waving placards reading "Watergate, Iran-Contra, and Monica?" and "He lied about sex. So what?"—gathered to hear from Barbra Streisand and Jack Nicholson, among others. Pronouncing herself "stupefied" by the impeachment proceedings, Streisand asked, "Who could have imagined that we would be living in a time when those we elected to office would turn their backs on the public and ignore the voices of the American people?" Nicholson sought to inject a sobering note by cautioning that the impeachment crisis was not entertainment, even though the rally was covered by TV's *Entertainment Tonight.* "We live in a television age. We're going to always live in a television age. These things regrettably sell a lot of soap," he said. "We can't confuse these issues."

Addressing a rally of artists and writers at New York University, the novelist E. L. Doctorow claimed that the impeachment of Clinton had "all the legitimacy of a coup d'état." Novelist William Styron rejoiced in the flexing of so much aesthetic political muscle. "Vietnam is almost the last moment I can think of until now when intellectuals, writers, and artists have really raised their voices in a chorus of protests," he declared.

In speaking out on Clinton's behalf many of these artists and thinkers on the left had to stifle their own inner qualms about his policies and his behavior. The *Nation,* in the same issue that was devoted in part to denouncing the impeachment effort, dismissed Clinton as a "lousy president" and condemned his bombing of Iraq. Dershowitz, who had himself written a scathing critique of Clinton's civil liberties policies, nevertheless opposed the "theocracy" seeking to impeach Clinton, on the grounds that impeachment represented even a greater threat to liberties guaranteed by the Constitution. As for Clinton the man, Dershowitz branded his conduct as "despicable" and declined to go along with those who claimed that what the president did was irrelevant politically. "It matters a lot," said Dershowitz. "I might not vote for him if he was running again. I think its constitutionally irrelevant, but it's politically relevant. I think people who cheat on their wives and who lie tend to be less trustworthy in other matters."

There is enough evidence that a good many other Americans share that view to oblige politicians to continue to take the character issue seriously. Much was made of the high approval ratings Clinton received in the polls for his job performance in the midst of the allegations of his sleazy behavior. A closer look at the various polls, though, suggests caution in accepting the notion fostered by some of Clinton's defenders that the public totally discounted the scandal. Rather, the picture that emerges is that of a citizenry conflicted, embarrassed, and uncomfortable with the behavior of the man they had chosen to be their leader.

Any analysis of polling results has to begin with an understanding of the limitations of the polling process. Polls tend to be more reliable about simple, explicit questions such as voting choices than about more complex and abstract issues such as marital fidelity, adultery, lying under oath, and the meaning of "high crimes and misdemeanors." "About some of these things people think very deeply in ways that cannot be caught by a polling question," points out the conservative cleric and social critic John Neuhaus. "About others they have not thought at all, which does not prevent them from having an 'opinion' to be registered."

Even so, the available data, whatever it may be worth, paints a more nuanced, enigmatic, and fluid impression of public opinion than has been commonly advertised. First of all, it needs to be remembered that judgments change. In October 1991, polls consistently showed Americans supporting the nomination of Clarence Thomas to the Supreme Court by a 2-to-1 ratio, even after Anita Hill's accusations. By similar numbers, Americans said they found Thomas to be more believable than Ms. Hill. One year after Thomas's confirmation, these numbers had practically reversed. Suddenly the public saw Ms. Hill as more credible.

Bolstering the possibility for some such shift in opinion about the case against Clinton are the sharp conflicts within the public about his behavior. According to a Fox News poll taken in the midst of Clinton's Senate trial, a majority of Americans believed the president had perjured himself before the grand jury the previous August. According to another poll, taken in January by John Zogby International, a majority of Americans also viewed perjury as an impeachable offense. Still other polls showed that most Americans opposed impeachment. In combination, all these polls suggested that Americans were against impeachment of Clinton for acts they considered impeachable. Similarly, in a survey conducted by the *Washington Post* in collaboration with Harvard University and the Henry J. Kaiser Family Foundation in the summer of the Lewinsky scandal, more than seven in ten people said adultery was unacceptable and "should not be tolerated." Yet fewer than half of those who said adultery "should not be tolerated" said Clinton's affair with Lewinsky was an important matter. The picture that emerges from this and other data is that of an electorate desperately seeking a reason not to remove Clinton from office.

Another finding in the survey conducted by the *Post* and its collaborators underlines the sharp divisions among Americans on the relevance of personal behavior to political performance—perhaps the central question raised by the Clinton scandal. Half of those interviewed said it is performance alone that counts in a president, agreeing that "as long as he does a good job running the country, whatever he does in his personal life is not important." But just as many disagreed: They said the president has a "greater responsibility" to set "an example with his personal life."

Given the closeness of these divisions, it is no wonder that the prime contenders for each party's presidential nomination in 2000, Republican George W. Bush and Democrat Al Gore, have set out to immunize themselves against the vagaries of the character issue.

Each man has a clear problem. In Bush's case the difficulty is his past, when he apparently lived a life free of care and discipline and by his own account drank more than was good for him. To help put distance between the two Bushes, today's presidential candidate Bush and yesteryear's sower of wild oats, Bush has tried to make the case that he has mended his unruly ways, a changeover he has underlined by his strict teetotalism and by his urgent proselytizing for sexual abstinence among young people. In announcing his candidacy in the summer following Clinton's acquittal, facing questions about his rumored use of drugs as a youth, Bush sought to link his makeover of himself to his view of the presidency. "When we put our hand on the Bible, we swear to uphold not only the laws but the dignity of the office to which we have been elected," the GOP presidential nomination front-runner said in his first stop in New Hampshire.

"It is a pledge I made to the voters of Texas and a pledge that I have upheld, so help me God," he said. "Americans are waiting for new hopes, new energy, new idealism," he declared when he moved on to Iowa. "We will give our country a fresh start after a season of cynicism. My first goal is to usher in the responsibility era, an era that stands in stark contrast to the last few decades, where our culture has said that if it feels good, do it; and if you've got a problem, just go ahead and blame somebody else. Each American must understand that we are responsible for the decisions that each of us makes in life."

Vice President Gore's problem is similar in a way, but also different. He too needs to separate himself from the past—not his own past, but rather that of the president whom he has served loyally for more than six years. Gore set about this task the night before his announcement speech, when in chatting with reporters he bemoaned "that awful year we went through,"—the year of Clinton's impeachment. "What was most upsetting about it," Gore told reporters, was "the wasted time."

"I'm even more anxious to move forward swiftly to make up for that waste of time," he went on. "We shouldn't have had to go through it."

The next day, in his formal announcement speech, Gore pledged to "bring a new wave of fundamental change to this nation," change that would include, he made clear, a fresh moral start in the Oval Office. "If you entrust me with the presidency, I will marshal its authority, its resources, and its moral leadership to fight for America's family," Gore said, with his own family, including his 87-year-old mother and his pregnant 25-year-old daughter, creating a tableau behind him. "I will take my own values of faith and family to the presidency."

In a television interview that aired later that same day, Gore called Clinton's behavior "inexcusable" no fewer than three times, contended that Clinton had compromised the dignity of the presidency, and accused Clinton of lying to him. That was more than the president wanted to hear about that. Through the medium of a leak to the *New York Times,* he let Gore know that he was "very upset." Said one close adviser: "This is not a passing thing."

But Gore seemed to shrug off the president's displeasure. He had little choice. No one knows whether voters will take a harsher view of presidential misconduct in the 2000 campaign than they seemed to adopt during the Lewinsky scandal. What became clear from the opening gambits of the Bush and Gore campaigns was that this is a risk no presidential candidate can afford to take.

Other evidence of the enduring political impact of the character issue came from First Lady Hillary Rodham Clinton, preparing to run for the U.S. Senate from New York, who suggested in a magazine interview that her husband's sexual behavior may have resulted from his troubled childhood. In response to criticism, she denied that she was trying to make excuses for the president. "I believe everyone of us is responsible for his or her behavior, including the president," she said. The presidency, and the nation, will have derived at least some benefit from her husband's recklessness if its consequences teach his successors to accept that premise.

A NOTE
ON SOURCES

Listed below, chapter by chapter, are the books that have served as my main sources for each of the presidents. In addition, for the post-Roosevelt presidents I have drawn on two of my own books, *None of the Above: Why Presidents Fail and What Can Be Done About It* (New York: New American Library, 1982) and *The Riddle of Power: Presidential Leadership from Truman to Bush* (New York: Dutton, 1991). For the more recent presidents, particularly those since John Kennedy, I have relied on the daily press, chiefly the *New York Times,* the *Washington Post,* and the *Los Angeles Times;* the newsmagazines *Newsweek* and *Time;* and my own reportage as a correspondent for *Newsweek,* from 1967 to 1972, and as national political correspondent for the *Los Angeles Times* since 1973, which includes personal interviews with six presidents and numerous candidates for the office.

Chapter 1

The academic research demonstrating the increasing salience of presidential character and values is Arthur H. Miller, Martin P. Wattenberg, and Oksana Malanchuk, "Schematic Assessments of Presidential Candidates," *American Political Science Review,* vol. 80, no. 2 (June 1986). For Greenberg's analysis of Dukakis's defeat, see Stanley B. Greenberg, "Reconstructing the Democratic Vision," *American Prospect* (Spring 1990).

Chapter 2

For background and debate on the constitutional convention, see Catherine Drinker Bowen, *Miracle at Philadelphia* (Boston: Little, Brown, 1966), and Richard B. Morris, *Witness at the Creation* (New York: Holt, Rinehart, 1985). The depiction of Washington is based mainly on two absorbing and accessible biographies: Richard Brookhiser, *Founding Father* (New York: Free Press, 1996), pp. 48–49, and Richard Norton Smith, *Patriarch* (New York: Houghton Mifflin, 1993). See also John R. Alden, *George Washington* (Baton Rouge: Louisiana State University, 1984), for Washington's early years, and Marcus Cunliffe, *The American Heritage History of the Presidency* (New York: Simon and Schuster, 1968), John Marshall, *The Life of George Washington* (Philadelphia: G. P. Wayne, 1807), and Arthur M. Schlesinger, *The Birth of the Nation* (New York: Knopf, 1969).

Chapter 3

For Jefferson, my greatest debt for an overall picture of the man and the politician is to Joseph J. Ellis, *American Sphinx* (New York: Knopf, 1997). Fawn M. Brodie, *Thomas Jefferson* (New York: Norton, 1974), is excellent for the scandals of the time. See also John T. Morse, *Thomas Jefferson* (New York: Chelsea House, 1980). For the general political climate of the time, I used Stanley Elkins and Eric McKitrick, *The Age of Federalism* (New York: Oxford University Press, 1993).

James C. Curtis, *Andrew Jackson and the Search for Vindication* (Boston: Little, Brown, 1976), was most important in shaping my understanding of Jackson. Also helpful were Herman J. Viola, *Andrew Jackson* (New York: Chelsea House, 1986), and Burke Davis, *Old Hickory* (New York: Dial, 1977).

David Herbert Donald's justly honored *Lincoln* (New York: Touchstone, 1995) was invaluable for the Great Emancipator. I also drew on Dwight G. Anderson, *Abraham Lincoln: The Quest for Immortality* (New York: Knopf, 1982); Gary Wills, *Lincoln at Gettysburg: The Words That Remade America* (New York: Touchstone, 1992); and Douglas L. Wilson, *Honor's Voice: The Transformation of Abraham Lincoln* (New York: Knopf, 1998).

For the presidents between Jackson and Lincoln and between Lincoln and Theodore Roosevelt, see Nathan Miller, *Star-Spangled Men: America's Ten Worst Presidents* (New York: Scribner, 1998), and Eugene H. Roseboom, *A History of Presidential Elections* (New York: Macmillan, 1957).

Chapter 4

For Theodore Roosevelt and his times, see H. W. Brans, *TR: The Last Romantic* (New York: Basic Books, 1997); David H. Burton, *Confident Imperialist* (Philadelphia: University of Pennsylvania Press, 1968); John Milton Cooper, *The Warrior and the Priest* (Cambridge, MA: Belknap Press, 1983); Richard Hofstadter, *The American Political Tradition* (New York: Vintage, 1961); Nathan Miller, *Theodore Roosevelt: A Life* (New York: William Morrow, 1992); Edmund Morris, *The Rise of Theodore Roosevelt* (New York: Coward, McAnn, 1979); and Henry F. Pringle, *Theodore Roosevelt: A Biography* (New York: Harcourt Brace, 1984).

Alexander and Juliette L. George, *Woodrow Wilson and Colonel House: A Personality Study* (New York: Dover, 1964), was essential for the section on Wilson. Also helpful were John Morton Blum, *Woodrow Wilson and the Politics of Morality* (Boston: Little Brown, 1956); Arthur S. Link, ed., *Woodrow Wilson: A Profile* (New York: Hill and Wang, 1968); and Edwin A. Weinstein, *Woodrow Wilson: A Medical and Psychological Biography* (Princeton: Princeton University Press, 1981).

Chapter 5

In its view of FDR, this chapter is reflective of my *Hard Bargain: How FDR Twisted Churchill's Arm, Evaded the Law, and Changed the Role of the American Presidency* (New York: Scribner, 1995). Patrick J. Maney, *The Roosevelt Presence* (New York: Twayne, 1992), was valuable for Roosevelt's early years. Raymond Moley, *After Seven Years* (New York: Da Capo, 1939), and Rexford G. Tugwell, *The Democratic Roosevelt* (Baltimore: Penguin, 1957), offer the best firsthand accounts of the start of the New Deal. Another useful eyewitness was James Farley, *Jim Farley's Story* (New York: McGraw-Hill, 1948). Geoffrey C. Ward's *A First-Class Temperament* (New York: Harper, 1989) and *Before the Trumpet* (New York: Harper, 1985) are unmatched for their insight into Roosevelt's complex psyche. James MacGregor Burns's *Roosevelt: The Lion and the Fox* (New York: Harcourt Brace, 1956) and Frank Freidel's *Franklin D. Roosevelt: A Rendezvous with Destiny* (Boston: Little Brown, 1990) and *Franklin D. Roosevelt: The Ordeal* (Boston: Little, Brown, 1954) are superb overall histories of the Roosevelt presidency. See also Hugh Gallagher, *FDR's Splendid Deception* (New York: Dodd Mead, 1985), for Roosevelt's efforts to conceal his paralysis, and Arthur Schlesinger Jr.'s, *The Crisis of the Old Order* (Boston: Houghton Mifflin, 1957), *The Coming of the New Deal* (Boston: Houghton Mifflin, 1959), and *The Politics of Upheaval* (Boston: Houghton Mifflin, 1960). For the "psychoanalyzed by God" quote, I am indebted to William Leuchtenburg, "The First Modern President," in Fred I. Greenstein, ed., *Leadership in the Modern Presidency* (Cambridge: Harvard University Press, 1988).

Alonzo Hamby, *Man of the People: A Life of Harry S. Truman* (New York: Oxford University Press, 1995) is the definitive work on the thirty-third president. Also valuable is Hamby's earlier "Harry S. Truman: Insecurity and Responsibility," in Fred Greenstein, ed., *Leadership in the Modern Presidency*. Robert Donovan's two volumes, *Conflict and Crisis: The Presidency of Harry S Truman, 1945–1948* (New York: Norton, 1977) and *Tumultuous Years: The Presidency of Harry S Truman* (New York: Norton, 1982), provide a comprehensive and balanced account. *Plain Speaking* (New York: Greenwich House, 1985) offers Truman's own lively if sometimes embellished recollections.

The most complete narrative of Dwight Eisenhower's life and presidency is Stephen Ambrose, *Eisenhower: Soldier, General of the Army, President-*

Elect (New York: Simon and Schuster, 1983) and *Eisenhower the President* (New York: Simon and Schuster, 1984). See also Kenneth S. Davis, *Soldier of Democracy* (New York: Doubleday, 1946); Peter Lyon, *Eisenhower: Portrait of the Hero* (Boston: Little, Brown, 1974); Piers Brendon, *Ike: His Life and Times* (New York: Harper and Row, 1986); and Richard Rovere, "Eisenhower Revisited," in Robert D. Marcus and David Burner, eds., *America Since 1945* (New York: St. Martin's Press, 1977).

Chapter 6

Arthur M. Schlesinger Jr., *A Thousand Days* (Boston: Houghton Mifflin, 1965), and Theodore C. Sorensen, *Kennedy* (New York: Harper and Row, 1965), are the most useful contemporaneous accounts of the Kennedy presidency. Henry Fairlie, *The Kennedy Promise: The Politics of Expectation* (Garden City, NY: Doubleday, 1973) is an early and notable revisionist view.

See also Thomas Brown, *JFK: History of an Image* (Bloomington: Indiana University Press, 1988); David Burner, *John F. Kennedy and a New Generation* (Boston: Little, Brown, 1988); James MacGregor Burns, *John Kennedy: A Political Profile* (New York: Avon, 1961); and David Halberstam, *The Best and the Brightest* (New York: Fawcett, 1973). Kennedy's 1960 drive for the presidency is best captured by John F. Kennedy, "The Speeches, Remarks, Press Conferences and Statements of Senator John F. Kennedy, August 1 through November 7, 1960," in *Freedom of Communications: Part I* (Washington, DC: U.S. Senate Commerce Committee, 1961).

Robert Caro's *The Years of Lyndon Johnson: The Path to Power* (New York: Knopf, 1982) is a penetrating narrative, though it sometimes suffers from its harsh view of its subject. Rowland Evans and Robert Novak, *Lyndon B. Johnson: The Exercise of Power* (New York: New American Library, 1968), is an exceptionally insightful book about Lyndon Johnson and American politics. Doris Kearns, *Lyndon Johnson and the American Dream* (New York: New American Library, 1976), is sympathetic yet candid. For transcriptions of Johnson's taped conversations, see Michael Beschloss, *Taking Charge* (New York: Simon and Schuster, 1997). Larry Berman, *Lyndon Johnson's War* (New York: Norton, 1989), captures the dilemmas that Johnson faced in Vietnam.

Chapter 7

Of all that has been written about Nixon, nothing is more revealing than Richard Nixon, *RN: The Memoirs of Richard Nixon* (New York: Grossett and Dunlap, 1978), perhaps the best memoir written by any modern president. Also of great value is an earlier Nixon memoir, *Six Crises* (New York: Doubleday, 1962). Nixon's own words, often much less elegantly phrased, are also on record in Stanley Kutler, *Abuse of Power* (New York: Basic Books, 1997), based on more than 200 hours of Watergate tapes, which Kutler won a court battle to make available. Of the abundant accounts by historians and journalists, I found the most useful to be Stephen E. Ambrose, *Nixon: The Education of a Politician* (New York: Simon and Schuster, 1987); Fawn M. Brodie, *Richard Nixon: The Shaping of His Character* (New York: Norton, 1981); and Rowland Evans Jr. and Robert D. Novak, *Nixon in the White House: The Frustration of Power* (New York: Random House, 1971).

Two of the most informative accounts of Gerald Ford and his presidency were written by aides: Robert T. Hartman, *Palace Politics* (New York: McGraw-Hill, 1989), and J. F. TerHorst, *Gerald Ford and the Future of the Presidency* (New York: Third Press, 1974). See also James Cannon, *Time and Chance: Gerald Ford's Appointment with History* (New York: HarperCollins, 1994); John Robert Greene, *The Presidency of Gerald Ford* (Lawrence: University Press of Kansas, 1985); and Gerald R. Ford, *A Time to Heal* (New York: Harper and Row, 1979).

For Jimmy Carter, I have drawn on my *Promises to Keep: Carter's First 100 Days* (New York: Crowell, 1977). Jimmy Carter, *Why Not the Best?* (New York: Bantam, 1976), is an informative and intriguing campaign autobiography, far superior to Carter's presidential memoir, *Keeping Faith* (New York: Bantam, 1982).

The best book-length attempts to explain the Carter presidency are Erwin Hargrove, *Leadership and the Politics of the Public Good* (Baton Rouge: Louisiana State University, 1988); Haynes Johnson, *In the Absence of Power* (New York: Viking, 1980); and Charles O. Jones, *The Trusteeship Presidency* (Baton Rouge: Louisiana State University, 1988). Two useful shorter pieces are Peter Bourne, "Jimmy Carter: A Profile," *Yale Review* (Fall 1982), and James Fallows, "The Passionless Presidency," *Atlantic*, May 1989.

Chapter 8

Two early journalistic accounts, Laurence I. Barrett, *Gambling with History* (New York: Penguin, 1984), and Lou Cannon, *Reagan* (New York: Perigee Books, 1982), are valuable chronicles of Ronald Reagan's fast start in the White House. Cannon's *President Reagan: The Role of a Lifetime* (New York: Simon and Schuster, 1991), is a solid study of the full eight years. Ronald Reagan, with Richard G. Hubler, *Where's the Rest of Me?* (New York: Duell, Sloan and Pearce, 1965), is a first-person, surprisingly candid account of Reagan's start in life and politics. Michael Rogin, *Ronald Reagan: The Movie* (Berkeley: University of California, 1987), is valuable for explaining the connection between Hollywood and Reagan's early years. For accounts of Reagan's personal strengths and limitations as chief executive from the varying perspectives of participants in his presidency, see Peggy Noonan, *What I Saw at the Revolution: A Political Life in the Reagan Era* (New York: Ivy, 1991); Martin Anderson, *Revolution* (New York: Harcourt Brace, 1988); and Dinesh D'Souza, *Ronald Reagan: How an Ordinary Man Became an Extraordinary Leader* (New York: Free Press, 1997).

Chapter 9

The literature on Bush and his presidency is as thin as the man himself and his record in office. This chapter depends heavily on contemporary newspapers and periodicals. Barry Bearak, "Bush: A Yearning to Serve," *Los Angeles Times*, November 22, 1987, is a 10,000 word overview of Bush's early life and how it tied into his career. In this area, see also Fitzhugh Green, *George Bush: An Intimate Portrait* (New York: Hippocrene, 1989). George Bush, *Looking Forward* (New York, Doubleday, 1987), provides a few revelatory nuggets. Colin Campbell and Bert A. Rockman, eds., *The Bush Presidency: First Appraisals* (Chatham, NJ: Chatham House, 1991), offers an early view that is generally accepting of Bush's own view of himself and the obligations of his office. Jack Germond and Jules Witcover, *Whose Broad Stripes and Bright Stars?* (New York: Warner, 1989), helps explain why Bush's election campaign left the country with such a bad taste. Bob Woodward and Carl Bernstein, *The Final Days* (New York: Simon and Schuster, 1976), p. 368, is the source for the anecdote about Bush's reaction to the decisive Nixon Watergate tape. For Gary Hart's reaction to the press corps' inquisitiveness, see E. J. Dionne, "Gary Hart: The Elusive Frontrunner," *New York Times*, May 3, 1987.

Chapter 10

For Clinton's unsolicited advice to Carter, see David Broder, "Carter Endorsed by Twenty Governors," *Washington Post*, July 9, 1979. David Maraniss, *First in His Class: The Biography of Bill Clinton* (New York: Simon and Schuster, 1993), examines Clinton's early life and prepresidential career. For a scholarly analysis of the links between Clinton's upbringing, his character, and his career, see Stanley A. Renshon, *High Hopes: The Clinton Presidency and the Politics of Ambition* (New York: New York University Press, 1996). Clinton's reference to his advice to Dukakis in the 1988 campaign is from a transcript of his remarks at the Chautauqua Institution, June 28, 1991, courtesy of the Chautauqua Institution. *Campaign for President: The Managers Look at 1992* (Hollis, NH: Hollis Publishing, 1992) offers a look at the shaping of strategy in the opposing camps in the election that sent Clinton to the White House. Bob Woodward, *The Agenda* (New York: Pocket Books, 1995), and Elizabeth Drew, *On the Edge: The Clinton Presi-*

dency (New York: Simon and Schuster, 1994), explain the contradictions of Clinton's first term. Paul Starr, "What Happened to Health Care Reform?" *American Prospect,* no. 20, is an objective and informed study of the failure of the centerpiece of Clinton's domestic agenda.

Chapter 11

For Clinton's outburst at his liberal critics, see Jann Wenner and Bill Greider, "The Rolling Stone Interview," *Rolling Stone,* December 9, 1993. Byron York, "Bill's Bad Lie," *American Spectator,* September 1996, drew the analogy between Clinton's golf game and his political style. See Joe Klein, "The Politics of Promiscuity," *Newsweek,* May 9, 1994, for Klein's misgivings about Clinton's character. Clinton's outrage over the premature disclosure of his new pet's name is from Howard Kurtz, *Spin Cycle: Inside the Clinton Propaganda Machine* (New York: Free Press, 1998). The quotation "The commander-in-chief is AWOL" is from Thomas L. Friedman, "Domestic Affairs," *New York Times,* June 12, 1997. For the loss of liberal moral superiority, see Michael Kelly, "Clinton's Legacy," *Washington Post,* October 30, 1997. The best narrative of the developing Lewinsky scandal is provided by Dan Balz, "The Story So Far," which ran every Sunday in the *Washington Post* from mid-January into March. See Catherine A. MacKinnon, "Harassment Law Under Siege, *New York Times,* March 5, 1998; Gloria Steinem, "Feminists and the Clinton Question," *New York Times,* March 22, 1998; Gwendolyn Mink, "Misreading Sexual Harassment Law," *New York Times,* March 30, 1998; Barbara Ehrenreich, "The Week Feminists Got Laryngitis," *Time,* February 9, 1998; and Molly Haskell, "We're All in Bed with Clinton," *National Observer,* March 2, 1998, for their respective views on Clinton from a feminist perspective. See Roger Simon, "Telling the Truth Slowly," *Chicago Tribune,* February 17, 1998, for Michael McCurry's deviation from the White House line. Mike Nichols's defense of Clinton is in James Kaplan, "True Colors," *New York,* March 2, 1998. Donna Smith's comparison of Clinton to Packwood is from Terry McDermott, "Packwood Inches Back to Esteem," *Los Angeles Times,* April 14, 1998. For the depiction of Clinton as a family man, see Dick Morris, *Behind the Oval Office* (New York: Random House, 1997), and Peter Rubin, "Family Man," *New Republic,* April 27, 1998. For Gertrude Himmelfarb's warning about Clinton's moral legacy, see Gertrude Himmelfarb, "Public Lives, Public Morality," *New York Times,* February 9, 1998.

Chapter 12

Clinton's election night reactions are from Stephen Braun ets al., "Pathway to Peril," Chapter VII, *Los Angeles Times,* January 31, 1999. Sources on Tom Delay are Eric Pianin and Kevin Merida, "How GOP's Enforcer Propelled the Process," *Washington Post,* Dec. 16, 1998, and Melinda Henneberger, "Impeachment: the Whip," *New York Times,* Dec. 17, 1998; on Henry Hyde, Kevin Merida, "The Judiciary Chairman's Trying Times," *Washington Post,* Dec.14, 1998, and Stephen Braun, "Hyde Was Driving Force Behind Day of Reckoning," *Los Angeles Times,* Dec. 20, 1998. The impact of the Starr report on the White House and on Senate Democrats is drawn from Bob Woodward, "A President's Isolation," by Bob Woodward, *Washington Post,* June 13, 1999. The bullish social indices are from Karl Zinsmeister et al., "Is America Turning a Corner?" *The American Enterprise*, January 1999. For more on Neuhaus's view of Clinton's character see Richard John Neuhaus, "Bill Clinton and the American Character," *First Things*, June 1999. The polling contradictions are cited by John J. Miller in "No Need to Hide," *New York Times*, Feb. 8, 1999. The results of the poll taken by the *Washington Post* et al., are from David Broder and Richard Morin, "Worries About Nation's Morals . . . " *Washington Post,* Sept. 8, 1998. Clinton's leak to the *New York Times* about Gore can be found in John M. Broder and Don Van Natta, Jr., "Aides Say Clinton Is Angered," *New York Times,* June 26, 1999.

INDEX